MW00576019

Within
Nietzsche's
Labyrinth

Within Nietzsche's Labyrinth

Alan White

ROUTLEDGE
NEW YORK & LONDON

Published in 1990 by

Routledge
An imprint of Routledge, Chapman and Hall, Inc.
29 West 35 Street
New York, NY 10001

Published in Great Britain by

Routledge
11 New Fetter Lane
London EC4P 4EE

Library of Congress Cataloging in Publication Data

White, Alan, 1951–
    Within Nietzsche's labyrinth / Alan White.
        p.   cm.
    Includes bibliographical references.
    ISBN 0-415-90327-0; ISBN 0-415-90328-9 (pbk.)
    1. Nietzsche, Friedrich Wilhelm, 1844–1900.   I. Title.
B3317. W453   1990
193—dc20   90-33265

British Library Cataloguing in Publication Data also available.

For Niko and Charlotte,
my favorite blond beasts

Table of Contents

III   Within the Labyrinth

Acknowledgments

In writing this book, I have benefited immensely from two resources that were not available to me as I wrote my earlier ones. Those I wrote while in Japan, far from philosophical colleagues and students; this one I have written in Massachusetts, in comfortable proximity to both. I thank Williams College for bringing me into that proximity, and for providing me with both the sabbatical during which the book was written and the support of its Center for the Humanities and Social Sciences.

Colleagues Philip Clayton, Dan O'Connor, and Mark Taylor have aided me by reading and commenting on earlier drafts of this book; their questions and suggestions have led to significant improvements. Students too numerous to name have aided me by being intrigued, provoked, inspired, perplexed, and infuriated as we have read Nietzsche together; again and again, they have forced me to re-examine my interpretations, and then either to alter them or to reformulate them more intelligibly. In addition, Kristian Omland read and commented helpfully on a draft of the book, and Kathy Ryan scrupulously checked page references and line numbers. Rachel Zuckert commented with magnificent ruthlessness on the page proofs (motivated, no doubt, by the gift-giving virtue rather than by the spirit of revenge). Finally, Anne Just—a friend, not a student—intervened, at the last minute, to bring at least a semblance of order to the chaos into which my index was threatening to deteriorate.

Other debts of gratitude predate my days at Williams. Were it not for the long-standing and continuing support of Stanley Rosen, Reiner Schürmann, and Thomas Seebohm, market conditions would likely have forced me to abandon the academy altogether; had I done so, this book would not have been written. A summer grant from the Earhardt Foundation allowed me to renew my study of Nietzsche. And Maureen MacGrogan has provided editorial expertise, support, and guidance, not for the first time and not, I hope, for the last.

I do not know what Jane, Niko, and Charlotte have had to do with the development of this book, but it would not seem right for me to acknowledge the aid of anyone else, on anything, without expressing my gratitude to them, for everything.

I gratefully acknowledge the permission granted me to quote from the following sources:

Excerpts from *If on a Winter's Night a Traveler* by Italo Calvino, copyright © 1979 by Giulio Einaudi editore s.p.a., Torino, English translation, copyright © 1981 by Harcourt Brace Jovanovich, Inc., reprinted by permission of Harcourt Brace Jovanovich, Inc.

Excerpt from *Invisible Cities* by Italo Calvino, copyright © by Giulio Einaudo editore s.p.a., Torino, English translation, copyright © 1974 by Harcourt Brace Jovanovich, Inc., reprinted by permission of Harcourt Brace Jovanovich, Inc.

Excerpt from *Mr. Palomar* by Italo Calvino, copyright © 1983 by Giulio Einaudi editore s.p.a., Torino. English translation, copyright © 1985 by Harcourt Brace Jovanovich, Inc., reprinted by permission of Harcourt Brace Jovanovich, Inc.

Excerpt from *tZero* by Italo Calvino, copyright © 1967 by Giulio Einaudi editore s.p.a., Torino, English translation, copyright © 1969 by Harcourt Brace Jovanovich, Inc. and Jonathan Cape Limited, reprinted by permission of Harcourt Brace Jovanovich, Inc.

From *The Book of Laughter and Forgetting*. By Milan Kundera. Translated by Michael Heim. Translation Copyright © 1980 by Alfred A. Knopf, Inc. Reprinted by permission of the publisher.

From *Life is Elsewhere*. By Milan Kundera. Translated by Peter Kussi. Translation Copyright © 1974 by Alfred A. Knopf, Inc. Reprinted by permission of the publisher.

Excerpts from *The Unbearable Lightness of Being* by Milan Kundera. Copyright © 1984 by Harper & Row, Publishers, Inc. Reprinted by permission of Harper & Row, Publishers, Inc., and of Faber and Faber Ltd.

A version of Chapter Two appeared in *International Studies in Philosophy* XIX/2 (1987), pp. 29–44.

A Note on Notes

No one way of handling footnotes is best for all books or for all readers. For this book, I have chosen the way that seems to me best for it, and while I do not doubt that my way will annoy some, I hope that it will please others. Page references are given parenthetically, but these are the only references that are apparent: no superscripted numbers interrupt the texts of the book's chapters, and no small print will be found at the bottoms of their pages. Notes are provided at the end, and readers who look to a chapter's notes only after reading all of the chapter itself (as I suspect most readers do) should have no difficulty in locating the passages to which the notes relate. On the other hand, readers who encounter passages they deem to require notes will discover whether notes are provided only by leafing to the end; that inconvenience to some will be offset, I hope, by the avoidance of unwelcome distractions to others. Readers interested in treatments of specific topics or authors should be able to locate them, in notes as well as in chapters, with the aid of the Index.

References to Nietzsche's Works

I have relied primarily on *Sämtliche Werke. Kritische Studienausgabe in 15 Bänden (KSA)*, ed. Giorgio Colli and Mazzino Montinari, 15 vols. (Berlin: de Gruyter, 1980). I have consulted, and often followed, the translations listed below. This list should clarify parenthetical references to Nietzsche's works. In all such references, the numbers refer to sections, not to pages; "P" designates the Preface or Prologue to a work.

A: *The Antichristian.* Translated by Walter Kaufmann as *The Antichrist.* In *PN* (see below).

BT: *The Birth of Tragedy.* SC designates the "Attempt at a Self-Criticism" added by Nietzsche to the second edition of *BT.* Translated by Walter Kaufmann. In *BW* (see below).

BW: *Basic Writings of Nietzsche.* Edited by Walter Kaufmann. New York: The Modern Library, 1968.

D: *Dawn.* Translated by R. J. Hollingdale as *Daybreak.* Cambridge: Cambridge University Press, 1982.

EH: *Ecce Homo.* Translated by Walter Kaufmann. In *BW.*

GM: *The Genealogy of Morals.* Translated by Walter Kaufmann. In *BW.*

HH: *Human, All Too Human.* Translated by R. J. Hollingdale. Cambridge: Cambridge University Press, 1986.

JS: *The Joyful Science.* Translated by Walter Kaufmann as *The Gay Science.* New York: Vintage Books, 1974.

N: *Nachlass.* References are keyed to the *Kritische Gesamtausgabe* (*KGA*), on which *KSA* is based. Most of the passages I refer to are from division VIII of the *KGA*, contained in volumes 12 and 13 of the *KSA*; when I cite from *KGA* division VII (*KSA* 10–11), I add the roman numeral. My references, in the form x[y] (or VII:x[y]), should allow the passages to be found easily in either *KGA* or *KSA.* In relating *KSA-KGA* passages to *WP* (see below), I have relied on the various concordances contained in *KGA.*

PN: *The Portable Nietzsche.* Edited by Walter Kaufmann. New York: Viking Press, 1954.

SE: *Schopenhauer as Educator.* Translated by R. J. Hollingdale. In *UM* (see below).

TI: *Twilight of the Idols.* Translated by Walter Kaufmann. In *PN.*

UM: *Untimely Meditations.* Translated by R. J. Hollingdale. Cambridge: Cambridge University Press, 1983.

WB: *Richard Wagner in Bayreuth.* Translated by R. J. Hollingdale. In *UM.*

WP: *The Will to Power.* Translated by Walter Kaufmann and R. J. Hollingdale. New York: Vintage Books, 1968.

Z: *Thus Spoke Zarathustra.* I provide part and section numbers, and then page and line numbers from volume 4 of the *KSA.* Translated by R. J. Hollingdale. Middlesex: Penguin Books, 1961. Also translated by Walter Kaufmann, in *PN.*

A girl came to see me who is writing a thesis on my novels for a very important university seminar in literary studies. I see that my work serves her perfectly to demonstrate her theories, and this is certainly a positive fact—for the novels or for the theories, I do not know which. From her very detailed talk, I got the idea of a piece of work being seriously pursued, but my books seen through her eyes prove unrecognizable to me. I am sure this Lotaria (that is her name) has read them conscientiously, but I believe she has read them only to find in them what she was already convinced of before reading them.

I tried to say this to her. She retorted, a bit irritated: "Why? Would you want me to read in your books only what you're convinced of?"

I answered her: "That isn't it. I expect readers to read in my books something I didn't know, but I can expect it only from those who expect to read something they didn't know."

Italo Calvino

I
Fish Hooks

1

Into the Labyrinth

Philosophy and Poetry

Within the past one hundred years, Nietzsche has inspired compositions by at least two hundred and nineteen musicians. This may not prove that he is a superior philosopher, but it does establish that he is an exceptional one: he is an exception to the general rule that philosophers do not inspire musicians.

To be exceptional in this literal sense is wholly characteristic of Nietzsche: he is an exception to virtually any rule one might introduce in attempting to say what a philosopher is. He is so exceptional that many philosophers and scholars—especially scholars—have taken him to have excepted his way out of philosophy entirely. In the noted philosophical journal *Saturday Review*, for example, music critic John Runciman has criticized composer Richard Strauss for squandering "time and expensive music paper" on Nietzsche's *Zarathustra*, and urged other composers to avoid "seeking inspiration in the uninspired pages of a mad German pseudo-philosopher" (Thatcher I, 285).

In this book, I attempt to develop a reading of Nietzsche revealing his pages as inspired as well as inspiring, and Nietzsche himself, when he wrote them, as neither mad nor a pseudo-philosopher (I merely mention Nietzsche's denial that he was German, for the sake of contradicting Runciman on every single point). Such a reading requires development because, for better or worse, most of what Nietzsche writes bears little resemblance to what has counted, throughout most of its history, as "philosophy," and even less resemblance to what is currently studied as "philosophy" in most graduate schools.

What "philosopher," besides Nietzsche, could have written,

Suppose truth is a woman [*Weib*]—what then? Are there not grounds for the suspicion that all philosophers, insofar as they were dogmatists, have been very inexpert about women? That the gruesome seriousness, the clumsy obtrusiveness with which they have tended to approach truth have been awkward and inappropriate methods for winning over a wench [*Frauenzimmer*]? What is certain is that she has not allowed herself to be won—and today every kind of dogmatism is left standing distressed and discouraged. (*BGE:P*)

Suppose truth is a woman. . . . Philosophy is the only academic discipline enshrined in our current curricula to be named neither for a well-defined subject matter (rocks, plants, etc.) nor for a product or method (the *logos* of biology and psychology, the *nomos* of astronomy and economics). Philosophy is named, instead, as an affect or emotion whose object is identified only vaguely: philosophy is the love of wisdom. And perhaps, Nietzsche suggests, the truth at the heart of the wisdom philosophers love does not respond to the "gruesome seriousness" and "clumsy obtrusiveness" of premises and conclusions; perhaps a different form of courtship might be more fitting. At the very least, it is safe to say that traditional forms of philosophy stand as "distressed and discouraged" today as they did when Nietzsche wrote. There is even a great deal of talk about the end or death of philosophy: our love for wisdom is doomed to remain unrequited, so why not give it up, and do something else? Something safer, more assured of success—and certainly more lucrative?

Is Nietzsche a philosopher? Is his main work, *Thus Spoke Zarathustra*, philosophical? Even though its spokesman offers only one argument, and that one is invalid? Is Nietzsche a philosopher? By whose standards? And what if the standards are poor ones? Is Nietzsche a philosopher? What's in a name? Nietzsche writes, "Whoever tries to place philosophy 'on a strictly scientific basis' first needs to stand not only philosophy but truth itself *on its head*—the grossest possible violation of decency in relation to two such venerable wenches!" (*GM*,III:24).

Is Nietzsche a philosopher? There is no question that he often calls himself a philosopher, and that he writes both of love and of wisdom. At the same time, much of his work seems to be in service not of love, but of hatred: hatred of priests, hatred of Christianity—and, to be sure, hatred of much of what has passed for philosophy. Is hatred for what one takes to be ignorance, dogmatism, error, cowardice, and pretension the same as love of wisdom?

There is no question that Nietzsche attacks these things and various others besides. I argue, however, that his attacks are in service not of hatred, but rather, precisely, of love, both of wisdom and of life. As a first step, I turn briefly to the attacks themselves, because the tones Nietzsche uses in them are among the sources of the suspicion that he is not a philosopher at all, but rather, perhaps, a demagogue, a prophet, or a lunatic.

What are we to make of Nietzsche's repeated attacks on much of what humanity, especially Western European humanity, has valued most, including philosophy? In his autobiographical *Ecce Homo*, Nietzsche describes his own project as, in part, an "attack on two thousand years of antinature [*Widernatur*] and desecration of humanity [*Menschenschändung*]" (*EH*,IV:4). He also stresses the violence of his attack:

One day there will be attached to my name the memory of something tremendous—a crisis without equal on earth, the most profound collision of conscience, a decision that was conjured up against everything that previously had been believed, demanded, hallowed. I am no man, I am dynamite. (*EH*,XIV:1)

What philosopher besides Nietzsche would describe himself as "dynamite"? Socrates call himself a gadfly—he stings—and a torpedo fish—he shocks. Nietzsche calls himself dynamite—he demolishes. In calling himself dynamite, Walter Kaufmann suggests, Nietzsche may allude to a review of *Beyond Good and Evil* sufficiently appealing to him that he quoted it at some length in a letter. The review reads, in part, "Spiritual explosives, like material ones, can do very useful work; it is not necessary that they be abused for criminal purposes. Yet one does well to label such stuff carefully: 'This is dynamite' " (*BW*:p. 782, n1).

The ambiguity of the term "dynamite," as applied to Nietzsche and his works, is both appropriate and characteristic. When dynamite is used, it is always used to blow something up; but it is often so used precisely in order to clear the way for something else, something intended to be an improvement. Similarly, hammers—mentioned in the subtitle of *Twilight of the Idols,* "How One Philosophizes With a Hammer"—can be used to build, to smash, or, as in *Twilight,* to tap on idols to reveal that they are hollow. Nietzsche, dynamite with a hammer, can therefore write:

I am by far the most terrible human being that has existed so far; this does not preclude the possibility that I shall be the most beneficial. . . . I am the first immoralist: that makes me the *annihilator* [*Vernichter*] par excellence. (*EH*,XIV:2)

"The annihilator par excellence"—sounds like a role for Arnold Schwarzenegger. But Nietzschean annihilation is both less bloody and more devastating than the Schwarzeneggerian variety:

What defines me, what sets me apart from the whole rest of humanity is that I *uncovered* [*entdeckt*] Christian morality. . . . The *uncovering* of Christian morality is an event without parallel, an actual catastrophe. He that is enlightened about that is a *force majeure*, a destiny—he breaks the history of mankind in two. Either one lives before him, or one lives after him. (*EH*,XIV:7–8)

I am necessarily . . . a man of catastrophe [*des Verhängnisses*]. For when truth enters into battle with the lies of millennia, we shall have upheavals, a convulsion of earthquakes, a moving of mountains and valleys, the like of which has never been dreamed of. The concept of politics will have emerged entirely within a war of spirits; all power structures of the old society will have been exploded—all of them are based on lies: there will be wars the like of which have never yet been seen on earth. It is only beginning with me that the earth knows *great politics*. (*EH*,XIV:1)

How will these wars be different from those seen heretofore on earth? Will they be bloodier? Perhaps; but would not those be wars of bodies rather than of spirits? So it seems. Perhaps, then, the wars that would characterize "great politics" are instead to be wars of the sort Nietzsche fights with *Human, All too Human*, of which he writes, retrospectively, "This is war, but war without powder and smoke, without warlike poses, without pathos and strained limbs" (*EH*,VI:1).

Nietzsche's war of spirits, I suggest, is a war not of guns and muscles— a war not for Schwarzeneggers and Stallones—but a war, rather, of words. And, as the passages I have quoted reveal, Nietzsche uses words of war masterfully. Yet words of war are not his only words, nor are they his most important. He has Zarathustra announce,

> With thunder and heavenly fireworks must one speak to slack and sleeping senses. But the voice of beauty speaks softly; it creeps only into the most fully awakened souls. (Z,II:5; 120.2–5)

Nietzsche's words of war are his thunder and fireworks. It is those words for which he is famous, often as demagogue, prophet, or lunatic: "God is dead"; "man is something that must be overcome"; "I teach you the overman"; "I am Europe's first complete nihilist."

Nietzsche's thunder and fireworks have, in at least some ways, functioned as intended: they have been heard and seen. Moreover, they have contributed to the awakening and tensing of many senses, no doubt including those of Nazis and fascists. The holocaust is not a part of the gift Nietzsche thought he was giving mankind—the "greatest gift" humanity has ever been given (*EH*,P:4)—but that is not to deny that it is a part of Nietzsche's legacy. Another part of that legacy, now, should be the knowledge that even the Nietzscheans among us—as opposed to the Nazis and fascists—must avoid the rhetorical excesses of Nietzschean thunder and fireworks: we have seen, as Nietzsche had not, how dangerous they can be.

The violence of much of Nietzsche's rhetoric is one of the features that distinguishes it from most of what generally counts as philosophical speech; there are others. A second is that Nietzsche provides remarkably little in the way of obviously unitary, coherent essays. Instead, he tends to give us aphorisms and poems, and to rely heavily on metaphor and hyperbole. His works appear fragmentary rather than systematic; indeed, he announces, "I mistrust all systematizers and I avoid them. The will to a system is a lack of integrity [*Rechtschaffenheit*]" (*TI*,I:26). Nevertheless, he stresses the deep unity of his own works:

> *That* I still cling to [my earlier ideas] today, that they have become in the meantime more and more firmly attached to one another, indeed entwined and

interlaced with one another, strengthens my joyful assurance that they might have arisen in me from the first not as isolated, capricious, or sporadic things but from a common root, from a *fundamental will* of knowledge, pointing imperiously into the depths, speaking more and more precisely, demanding greater and greater precision. For this alone is fitting for a philosopher. We have no right to *isolated* acts of any kind: we may not make isolated errors or hit upon isolated truths. Rather do our ideas, our values, our yeas and nays and ifs and buts, grow out of us with the necessity with which a tree bears its fruit—related and each with an affinity to each, and evidence of one will, *one* health, *one* soil [*Erdreich*], one sun.—Whether you like them, these fruits of ours?—But what is that to the trees! What is that to *us*, us philosophers! (*GM*,P:2)

Nietzsche tells us that the will to a system is a symptom of corruption, but also that the philosopher's thoughts should develop with "the necessity with which a tree bears fruit." Does he contradict himself? Many have thought that he does so, here and often elsewhere (a standard joke among Nietzsche scholars, funny only by scholarly standards: Pick any statement Nietzsche makes; if you cannot find a passage where he contradicts it, that is because you have not looked hard enough).

Does he contradict himself? Are we ripe for his fruit? A will to system can be quite different from a will to truth, a will to knowledge, or a will to grow. To say that the tree bears its fruit with necessity is not to say that the tree should be systematic, or that it should strive to be systematic. The young Schelling exhibited the "will to a system": presupposing that the world itself must be systematic, he struggled to discover that system. Nietzsche, more deeply philosophical, questions the assumption. Suppose truth is a woman (or a man, or a tree)—what then?

So far, I have suggested at least the following: Nietzsche gives us little by way of deductive argument, but that does not prove that he does not love wisdom or, therefore, that he is not a philosopher; Nietzsche often seeks to demolish, but that is not to say that he never builds; Nietzsche does not strive to be systematic, but that does not mean that he is incoherent. As the passages I have cited should also reveal to any who may not already have known, he is an extraordinarily gifted writer, one who is, at the very least, fascinating as well as provocative, one who leads his readers to curse, but also to laugh, often at the same time. "Laughter I have pronounced holy," Zarathustra announces; "you higher humans, *learn from me* to laugh" (Z,IV:13.20; 368.2–3).

"Philosophers," these days, rarely make us either laugh or curse; more often, I suspect, they lull us to sleep (we lull others, and each other, to sleep) by sifting through the minutiae either of abstruse puzzles or of archaic texts. In making us laugh and curse, as in writing aphorisms and even verses, as in creating characters and stories, Nietzsche seems more poet than philosopher.

The quarrel between philosophy and poetry was already old, Plato tells us, in his time. The quarrel is often portrayed as being between two types of human beings, but it is more accurately seen, I believe, as a struggle within the individual. To the extent that poetry and philosophy are taken to be mutually exclusive, poetry is viewed as an activity purely of creating or inventing (*poiesis*, making), philosophy, as an activity purely of learning (*mathesis*) or seeing (*theorein*). Poets are taken to produce, actively, what had not been at all, philosophers to apprehend, passively, what must always be. This is why philosophers have been taken, by some, to have access to the truth: they are supposed merely to take in what they view, not to alter it by viewing.

This opposition between making and learning—and, therefore, the mutual exclusion of poetry and philosophy—is a false one. As for making, no matter how creative the poet, the poem created is conditioned by the poet's language and experience: the creation is not *ex nihilo*. It may be less apparent that the philosopher's learning cannot be a matter of wholly passive receptivity— I argue below that it cannot be—but even if it were, the receptivity could not go beyond a mute apprehension. As soon as the philosopher begins to speak or to teach, the philosopher begins to make or produce: the philosopher becomes poet.

If the philosopher is not to remain immersed in silent vision—in which case, I suggest, he cannot be distinguished, by himself or by others, from the lunatic—then the philosopher must produce a linguistic account, thereby becoming a poet. But even if this similarity between the activities of poet and philosopher is granted, does there not remain a distinction in terms of what is produced? Philosophers attempt to express truths; does this not distinguish them from poets, who attempt instead to produce works of art, things of beauty? But what is a work of art, and what is beautiful? In a conversation between Jordan Elgrably and novelist Milan Kundera, we find the following exchange:

J. E.: You quote Hermann Broch as having said the novelist's only obligation is the quest for knowledge. Doesn't this somehow suggest that a work of art may, rather than providing aesthetic pleasure, have a quality which is void of a certain beauty?

M. K.: But what is aesthetic pleasure? For myself, it is the surprise I experience before something which hasn't already been said, demonstrated, seen. Why is it that *Madame Bovary* never fails to enchant us? Because even today this novel surprises us. It *unveils* that which we are not in a position to see in our daily lives. We have all met a Madame Bovary in one situation or another, and yet failed to recognize her. Flaubert unmasked the mechanism of sentimentality, of illusions; he showed us the cruelty and the aggressiveness of lyrical sentimentality. This is what I consider the knowledge of the novel. The author unveils a realm of reality that has not yet been revealed. This unveiling causes surprise and the surprise aesthetic pleasure or, in other words, a sensation of beauty. (Elgrably, 5–6)

Can one seek to "unmask the mechanism of illusions," yet have no interest in truth, knowledge, or wisdom? If the novelist's "only obligation is the quest for knowledge," the novelist can be poet *rather than* philosopher? Must not the novelist—the novelist Broch, in any case, and the novelist Kundera—be philosopher *as well as* poet? Some poets may overwhelm us with flights of fantasy, some may seem to teach us nothing; but is there less to be *learned* from Kundera, Proust, or Tolstoy than from, say, Donald Davidson, Michael Dummett, or Bertrand Russell?

I do not mean to suggest that no distinction between philosophy and poetry may or should be drawn; I do mean to suggest that any distinction that would make of every writer *either* a philosopher or a poet is misleading. The best writers, in my judgment—the most interesting, the most illuminating, the most informative, the most aesthetically pleasing—are philosophical poets or poetic philosophers. Nietzsche is among them.

A Path Within the Labyrinth

Among philosophers, Nietzsche writes exceptionally well. He also wrote exceptionally much: a book a year for sixteen years, plus volumes of unpublished notes. In what follows, I make no attempt to treat his writings exhaustively. In the metaphorical terms introduced in my title, and to be developed throughout this study, Nietzsche's text, like any other text, is a labyrinth: there is no single path within it. In the hope of encouraging readers to follow my path, I now provide some of my reasons for following it, and sketch a map charting its course. Like all maps, mine is an abstraction; I hope that readers unfamiliar with some of its terminology will not be dissuaded from following the path it charts. Unless I have simply failed, the path itself should be accessible to philosophical poets as well as to poetic philosophers.

I make no attempt to discuss all of Nietzsche's writings; instead, I move toward, and then concentrate on, a single one of them, *Thus Spoke Zarathustra*. The most powerful reason for this emphasis may well be that *Zarathustra* is, among Nietzsche's works, my favorite (perhaps because it is his most poetic). This is a reason Nietzsche would appreciate, but one hardly sufficient as a justification for a philosophical treatise (poetic or not). I therefore provide a second, more scholarly authorization for my concentration on *Zarathustra*: Nietzsche consistently deems it his most important work. He writes, retrospectively (and, as often, hyperbolically):

Among my writings my *Zarathustra* stands apart [*für sich*]. With it I have given mankind the greatest gift that has ever been made to it so far. This book, with

a voice bridging centuries, is not only the highest book there is, the book that
is truly characterized by the air of the heights—the whole fact of humanity lies
beneath it at a tremendous distance—it is also the *deepest,* born out of the
innermost wealth of truth, an inexhaustible well to which no pail descends
without coming up again filled with gold and goodness. (*EH,P*:4)

This work stands altogether apart. Leaving aside the poets: perhaps nothing
has ever been done from an equal excess of force. My concept of the "Dionysian"
here became a *supreme deed;* measured against that, all the rest of human
activity seems poor and conditioned. (*EH*,IX:6)

The reason Nietzsche gives for deeming *Zarathustra* his most important
book is that it is the one in which the "yes-saying" part of his task is
completed; his later works are all "fish hooks," designed to pull readers out
of the sea of dogmatic opinion and onto the shore from which they may
begin their ascent of Zarathustra's mountain. Nietzsche admits that his fish
hooks caught nothing, but denies that their failure establishes his incompe-
tence as a fisherman; the problem, he insists, is that "there were no fish"
(*EH*,X:1).

If we are to be fish for Nietzsche, if we are to be ripe for his fruit, we must
read and think in ways to which we may not be accustomed. Nietzsche
writes, "thinking wants to be learned like dancing, as a kind of dancing. . . .
One cannot subtract dancing in every form from a noble education—to be
able to dance with one's feet, with concepts, with words . . ." (*TI*,VIII:7).
Such thinking, thinking as dancing, may be alien to many of us, as it is,
according to Nietzsche, to Germans generally. Of Germans, he writes:

I cannot endure this race . . . that has no fingers for nuances—alas, I am a
nuance—[this race] that has no *esprit* in its feet and does not even know how
to walk.—The Germans ultimately have no feet at all, they have only legs.
(*EH*,XIII:4)

My primary concern is with Nietzsche's love of wisdom and of life, his
yes-saying teachings, the teachings spoken with "the voice of beauty," and
spoken to those with "fingers for nuances"; I therefore take my bearings by
the single one of his books that, he tells us, expresses those teachings. My
concern is theoretical, but also practical. To put it one way: few who are
even vaguely sympathetic to Nietzsche would deny his skill as a diagnostician
of modernity—he knows, for the most part, what ails us. At the same time,
many even of those who are powerfully drawn to Nietzsche doubt his skill
as a therapist: he has recognized our malady, but it is not clear that he knows
how to treat it. It is the treatment that concerns me chiefly.

For these various reasons, I take my bearings by *Zarathustra;* but I move
to *Zarathustra* rather than beginning with it. I do so, first, because we cannot
evaluate Nietzsche's prescribed treatment for the illness of modernity if we

are unfamiliar with the disease. In addition, although I take *Zarathustra* to be Nietzsche's most intriguing work, I also recognize it as his least accessible (chiefly because it is his most poetic); my initial considerations of other texts are intended to facilitate the central exploration. In moving toward *Zarathustra* as in moving within it, I attempt to remain sensitive to the tension between philosophy and poetry, between learning and making. In presenting Nietzsche as at once poet and philosopher, I attempt to avoid two influential ways of reading him. Until the 1960's, Nietzsche was generally read as having an unambiguously determinable teaching accessible to scholars practiced in reading the likes of Aristotle and Kant; the Nietzsche that emerged was most often an advocate of power politics, devoted to producing supermen who would rule the world. Since the early 1970's, this reading—which I now christen with the two names "Germanic" and "metaphysical" (it might also be called "modern," "positivistic," "objectivistic," "realistic," or "angelic")—has been countered, initially in France, by an impressive array of thinkers who have seen Nietzsche's works as undermining the very possibility of the communication, indeed even of the possession, of unambiguously determinable teachings. The Nietzsche that emerges from these readings—to which I henceforth refer as "postmetaphysical" and "French" (options would include "postmodern," "relativistic," "idealistic," and "diabolical")—is an advocate not of totalitarian cosmos but rather, in extreme cases, of anarchic chaos.

In reading Nietzsche—as, I think, in reading anything else—I reject what I have dubbed the Germanic or metaphysical position, but also the most extreme version of the French or postmetaphysical alternative. I want to have feet, but I don't want to trade in my legs in order to get them.

In terms elaborated in Chapter Two, Nietzsche is viewed by my "metaphysicians" as a religious nihilist seeking to win the faith of others, and by my "postmetaphysicians" as a radical nihilist concerned only with destruction; I argue that Nietzsche's attempt to complete nihilism leads him away from both of these positions. In Chapter Three, I introduce the Dionysian perspective from which Nietzsche seeks to affirm the human condition as it is; I oppose this perspective both to the "metaphysical" Apollinian and Socratic positions, which seek to perfect the human condition, and to the "postmetaphysical" Silenian standpoint, from which human life appears as not worth living. The conflict among positions or standpoints is considered more closely in Chapter Four, wherein I attribute to Nietzsche a perspectivism that avoids both the metaphysical extreme of objectivism or positivism—the insistence that we make epistemic progress by relying on facts while avoiding interpretations—and the postmetaphysical alternative of relativism or idealism—the claim that there are no facts, there are only interpretations. Chapters Five through Seven develop an account of the human being who registers facts and hazards interpretations, who has a perspective—a self that is neither a metaphysical, substantial subject nor a postmetaphysical nullity. Chapters Eight and Nine, finally, sketch the ethical and political implications of the position that has developed: my Nietzsche rejects political totalization and moral absolutes, but also the antipolitical chaos of unbridled egotism.

This sketch may suggest that my Nietzsche is a moderate, attempting again and again to steer between extremes; this suggestion is misleading. As I argue explicitly in my discussion of nihilism, and implicitly thereafter, Nietzsche's logic is not one of mediation, either in the quasi-mathematical Aristotelian sense of avoiding extremes, or in the dialectical Hegelian sense of preserving distinctions while overcoming contradictions. To anticipate: the position I term "metaphysical," and which Nietzsche often characterizes as "Christian-moral," requires that one accept a premise or set of premises (e.g., "God is good," "the world has a goal") as true; the position I term "postmetaphysical" emerges when that premise or set of premises is deemed false. Nietzsche argues that the premises in question are neither true nor false, but rather meaningless and/or irrelevant. In a relatively early passage, Nietzsche applies this logic to the opposition between (metaphysical) optimism and (postmetaphysical) pessimism:

> *Discredited words.*—Away with the tediously abused words "optimism" and "pessimism"! For the inducement for using them weakens from day to day: only jabberers [*die Schwätzer*] continue to find them unavoidably necessary. For why in all the world would anyone want to be an optimist if he did not have to defend a God who *must* have created the best of worlds if he himself is to be good and perfect? And what thinker still finds the hypothesis of God necessary?
>
> But there is also lacking every inducement for a confession of pessimistic faith if one has no interest in annoying God's advocates, the theologians or the theologizing philosophers, by forcefully presenting the counterposition: that evil rules, that pain is greater than pleasure, that the world is poorly made [*ein Machwerk*], the appearance of an evil will to life? But who still cares now about the theologians—except for the theologians?
>
> Aside from all theology and the fight against it, it is clear that the world is not good and not evil, not the best or the worst, and that these concepts "good" and "evil" have meaning only in relation to human beings, and indeed perhaps even then are not used justifiably when they are used as they generally are. In any case, we must cease viewing the world with an eye either to abuse or to extol it. (*HH*,I:28)

The Risk of Interpretation

To conclude this introductory chapter I return, briefly, to the problem of reading Nietzsche's philosophical poetry or poetic philosophy. The second chapter of *Zarathustra*'s Part III, "Of the Vision and the Riddle," describes not only the vision and riddle mentioned in its title, but also the audience to whom Zarathustra relates them. Zarathustra will not present his riddles to just anyone. Neither will Nietzsche present his teachings to just anyone, although his books are there for all to read (*Zarathustra* is subtitled "A Book For Everyone and No One"). Instead, he writes in *Ecce Homo*, "In the end, I could not say better to whom alone I am speaking at bottom than Zarathustra said it: to whom alone will he relate his riddle?" (*EH*,III:3). Zarathustra describes his—and Nietzsche's—ideal audience as follows:

> To you, the bold searchers, researchers, and whoever embarks with cunning sails on terrible seas—
> to you, drunk with riddles, glad of the twilight, whose souls flutes lure astray to every whirlpool [*Irr-Schlund*],
> because you do not want to grope along a thread with cowardly hand; and where you can guess [*errathen*], you hate to *deduce* [*erschliessen*]—
> to you alone will I tell the riddle that I saw—the vision of the loneliest. (Z,III:2.1; 197.17–25).

Drunk with riddles, not soberly tackling problems; glad of twilight, not longing for Platonic sunlight; lured by flutes rather than harboring Platonic suspicions of music; not groping, with Theseus, along threads of deductions, but rather guessing and probing, with Dionysus—so must we be and so must we proceed, according to Nietzsche, if we are to understand him; so must we be if we are to hear the "voice of beauty."

Those who guess and probe rather than deduce and prove must give up what Nietzsche calls the "venerable philosopher's abstinence," the "intellectual stoicism" that leads its possessor "to halt before the factual, the *factum brutum.*" Instead of attempting to halt before the fact, we must risk interpretation, and with it "forcing, adjusting, abbreviating, omitting, padding, inventing, falsifying, and whatever else is of the essence of interpreting" (*GM*,III:24). In this study, I risk an interpretation. For reasons introduced above and elaborated below, I take the bearings for my interpretation by locating *Zarathustra* centrally within it. No doubt, quite different readings of Nietzsche emerge for those who take their bearings from other works. Heidegger and Müller-Lauter, among others, have concentrated on the unpublished notes from the late 1880's, and have produced interpretations of Nietzsche that are both powerful and intriguing, but that are not tenable, I argue, if judged in terms of the teachings that emerge from the careful reading of *Zarathustra*. The reading I develop is not the only possible reading but, I argue, it is better than many others; I do so by providing reasons for selecting the works and passages I have selected, and for interpreting those works and passages as I do. This practice is in full accordance with what I take to be a good Nietzschean principle, one I attempt to explain and defend in what follows: there is no perfect interpretation of anything as complex as

Nietzsche's thought, or of any of his works, but some interpretations are better than others.

There is no one path within any labyrinth. In addition, as my title's preposition suggests, there is no path *through* Nietzsche's labyrinth, there are only paths *within* Nietzsche's labyrinth. The reason for this is that Nietzsche's labyrinth is our labyrinth, the labyrinth of the human condition; to affirm human life is to value living within this labyrinth, rather than to attempt to escape from it. This is the affirmation that completes nihilism, surpassing both the religious nihilist's desperate conviction that there must be a way out, and the radical nihilist's vilification of a labyrinth from which there is no exit.

There are many paths within any labyrinth. Some paths may be more interesting than others, more ambitious, more informative, more challenging, even more dangerous. Following the path I here follow, I have, it seems to me, learned about the labyrinth that is *Zarathustra*, the labyrinth that is Nietzsche, and the labyrinth that is life. I hope that others may learn by exploring my path as they move, along their own paths, through this book.

2

Nihilism

In recent centuries, the term "nihilism" has been used as a synonym for idealism, but also for materialism; for Christianity, but also for atheism; for solipsism, but also for pantheism; and, for good measure, for the likes of pessimism and skepticism. There is no coherent history of its various uses, largely because its users have often been unaware of their predecessors. Turgenev claimed credit for coining the term in 1861, and his claim has been accepted by many. Other scholars, however, have determined that he was well over a century too late.

I make no attempt to reconstruct the history of how the term "nihilism" has been used, because that history is of negligible importance both for Nietzsche and for philosophy. What makes the term "nihilism" philosophically vital is not its history, but rather its use by Nietzsche. Nihilism becomes philosophically vital when it is presented not as one position among many, a doctrine some may chance to espouse, but rather as the necessary consequence of the Western philosophical tradition. In his own time and for the two centuries to follow, Nietzsche tells us, thoughtful human beings must of necessity be nihilists—and the thoughtless as well, although they are less likely to know it.

What then is this "nihilism" Nietzsche presents as unavoidable? Readers familiar only with works Nietzsche published or prepared for publication might recall no references to it at all. *Beyond Good and Evil* (1886) is the first published work in which it even appears, and while it is found in most of the later works Nietzsche edited for publication (all save the two on Wagner), it is central to none. Nevertheless, various posthumously published outlines—some published only within the last twenty years—reveal that it was to have been a focal point of *The Will to Power*. Appropriately, the term is prominent in the version of *The Will to Power* that became standard. That version not only contains various definitions of "nihilism" per se, it also introduces bewilderingly many specific types of nihilism. "Active" and "passive" nihilism are paired, as are "theoretical" and "practical" nihilism, and "complete" and "incomplete" nihilism. Other forms appear in relative isolation, including "authentic" nihilism, "contagious" nihilism, "ecstatic" nihilism, the "most extreme" nihilism, "first" nihilism, "final" nihilism, "fundamental" nihilism, "genuine" nihilism, "philosophical" nihilism, "radical" nihilism, "religious" nihilism, "tired" nihilism, and "suicidal" nihilism.

Commentators have further complicated matters: Heidegger has added "classical" nihilism as though it were a Nietzschean term, Deleuze "reactive" nihilism, and Rosen the opposition, to which he refers as "Nietzsche's fundamental distinction," between "base" and "noble" nihilism.

Nihilism, according to Nietzsche, is our heritage, our fate. If we grant, provisionally, that he may be right about that, then it certainly makes sense to ask: which nihilism? And whichever it is, terminologically, what is it, what does it mean? Is it a blessing, or a curse? Is it a peak we have ascended, or an abyss into which we have plunged? *The Will to Power* does not answer these questions, for it does not systematically interrelate the various forms of nihilism (nor do the works of Heidegger or Deleuze, or, as far as I know, of other commentators); indeed, the standard version obscures Nietzsche's thought by mangling several important texts. Nevertheless, comprehension of Nietzschean nihilism requires some such interrelation. I here attempt to clarify Nietzsche's notion of nihilism by relating his various forms to three fundamental levels that I, adapting Nietzschean terms, name "religious," "radical," and "complete" nihilism. I suggest that virtually all other forms Nietzsche identifies fall on what I term the level of "radical" nihilism; the distinctions among them are less important, it seems to me, than those among the levels themselves. That this is the case I indicate by introducing some questions my distinction among levels suggests, questions whose answers I take to be of central importance for the comprehension and evaluation of Nietzsche's affirmative teachings. I seek answers for the questions in the following chapters of this book.

Transformations of Nihilism

I take as my starting point Nietzsche's assertion that the emergence of nihilism as a "psychological state" is bound up with the failure of the attempt to endow the world with value by attributing to it an ultimate "purpose," "unity," or "truth" (*N*:11[99] / *WP*:12). This failure leads to nihilism as "the radical rejection of value, meaning, and desirability" (*N*:2[127] / *WP*:1). These descriptions suggest that nihilism has its origin in a negation, i.e., in the failure of an attempt, or in the rejection of a purported value. Yet neither of these negations can be the first step towards nihilism, because neither is a first step at all. The failure of an attempt presupposes that it has been made, and any rejection presupposes either prior acceptance or, at least, prior awareness of a question.

I therefore suggest that the first step towards nihilism—a step that, in Nietzsche's view, leads historically to the second—is the step taken with the judgment that the existence of our world of becoming would be justified only through a *purpose* that guides it, through an "infinitely valuable" *unity* that underlies it, or through another world, a "true world" or "world of *being*" that is accessible through it (*N:*11[99] / *WP:*12). This step, like the step to rejection, is a negation in that it contains, at least implicitly, the judgment that our "world of becoming" as it presents itself, in isolation from such purpose, unity, or truth, "ought not to exist" (*N:*9[60] / *WP:*585). The step presupposes the judgment that without some such source of worth, which cannot be contained within the flux of a "world of becoming," that world—our world—would be worthless.

Is the person who has taken this first step—who has judged that the world requires justification—a nihilist? Certainly not an avowed one: this person will use the appellation "nihilist," if at all, only for others. Nevertheless, this person is "nihilistic" in a way that one who simply accepts the world of becoming is not. From the Nietzschean perspective, those who posit the extraneous source of value are nihilists in that (1) they judge of our world that it ought not to be (on its own), and (2) they believe in a world that is, despite their beliefs to the contrary, "fabricated solely from psychological needs," a world to which we have "absolutely no right" (*N:*11[99] / *WP:*12). To be sure, they are not aware that the world of their belief is a mere fabrication; that is why they will deny being nihilists. For this reason, if it is appropriate to term them "nihilists" at all, an essential qualification must be added: their nihilism is unconscious. Or, to adopt a more Nietzschean term, they are religious nihilists: their affirmation of another world or source of value is a consequence of their denial of our world as bearer of its own value.

Nihilism becomes conscious—avowed or, in a Nietzschean term, "radical"—with a second step, the step taken with the judgment that the sources of value are absent, that the three categories of value (purpose, unity, and truth) remain uninstantiated. "Radical nihilism," in Nietzsche's explicit definition, is

> the conviction of an absolute untenability of existence when it is a matter of the highest values that one recognizes; plus the insight that we have not the slightest right to posit a being or an in-itself of things that would be 'divine' or incarnate morality. (*N:*10[192] / *WP:*3)

These "highest values" themselves are not denied by the radical nihilist; the problem is that nothing in our world—the only world to which we have "the slightest right"—corresponds to them.

If I am not mistaken, this is the only passage in which Nietzsche uses the term "radical nihilism." Nevertheless, in various passages where he uses the term "nihilism" without a qualifying adjective, I take him to be speaking of that same general position, i.e., the position one reaches when "all one has left are the values that pass judgment [*die richtenden Werte*]—and nothing more" (*N:*9[107] / *WP:*37). The radical nihilist *retains* "belief in the rational categories," belief that the world could have value only if it either had a purpose, exhibited an "infinitely valuable" unity, or were related to another, "true" world of "being" (N:11[99] / WP:12). Radical nihilists continue to judge the world as a whole in terms of the traditional categories of value; they are then horrified by the verdict they are forced to draw, a verdict of absolute condemnation. In accepting that verdict, they become avowed nihilists.

If this nihilism were truly "radical," one would expect it to be the final form of nihilism; one would expect it to go to the root of nihilism. But if it were the final form, why should Nietzsche present it as a position of "conviction" that the supposed "highest values" are not present in our world (N:10[192] / WP:3), rather than, say, of "recognition" or "insight"—terms he often uses when speaking of other matters? Perhaps Nietzsche's use of "conviction" here is merely accidental, or perhaps Nietzsche intends no pejorative overtones; but I see few reasons to think so, and many reasons to think not. Passages already introduced reveal that he characterizes this position not only as "conviction," but also as "belief." Examination of other relevant texts reveals that he is quite consistent in describing the nihilism of those who "retain the values that pass judgment" in such terms (my emphases throughout): nihilism is "*belief* in valuelessness" (N:7[8] / WP:8); "the *belief* in the absolute immorality of nature, its aimlessness and meaninglessness" (N:5[71] / WP:55); "*belief* in absolute worthlessness, i. e., meaninglessness" (N:7[54] / WP:617); "the penetrating *feeling of*—'nothingness' " (N:11[228] / WP:1020). It is the position of one "who *judges* of the world as it is that it ought not to be, and of the world as it ought to be that it does not exist" (N:9[60] / WP:585).

All these terms I have emphasized are, traditionally, epistemologically loaded ones: all indicate conviction as opposed to knowledge, opinion as opposed to truth. Moreover, the belief is not necessary:

> The "meaninglessness of events": belief in this is the consequence of an insight into the falsity of previous interpretations, generalization of discouragement and weakness—not a necessary belief.
> The immodesty of man: to deny meaning where he sees none. (N:2[109] / WP:599)

Here, Nietzsche presents the radical nihilist's position as having a solid epistemological basis—"an insight into the falsity of previous interpretations"—but stops short of asserting that there can be "insight" into the "truth" of the position itself. If we could have insight into its truth, it would qualify, perhaps, as a "necessary belief." But it does not; those who hold it are described not as perspicuous, but rather as "immodest."

The nihilist's immodesty is a form both of sickness—"what is pathological [in the nihilist] is the monstrous [*ungeheure*] generalization, the conclusion that there is no meaning at all" (*N:9[35] / WP:*13)—and of inconsistency:

> A nihilist is a man who judges of the world as it is that it ought not to be, and of the world as it ought to be that it does not exist. According to this view, our existence (action, suffering, willing, feeling) has no meaning: the pathos of "in vain" is the nihilists' pathos—at the same time, as pathos, an inconsistency on the part of the nihilists. (*N:9[60] / WP:*585)

For this nihilist, all pathos is "in vain," "has no meaning," so the nihilist's own pathos is no more significant than any other pathos, including that of religious conviction.

In addition to being immodest and inconsistent, radical nihilists of one sort are also "illogical": active nihilists do not merely believe that all values are crumbling, they also attempt to hasten their destruction. "That is, if you will, illogical: but the nihilist"—in my terms, the radical nihilist—"does not believe in the necessity of being logical" (*N:*11[123] / *WP:*24; cf. *N:*9[35] / *WP:*22–23).

The inclusion of active nihilism as a form of radical nihilism is, I suspect, the feature of my typology most likely to raise questions. This placement is initially disturbing in that "active" and "passive" are the forms of nihilism Nietzsche himself most explicitly opposes to one another. That suggests that he sees this distinction as the primary one, so that one should take one's typological bearings by it, rather than by anything like my three levels.

My strongest reason for subordinating both active and passive nihilism to what I call radical nihilism is that both exhibit the latter's distinctive feature, i.e., pessimism. Religious nihilists are not pessimistic, for their faith in some ultimate unity, purpose, or being guarantees for them that all must be for the best. Nor are complete nihilists pessimistic; the "experimental philosophy" they will practice does not intend to "halt at a no, a negation, a will to negation. It wants rather to cross over to the opposite of this—to a Dionysian affirmation of the world as it is" (*N:*16[32] / *WP:*1041).

If pessimism is characteristic of the genus "radical nihilism," then not only active and passive nihilism, but also what Nietzsche calls "genuine nihilism" are included among its species. In a note entitled "Overall insight," Nietzsche asserts, "It could be the sign of a crucial and most essential growth, of the transition to new conditions of existence, that the most extreme form of pessimism, genuine nihilism, would come into the world" (*N:*10[22] / *WP:*112). It could be a sign of growth, but it need not be: nihilism is ambiguous, for it can be a sign either of "increased power of spirit"—"*active nihilism*"—or of "weakness," of "decline and recession of the power of spirit"—"*passive nihilism.*" Nihilism can be a sign of strength: the force of spirit can have grown so strong that previous goals ("convictions," articles of faith) have become incommensurate. . . .

On the other hand, a sign of strength that is insufficient for the productive positing of a new goal, a why, a belief for itself.

It attains its maximum of relative force as a violent force of destruction: as active nihilism. Its opposite would be tired nihilism, which no longer attacks: its most famous form, Buddhism: as passive nihilism.

. . .the force of spirit can be tired out, *exhausted,* so that *previous* goals and values are inappropriate and can no longer arouse faith. (N:9[35] / WP:22,23)

Active nihilism, as a form of "radical nihilism" and a force only of destruction, can represent a maximum only of relative strength; the force it can exert is limited by the strength of what is present for it to destroy. Active nihilists cannot take the step from destruction to creation.

The immediate continuation of the passage I have been discussing is separated from it in *The Will to Power* (there, it is found in 13, whereas what precedes it is in 23). When it is put in place, it offers strong support for my contention that active nihilism remains on the intermediate level, for after having presented nihilism as "ambiguous"—as either active or passive—Nietzsche turns to the species of nihilism that contains these two subspecies, describing it as "a pathological transitional stage" (N:9[35] / WP:13).

The various passages I have cited, taken in conjunction, indicate that radical nihilists, whether active or passive, possess belief rather than knowledge, are governed by feeling rather than by rationality, and rely on judgment rather than insight; they are also immodest, inconsistent, and illogical. Perhaps, of course, there is nothing wrong with any of that, at least in Nietzsche's view. After all, his writings contain various polemics against logic and rationality and their demands for consistency, and against the traditional philosophical view that "passion" is inferior to "reason." Perhaps the terms I have been emphasizing are pejorative only in the view of the philosophical tradition, a tradition Nietzsche emphatically rejects. Perhaps, but I think not, and for a variety of reasons. I briefly present three of them:

(1) N:2[109] / WP:599, quoted above, characterizes the position taken by the radical nihilist as "a generalization of discouragement and weakness"; Nietzsche would be the last to advocate acceptance of such a generalization.

(2) Nietzsche objects to what he takes to be the Christian project of extirpation of "feeling"; but he objects equally strenuously to the rule of feeling (N:11[353] / WP:928; N:9[139] / WP:933; N:10[2] / WP:1021).

(3) In other passages, Nietzsche uses the term "logic" positively rather than negatively, precisely when speaking of nihilism; but the nihilism he is then speaking of is not what I have characterized as radical nihilism, and, I would say, he is not speaking in those passages as a radical nihilist. Consider

the following: nihilism is "the logic of our great values and ideals, thought through to its end" (N:11[411] / WP:P), "the logic of decadence" (N:14[86] / WP:43; see also N:9[126–7] / WP:10); nihilism means "that the highest values devalue themselves" (N:9[35] / WP:2); "it is our previous values themselves that draw their final conclusion in [nihilism]" (N:11[411] / WP:P). The assertion that the highest values devalue themselves is particularly suggestive. The nihilism that follows recognition of that devaluation cannot be radical nihilism, because the radical nihilist continues to accept the value of the values.

All of this suggests that radical nihilism remains "something to be overcome." The questions arise: by whom, and how? A passage already introduced provides a hint concerning the first. What I have been calling radical nihilism results when "all one has left are the values that pass judgment." This suggests that one for whom those values have "devalued themselves" must be left with nothing at all. Etymologically, it would certainly make sense to call such a person a "nihilist." In addition, Nietzsche suggests that one who is left with nothing in this manner has gained rather than lost. In denying that the world requires "purpose," "unity," or "truth" of the sort posited by religious nihilists and despaired of by radical nihilists, one may regain the world of becoming in its original innocence:

> one cannot judge, measure, compare, or even deny the whole! Why not?—For five reasons, all accessible even to modest intellects; for example, because there is nothing besides the whole [weil es nichts gibt ausser dem Ganzen]. . . . And, once again, this is a tremendous restorative, for herein lies the innocence of all existence. (N:15[30] / WP:765; cf., TI,VI:8)

The Nietzschean term that suggests itself for the resulting position is "complete [vollendeter] nihilism," but this term must be used with care. I take it from Nietzsche's description of himself as "Europe's first complete nihilist, who, however, has himself already lived nihilism through to its end, within himself—who has it behind him, beneath him, outside of him" (N:11[411] / WP:P). The wording of this passage indicates that Nietzsche, although Europe's first complete nihilist, is no longer a nihilist. I will nevertheless characterize this position as "complete nihilism" in the sense of completed nihilism, nihilism that has been lived through entirely, "the logic of our great values and ideals, thought through to its end" (N:11[411] / WP:P).

My use of the term receives some justification from Nietzsche's claim of having brought nihilism to its end, albeit only within himself; its advent within the world at large, he tells us, is to dominate "the history of the next two centuries." Following those two centuries, "in some future or other," there will be a countermovement, a transvaluation, that will "absolve [ablö-

sen] this complete nihilism" (*N*:11[411] / *WP:P*). If Nietzsche cannot accomplish this transvaluation, he can at least foresee it, and thereby, within himself, bring nihilism to its end. But, again, he can be aware of doing so, he can be aware that the end is end, only if he is beyond the end, only if he sees that what follows the end is no longer nihilism. One is a complete nihilist only when one has completed nihilism, thereby ceasing to be a nihilist. And indeed, in the continuation of the passage defining nihilism as the condition of one who has left only "the values that pass judgment—nothing else," Nietzsche describes the "problem of strength and weakness" in terms that clearly place the strongest beyond the so-defined nihilism:

(1) the weak collapse
(2) the stronger destroy what does not collapse;
(3) the strongest overcome the values that pass judgment. (*N*:9[107] / *WP*:37)

The religious nihilist, unlike the radical nihilist, denies being a nihilist; what about the complete nihilist? Certainly, the latter acknowledges that our world does not correspond to the traditional "highest values," and that we "have no right" to any other world; but this acknowledgment is paired with the denial that any other world "ought to be," and that our "world of becoming" ought not to be. For the complete nihilist, denigrating the world for its lack of purpose is as senseless as denigrating a philosophical treatise for its lack of plot, a symphony for its lack of text, or a painting for representing, rather than containing, motion or depth. In non-Nietzschean terms: the complete nihilist considers nihilism itself to be the result of a category mistake. The complete nihilist thus returns to a position abandoned with the step to religious nihilism: the complete nihilist "deifies becoming and the apparent world as the only world, and calls them good" (*N*:9[60] / *WP*:585).

Like the religious nihilist, then, the complete nihilist will deny being a nihilist; according to Nietzsche, the denial of the former is mistaken— "*Nihilist und Christ* ['nihilist' and 'Christian'] rhyme, and not only rhyme" (*A*:58)—whereas that of the latter is not: the "complete nihilist" is an antinihilist (see *GM*,II:24). "Complete nihilism" merely appears nihilistic, from other—lower—perspectives, in that it insists on the valuelessness of the highest values. But despite this externality of the appellation, "complete nihilism" remains intrinsically related to nihilism, as does what I have called "religious nihilism". Whereas "religious nihilism" is the immediate and necessary predecessor of "radical nihilism," "complete nihilism" is its logical result, albeit not necessarily its historical one (the human race may deteriorate to what Zarathustra calls the "last human"). All three positions are "nihilistic" in important senses, but only those holding the second acknowledge their nihilism.

Completing Nihilism

To the extent that my typology of Nietzschean nihilism is plausible, it may raise more questions than it answers. I introduce the questions I take to be the most important.

My first question concerns the step from radical to complete nihilism. I have presented this step as a logical one, not only in that Nietzsche asserts that it is a "logical" result, but also in that it is accomplished through thought alone. It is taken when one concludes that either the affirmation or the denial of the proposition that the whole is purposive or meaningful yields what Hegel calls an "infinite judgment". Our world is not among the subjects of which the likes of "purpose" and "meaning" can be correctly predicated, either positively or negatively; the proposition "the world has no purpose" is no more informative than, to choose a Hegelian example, "spirit is not red."

Nietzsche, too, speaks of a "logic" of the devaluation of the highest values. But he does not present the step from radical to complete nihilism simply as an intellectual one, one that is made wholly on the basis of thought or of logical insight. For Nietzsche, the step requires strength, not mere logic: we remain in the "intermediate period of nihilism"—the period of radical nihilism—until there is present "the strength to reverse values and to deify becoming and the apparent world as the only world, and to call them good" (N:9[60] / WP:585; cf. N:9[107] / WP:37; N:11[150] / WP:56). The question is, why should the step require strength? I begin to answer this question in the following chapter, which treats *The Birth of Tragedy*. I develop the answer further in Chapters Five and Six.

My second question concerns the logic and rationality Nietzsche seems both to accept and to condemn. Both are rejected by the radical nihilist, who "does not believe in the necessity of being logical" (N:11[123] / WP:24). Nevertheless, nihilism itself is "the logic of our great values and ideals, thought through to its end" (N:11[411] / WP:P). These passages, taken in conjunction, suggest that Nietzsche's polemics against logic and rationality may be addressed from the standpoint of radical nihilism, against the standpoint of religious nihilism, where "logic" and "rationality" are used to shore up arguments for either the necessity or the accessibility of a purpose or unity for a world, or for a relation between it and a "true" world of "being." Nietzsche himself relies on something he calls "logic" in asserting the necessity of the advent of nihilism. The question then becomes: does Nietzsche develop such a logic? In Chapter Four, "Genealogies," I argue that he does.

My third question arises from the fact that, in my analysis, the entire development to and through nihilism revolves around the question of the relevance of the "categories of value" to the world of becoming as a whole. On the levels of religious and of radical nihilism, the assumption is made that any part can be meaningful or have a purpose only if the whole is meaningful or purposive. But on both those levels, it is also assumed that the world requires justification. The complete nihilist, on the other hand, deems the question of the justification of the world senseless. To put the matter one way: justification is always in terms of a beyond, there can be no beyond for the whole, and, for Nietzsche, becoming is the whole.

What, then, is to be said about the parts? If the question of justification or purpose or meaning is irrelevant to the whole, does it follow that it is irrelevant to the parts? If I acknowledge that it makes no sense to ask about the purpose or meaning of the world, must I also hold that it makes no sense to ask about the purpose or meaning of, let us say, the fact that I am pursuing philosophy rather than herpetology? The Doctor in Camus's *The Plague* certainly denies that there is meaning or purpose to the world as a whole. He also realizes that he cannot save all little children from suffering; but he proposes to save some from suffering. Does the denial of purpose or meaning to the whole make that position ethically indistinguishable from that of one who, while unable to torture all little children, vows to torture all that he can?

Differently stated, is it not the case that, in the words of Ivan Karamazov, "If God is dead, then all is permitted," or, in Nietzsche's own words, "Everything is false! Everything is permitted!" (*N*,VII:25[505] / *WP*:602; cf. *N*,VII:25[304], *N*:26[25], *N*:31[51], *N*:32[8(34)])? My answer—introduced in the chapter devoted to *Zarathustra,* and developed in those that come thereafter—is that everything is indeed permitted, but that universal permissibility does not make ethical reflection impossible or trivial. On the contrary, it makes such reflection all the more pressing. Simply put: to say that everything is permitted is to say, at least, that there is no one—better, no One—around to forbid or prohibit anything. It is not to say that we cannot make distinctions, that all acts are equally admirable, or honorable, or desirable. If we take our ethical bearings by what is permitted and what is forbidden, we may pay little attention to what is noble. Likewise, even if everything is permitted, that does not mean that all answers to the question, "What should I do," are equally good. Instead, it makes the question more complicated, more difficult, and more interesting.

As I attempt to decide what I am to do, how I am to live my life, it makes little difference whether "everything is permitted" or not. If some ways of living were prohibited, I would still have to decide which of the remaining ways to adopt as my own. If no ways are prohibited, the question becomes the more important—even if all ways are somehow open, I must still decide which I am to follow.

Moreover, just as acceptance of a universal moral code—denial that "everything is permitted"—does not entail decent or admirable behavior, neither does the denial of such codes entail indecent of despicable behavior. We have all, I suspect, encountered moral absolutists who, while adhering strictly to their accepted laws, allow themselves extraordinary latitude with respect to acts not specifically covered by the codes. Appropriately, Nietzsche insists explicitly that just as the identification of prohibitions does not guarantee admirable behavior, the denial of prohibitions does not preclude it:

> I deny morality as I deny alchemy, that is, I deny their premises: but I do *not* deny that there have been alchemists who believed in these premises and acted in accordance with them.—I also deny immorality: *not* that countless people *feel* themselves to be immoral, but that there is any *true* reason so to feel. It goes without saying that I do not deny—unless I am a fool—that many actions called immoral ought to be avoided and resisted, or that many called moral ought to be done and encouraged—but I think the one should be encouraged and the other avoided *for other reasons than hitherto.* (D:103)

This discussion of morality and permissibility points back toward my first question. If some things are not permitted, then avoidance of those things—called "morality"—may be based in fear of the consequences of transgression. If everything is permitted, then doing what nobility requires—which Nietzsche refuses to call "morality"—cannot be a matter of such fear. It may instead be a matter of strength. The problem of strength and weakness, introduced above, "constitutes the tragic age" (N:9[107] / WP:37). The problem therefore leads us to *The Birth of Tragedy.*

3
Tragedy

It is an eternal phenomenon: the insatiable [*gierige*] will always finds a way, by means of an illusion spread over things, to detain [*festzuhalten*] its creatures in life and to compel them to live on. One is chained by the Socratic joy of knowing and the delusion of being able thereby to heal the eternal wound of existence; another is ensnared by art's seductive veil of beauty fluttering before his eyes; yet another by the metaphysical consolation that beneath the whirl of appearances eternal life flows on indestructibly—to say nothing of the more common and almost more forceful illusions the will has at hand at every moment. (*BT*:18)

Thus writes Nietzsche in the 1872 version of *The Birth of Tragedy*. By 1886, when he appends an "Attempt at a Self-Criticism" to the book's second edition, he has concluded that the "insatiable will" is an unfortunate holdover from Schopenhauer's metaphysics (*BT*,SC:6), and that "metaphysical consolations," which earlier he had praised, should be "sent to the devil" along with metaphysics itself (*BT*,SC:7), Socrates's "delusion," and "art's seductive veil." Despite these reservations, however, the later Nietzsche continues to endorse *The Birth of Tragedy*'s attempt "to view science through the lenses [*unter der Optik*] of the artist, and art through those of life" (*BT*,SC:2), and to raise the yet more difficult question, "viewed through the lenses of life, what is the significance of morality?" (*BT*,SC:4).

Because my central concern is with *Zarathustra*, I make no attempt, as I examine *The Birth of Tragedy*, to remove the lenses provided by Nietzsche's later works. On the contrary, I approach it explicitly through the "Attempt at a Self-Criticism." In so doing, I attempt to excise the elements of Wagnerian romanticism and Schopenhauerian pessimism pervasive in the 1872 text but disavowed by the Nietzsche of 1886 (*BT*,SC:6); I seek thereby to expose some of the features Nietzsche's mature affirmation will have to avoid, and some it will have to exhibit.

The Tragic Disposition

When he first published *The Birth of Tragedy*, Nietzsche was known (to those who knew of him at all) as a classical philologist. His academic colleagues expected from his first book an erudite treatise, full of scholarly footnotes, on the development of a literary genre. That is not what they found: for Nietzsche, tragedy is not primarily a literary genre, and the question of its birth not an antiquarian issue.

That tragedy is not simply a form of drama is indicated by a question early in the "Self-Criticism":

> The most successful [*wohlgerathenste*], most beautiful, most envied type of humanity to date, those most apt to seduce us to life, the Greeks—what then? They of all people should have found tragedy necessary [*hatten die Tragödie nötig*]? Even more—art [*Mehr noch—die Kunst*]? What was Greek art for [*Wozu—griechische Kunst*]? (*BT*,SC:1)

The Greeks required not only tragedy, Nietzsche tells us, but also art. This suggests that some form of tragedy is independent from art; in *Richard Wagner in Bayreuth* (1876), Nietzsche names this form the tragic disposition [*Gesinnung*]:

> if humanity itself must someday die out—and who can doubt that!—it has as its highest task for all coming ages the goal of maturing, individually and as a whole, in such a way that it meets its incipient demise [*Untergange*] with a *tragic disposition;* within this highest task lies everything ennobling about humanity; from its ultimate rejection [*Abweisen*] would result the most dismal [*trübste*] picture any friend of humanity could place before his soul. . . . There is only one hope and one guarantee for the future of humanity: it is that the tragic disposition not die out. (*WB:*4)

Given that "tragedy," for Nietzsche, does not merely identify a literary genre—given that the "tragic disposition" is a feature of whatever in humanity Nietzsche deems noble—it should come as no surprise that Nietzsche, in considering the birth of tragedy, is not pondering a question for literary historians. His deeper concerns are introduced with a question: "Is pessimism necessarily the sign of decline, decay [*Verfall*], failure [*Missrathensein*], of exhausted [*ermüdeten*] and weakened instincts?—as it was for the Indians, as it certainly appears to be for us, 'modern' men and Europeans?" (*BT*,SC:1).

Taken together, the passages I have cited introduce the problem that motivates *The Birth of Tragedy:* the situation in Nietzsche's Europe is compared to the historico-social developments of ancient Greece and of ancient India. The basis for the association of the three is a feature common to all: pessimism. According to Nietzsche, Indian pessimism is symptomatic of exhaustion, decline, and failure, whereas its Greek counterpart is among the features of "the most successful [*wohlgerathenste*] . . . type of humanity to date." Nietzsche suggests the fundamental difference between the two pessimisms through yet another series of questions:

Is there a pessimism of strength? An intellectual predilection for the hard, gruesome [*schauerliche*], evil, problematic aspects of existence that arises from well-being [*Wohlsein*], overflowing health, from the fullness of existence? ... A seductive, striving [*versücherische*] courage that sees clearly [*des schärfsten Blicks*] and demands the fearsome as the enemy, the worthy enemy on whom it can test its strength? from whom it wants to learn what it means "to be afraid"? (*BT*,SC:1)

Pessimism—like the radical nihilism with which it is so closely related—may be a sign of strength or of weakness, of health or of sickness. Hence, Nietzsche's non-antiquarian concern: assuming that Europe is becoming increasingly pessimistic, what does its pessimism signify? It "certainly appears to be" a sign of morbidity, but even if it now is, must it remain so? Whether or not it must so remain, it will so remain, Nietzsche fears, unless the tragic disposition can come to flourish in Europe, as it did in Greece but not in India. What is required is a rebirth of tragedy. Hence, Nietzsche's concern with the birth of tragedy, not as a unique occurrence now past, but rather as a recurring possibility.

If we are to resurrect tragedy, Nietzsche suggests, we must first understand it, comprehending both its birth from "the tragic myth" and "the extraordinary phenomenon of Dionysus," and its death, caused by "the Socraticism of morality, dialectic, satisfaction [*Genügsamkeit*], and the equanimity [*Heiterkeit*] of the theoretical man" (*BT*,SC:1). I reconstruct Nietzsche's circumscription by returning to the passage that opens this chapter, in order now to examine it in detail.

It is an eternal phenomenon: the insatiable will always finds a way, by means of an illusion spread over things, to detain its creatures in life and to compel them to live on. One is chained by the Socratic joy of knowing and the delusion of being able thereby to heal the eternal wound of existence; another is ensnared by art's seductive veil of beauty fluttering before his eyes; yet another by the metaphysical consolation that beneath the whirl of phenomena eternal life flows on indestructibly—to say nothing of the more common and almost more forceful illusions the will always has at hand. (*BT*:18)

The first three forms of illusion are reserved for the "more nobly endowed natures" who have perceived "the burden and gravity of existence with deep displeasure." Less reflective or insightful humans are more easily satisfied: in Schopenhauer's words, "Human life, like all bad merchandise, is covered over by a gaudy paint job" (*WWR*,I:58). Those who are taken in by the paint job find life simply worth living, they require no further justification. Nietzsche's nobler natures, on the other hand, recognize that life is burdensome, but also that their choice is between life and nothing; illusions are required if they are to be "detained in life."

Differently put: the nobler natures are those who are aware, at least subliminally, of the wisdom of Silenus, which Nietzsche identifies as reflecting "Greek folk wisdom." Silenus, a companion of Dionysus, is captured by King Midas and forced to reveal "the best and most desirable of all things for man." His answer:

> Oh, wretched ephemeral race, children of chance and misery, why do you compel me to tell you what it would be most expedient for you not to hear? What is best of all is utterly beyond your reach: not to be born, not to be, to be nothing. But the second best for you is—to die soon. (*BT*:3 [Sophocles, *Oedipus at Colonus*, 1224ff])

Silenus tells us we do best by dying as soon as possible. Why do we reject his advice? All of us, some of the time, some of us, all of the time, and most of us, most of the time, are presumably taken in by life's gaudy paint job, or perhaps by promises of afterlives. Nietzsche suggests that those of us who are not, when we are not, rely, respectively, on three forms of illusion: some embrace the Socratic delusion, some focus on an Apollinian veil, some resign themselves to Silenian consolation.

Socratic Delusion

The first justificatory illusion listed by Nietzsche in the passage under consideration, the Socratic delusion, is historically the last; as I have indicated, Nietzsche attributes the death of tragedy to "the Socraticism of morality, dialectic, satisfaction [*Genügsamkeit*], and the equanimity [*Heiterkeit*] of the theoretical man" (*BT*,SC:1). With the emergence of Socraticism, art and beauty are displaced within the hierarchy of cultural values, subordinated on the one hand to morality and goodness, on the other to theory (or science) and truth. In that this subordination remains in effect in Nietzsche's own time (as in ours), its examination is central to Nietzsche's non-antiquarian project:

> what does all science *signify*, viewed as a symptom of life? . . . Where is science going; worse yet, where did it come from? . . . Is the scientific spirit perhaps only a fear of, a fleeing from pessimism? A subtle last resort against—the truth? And, in moral terms, something like cowardice and falsity? In non-moral terms, a ruse [*Schlauheit*]? Socrates, Socrates, was that perhaps your secret? (*BT*,SC:1)

What is the secret? Art is generally supposed to be concerned with beauty, science with truth, and morality with goodness. Yet Nietzsche suggests, directly, that science may be a defense against truth, an attempt to disguise the truth. He also suggests, indirectly, that morality may be a defense against goodness, an attempt to avoid acknowledging what true goodness would require. The mechanism that allows these defenses to work is a "new and unprecedented treasuring [*Hochschätzung*] of knowledge and insight" (*BT*:13). Clear evidence for the novelty of this valuation is provided by Socrates's admission of his own ignorance, and his amazement that others— great statesmen, orators, poets, and artists—are governed by instinct rather than by knowledge:

> "Only from instinct": with this expression, we touch the heart and midpoint of the Socratic tendency. With it, Socraticism condemns existing art as well as existing ethics: wherever he directs his examining glance, he sees the lack of insight and the power of delusion [*Wahn*]; from this lack, he concludes that what exists is internally perverse [*verkehrt*] and reprehensible [*verwerflich*]. (*BT*:13)

In condemning all that exists, including current art and ethics, Socrates condemns both what is and what has been. Given this rejection of past and present, he can be "detained in life" only by the delusion that he can make the future radically different. He consequently views his own task as one of therapy; he is to "heal the wound of existence" by "correcting existence" (*BT*:13). This correction or healing is a practical project, but it requires a theoretical foundation: the replacement of custom by morality presupposes a replacement of instinct with knowledge. The result of the two replacements is a transformation of pessimism into optimism:

> Socrates is the prototype [*Urbild*] of the theoretical optimist who, with his already characterized faith in the fathomability [*Ergründlichkeit*] of the nature of things, ascribes to knowledge and cognition the force of a panacea, and conceives error as evil in itself. To penetrate into every ground [*Grund*] and to separate true cognition from semblance and from error strikes the Socratic man as the most noble human calling, indeed the only truly human calling. (*BT*:15)

The Socratic legacy—hence, the functioning of the Socratic illusion—is clearest in the paradigm [*Typus*] of a form of existence unheard of before Socrates: that of the theoretical man, who embraces Socrates's project, "to make existence appear comprehensible and thereby as justified" (*BT*:16), and thereby also Socrates's "profound delusion [*Wahnvorstellung*]," the "unshakable faith that thinking, following the guideline of causality, reaches into the deepest abysses of being, and that thinking is in a position not merely to know being, but even to correct it" (*BT*:15). The "essence of the spirit of science," then, combines "faith in the fathomability [*Ergründlichkeit*] of nature and in knowledge as panacea [*an die Universalheilkraft des Wissens*]" (*BT*:17). Life is worth living, for those possessed of this spirit, only because it is perfectible.

Apollinian Veil

In order to grasp the functioning of his second justificatory illusion, the Apollinian veil, Nietzsche deems it necessary to deconstruct [*abtragen*] Apollinian culture "stone by stone, as it were," in order to expose its foundation in the "magnificent figures of the Olympian gods." How this culture of gods serves as illusion is suggested by the description Nietzsche provides in distinguishing it from the Christian perspective: "Nothing here reminds us of asceticism, spirituality, or duty; here, only an exuberant, indeed triumphant existence speaks to us, one in which *everything present, whether good or evil, is deified*" (*BT*:3).

The present, condemned by Socrates, is deified by the Apollinian. This is perplexing, however, in that the deification of the present is characteristic, according to the later Nietzsche, not of the Apollinian but of the Dionysian, and thus of the perspective he himself attempts to take. Consider:

> An experimental philosophy [*Experimental-Philosophie*] such as I live anticipates experimentally [*versuchsweise*] even the possibilities of fundamental [*grundsätzlichen*] nihilism; but this is not to say that it must halt at a no, a negation, a will to the no. It wants rather to continue on to the reverse of this [*bis zum Umgekehrten hindurch*]—to a Dionysian affirmation of the world as it is, without subtraction, exception, or selection—it wants the eternal circulation [*Kreislauf*],—the same things, the same logic and illogic of entanglements [*Knoten*]. The highest state a philosopher can attain: to stand in a Dionysian relationship to existence—my formula for this is *amor fati*.
>
> This requires conceiving the previously denied aspects of existence not only as necessary, but as desirable [*wünschenswert*]: and not only as desirable in relation to the previously affirmed aspects (perhaps as their complements or preconditions), but for themselves [*um ihrer selber willen*], as the more powerful, more fruitful, truer aspects of existence, within which its will speaks out more distinctly. (*N:*16[32]; *WP:*1041)
>
> My formula for what is great in humanity is *amor fati:* that one wants nothing otherwise, not forward, not backward, not in all eternity. Not merely to bear what is necessary, still less to conceal it—all idealism is mendacity in the face of what is necessary—but rather to *love* it. (*EH,*II:10)

The Apollinian veil, like Nietzschean *amor fati,* involves affirming existence rather than disguising or attempting to heal it; but it stops short of *amor fati* in that it does not involve the affirmation of *all* of existence, "without subtraction, exception, or selection." Returning to *The Birth of Tragedy:* "How is the world of the Olympian gods related to this folk wisdom [i. e., the wisdom of Silenus]? Even as the rapturous [*entzückungsreiche*] vision of the tortured martyr to his torments" (*BT*:3).

The Apollinian, like the Christian martyr but unlike the Dionysian, turns away from this world and looks to another: "The Greek knew and felt the terror and horror of existence; in order to be able to live at all, he had to interpose between himself and life the radiant dream-birth of the Olympians" (*BT*:3). To the extent that the "terror and horror of existence" are affirmed, they are affirmed not "for themselves," but rather—like the martyr's torments—for sake of the visions they make possible. The "terrors and horrors" are revealed in the pre-Olympian myths that inspire the great tragedians. The Olympians provide the Apollinian veil that, "interposed" between the Greeks and life, shields them from the horrors:

> That overwhelming dismay in the face of the titanic powers of nature, the Moira enthroned inexorably over all knowledge, the vulture of the great lover of mankind, Prometheus, the terrible fate of the wise Oedipus, the family curse of the Atridae, which drove Orestes to matricide: in short, that entire philosophy of the sylvan god [i. e., Silenus (see *BT*:7)], with its mythical exemplars, which caused the downfall of the melancholy Etruscans—all this was again and again overcome by the Greeks with the aid of the Olympian middle world [*Mittelwelt*] of art; or at any rate it was veiled and withdrawn from sight. (*BT*:3)

> The gods justify human life by living it themselves—the only satisfactory theodicy! Existence under the bright sunshine of such gods is perceived [*empfunden*] as desirable in itself, and the real pain of Homeric man is caused by parting from it, especially by early parting; so that now, reversing the wisdom of Silenus, we might say of the Greeks that "to die soon is worst of all for them, the next worst—to die at all." (*BT*:3)

Whereas life is the worst for the Silenian, death is the worst for the Apollinian. But as long as either life or death is condemned, human existence cannot be affirmed. The Apollinian affirms all that is present, but only as present, only as permanent. Mortality, the horror the Apollinian cannot affirm, must be disguised; it is concealed behind the Olympian veil.

Silenian Consolation

Whereas the Apollinian perspective resembles Nietzsche's own, *The Birth of Tragedy's* third illusion, which I have termed "Silenian consolation," embodies one of its early forms, later to be rejected. As of 1872, Nietzsche insists that any affirmative perspective will require a "metaphysical consolation":

> Let us imagine a coming generation with such intrepidity of vision, with such a heroic penchant for the tremendous; let us imagine the bold stride of these dragon-slayers, the proud audacity with which they turn their back on all the weakling's doctrines of optimism in order to "live resolutely" in wholeness and fullness: would it not be necessary for the tragic man of such a culture, in view

of his self-education for seriousness and terror, to desire a new art, the art of metaphysical consolation, to desire tragedy as his own proper Helen, and to exclaim with Faust, "Should not my longing overleap the distance, and draw the fairest into existence?" (*BT*:18)

In the 1872 text, the closing question is rhetorical, its answer implicitly but clearly positive. By 1886, Nietzsche's perspective has developed. Quoting this passage in his "Self-Criticism," Nietzsche acknowledges that to answer it positively would be to sink into romanticism, but then provides his current response: "No, three times no!" Rejecting the demand for "metaphysical consolation" as incipiently Christian, the Nietzsche of 1886 insists:.

You should first learn the art of earthly [*diesseitigen*] consolation,—you should first learn to laugh, my young friends, if you want to remain pessimists; perhaps then, as laughers, you will some day send all metaphysical consolations to the devil—and metaphysics first of all. (*BT*,SC:7)

The later Nietzsche sends metaphysical consolations to the devil, but he does not send Dionysus along with them, although he originally presents such consolation as Dionysian. On the contrary, whereas he argues in 1872 that tragedy requires the combination of Dionysian intoxication with Apollinian vision, his "Self-Criticism" makes no mention of Apollo, and by 1888 he has concluded that the very idea of such a synthesis "reeks repellently of Hegelianism" (*EH*,IV:1).

The later Nietzsche, then, rejects Apollo for Dionysus, and metaphysical consolation for earthly affirmation. This might seem to suggest that nothing concerning his later positive teachings may be gleaned from *The Birth of Tragedy*, but mine is an alternative suggestion; that is why I have termed *The Birth of Tragedy's* consoling illusion "Silenian" rather than "Dionysian." My suggestion is that Nietzsche's descriptions, in 1872, are richer than his terminology. Specifically: whereas the primary terminological distinction is between the Apollinian and the Dionysian, an additional and important descriptive distinction is suggested, within what Nietzsche terms simply the "Dionysian," between what I term the "Dionysian" and the "Silenian." The Dionysian, in my narrower sense, points in the direction of what Nietzsche continues to affirm, the Silenian, towards what he comes to deny.

I move in the direction of my distinction between the Silenian and the Dionysian by first considering another famous and problematic teaching from *The Birth of Tragedy*: "it is only as an aesthetic phenomenon that existence and the world are eternally justified" (*BT*:5; cf. *BT*:24, SC:5). In the course of the text, two distinct "aesthetic justifications" are described, and a third suggested. Although Nietzsche presents all as Dionysian, the first of the explicit justifications is better termed Schopenhauerian, the second, Silenian; the one merely suggested points towards the specifically Dionysian. Nietzsche describes his first version of an aesthetic justification of existence in *The Birth of Tragedy*'s opening section:

> Man is no longer artist, he has become work of art: the artistic power of all of nature reveals itself here, in these paroxysms [*Schauern*] of intoxication, for the highest gratification [*Wonnebefriedigung*] of the primordial one [*Ur-Einen*]. The noblest clay, the most costly marble, man, is here kneaded and cut, and to the sound of the chisel strokes of the Dionysian world-artist rings out the cry of the Eleusinian mysteries: "Do you prostrate yourselves, millions? Do you sense your maker, world? " (*BT:1*)

The clearly Schopenhauerian element in this description is the *Ur-Einen*, the "primordial one" for whose gratification alone the earthly drama unfolds. Its putative role is described with increasing clarity as Nietzsche's essay develops:

> the more clearly I perceive in nature those omnipresent artistic impulses, and in them an ardent longing for illusion, for redemption through illusion, the more I feel myself impelled to the metaphysical assumption that the truly existent primal unity, eternally suffering and contradictory, also needs the rapturous vision, the pleasurable illusion, for its continuous redemption. (*BT:4*)

> Insofar as the subject is artist, it is already redeemed from its individual will and has become, so to speak, a medium through which the one truly existent [*wahrhaft seiende*] subject celebrates its redemption in illusion. For to our humiliation and exaltation, one thing above all must be clear to us. The entire artistic comedy [*Kunstkomödie*] is not performed for our betterment or education, nor are we the true creators of this art world. On the contrary, we may assume that we are merely images and artistic projections for the true creator, and that we have our highest dignity in our significance as works of art—for it is only as an aesthetic phenomenon that existence and the world are eternally justified—while of course our consciousness of our own significance hardly differs from that which the soldiers painted on canvas have of the battle represented on it. (*BT:5*)

For this "aesthetic justification" to succeed, we must exist as individuals; yet this vision provides no justification for us, as individuals. If I avoid "dying soon," I do so not for my own gratification, but rather for that of the "primal one." Why we should submit to such prostitution is unclear; Schopenhauer's alternative suggestion that we thwart the *Ur-Einen* through will-less self-destruction seems, at worst, no less appealing.

From the Schopenhauerian perspective, then, we merely perform for the primal one, and only for the primal one is existence justified; the Silenian position retains the metaphysical elements of the Schopenhauerian, but is somewhat more attractive in that it provides us with the hope that we too may enjoy the voyeuristic pleasure of the primordial being. Nietzsche relates this pleasure to the satisfaction provided to the spectators of tragic dramas:

> The metaphysical consolation [*Trost*]—with which, I am suggesting, every true tragedy leaves us—that life is at the bottom [*Grunde*] of things, despite all the changes of appearances, indestructibly powerful and pleasurable [*mächtig und lustvoll*], this consolation appears in corporeal clarity as the chorus of satyrs, as the chorus of natural beings who live ineradicably, as it were, behind all civilization and remain eternally the same, despite the changes of generations and of the history of peoples. (*BT*:7)

The Silenian perspective offers a form of eternity, a merging with the primordial; but this eternity is gained, for the individual human being, only at the price of individuality: "Dionysian art, too, wants to convince us of the eternal pleasure of existence; but we are to seek this pleasure not within the appearances, but rather behind the appearances" (*BT*:17). We see that all that comes to be must pass away, but a "metaphysical consolation" saves us from the bustle of changing appearances before we become "rigid with fear [*erstarren*]":

> We are really, for a brief moment, the primordial being itself, feeling its raging desire for existence and joy in existence. . . . We are pierced by the maddening sting of these pains just when we have become, as it were, one with the infinite, primordial joy in existence, and when we get an inkling [*ahnen*], in Dionysian ecstasy, of the indestructibility and eternity of this joy. In spite of fear and pity, we live happily [*sind die glücklich-Lebendigen*], not as individuals, but rather as the one that lives [*das eine Lebendige*], into whose creative joy we are melted down [*mit dessen Zeugungslust wir verschmolzen sind*]. (*BT*:17)

Dionysian Affirmation

If we send metaphysics to the devil, then we send the Schopenhauerian and Silenian perspectives, with whatever consolation or justification they may provide, along with it: we reject the presupposition, on which both perspectives depend, that there is a "primordial will" "behind the appearances." But if we reject this presupposition and thus these perspectives, to what are we to turn? Not to a forgetting of Silenian wisdom; that leads back to Schopenhauer's cheap, gaudy paint job. Nor to the Socratic delusion of individuality transformed, of life following the healing of the wound of existence; that is another form of metaphysical consolation. Nor, finally, to the Apollinian vision of individual immortality; we cannot affirm human life without also affirming death. What we must affirm is the existence of the world as it is rather than as we might wish it (Socrates), of an individuality neither destroyed (Silenus) nor made permanent (Apollo), but rather lived.

This is the perspective, the life that, according to Schopenhauer, is impossible: "If one were to reveal to anyone the terrible pains and tortures to which his life is constantly exposed, this person would be overcome by horror" (*WWR*,I:58). The source of this horror is not the pains and tortures we actually suffer; many of us, much of the time, suffer few. But only life's gaudy paint job, or the Socratic delusion that the wound of existence is being healed, can blind us to the fact of our *exposure* to pains and tortures; suffering is occasional, exposure to it constant.

Constant exposure to suffering, accompanied by the constant possibility of joy, is shared by humans with Dionysus, the god of whom, according to Nietzsche, all pre-Euripidean Greek heroes are masks:

> the one true, real Dionysus appears in a multiplicity of figures, in the mask of the struggling hero and, so to speak, enmeshed in the net of individual will [*Einzelwillen*]. As the appearing god now speaks and acts, he resembles an erring, striving, suffering individual. . . . In truth, however, the hero is the suffering Dionysus of the mysteries, the god experiencing in himself the agonies of individuation, of whom wonderful myths tell that as a boy he was torn to pieces by the Titans and now is worshiped in this state as Zagreus. (*BT*:10)

And what is the perspective of Dionysus, the perspective from which such an existence is justified, such a life worth living? The Nietzsche of 1872 provides us with no more than a hint:

> In Dionysian art and in its tragic symbolism the same nature speaks to us in its true, undisguised voice: "Be as I am! Amid the ceaseless flux of appearances the eternally creative, primordial mother, eternally impelling to existence, eternally finding satisfaction in this change of phenomena." (*BT*:16)

It is not clear that Nietzsche recognizes this as a position distinct from what I have called the Silenian. Indeed, in the very next section (in a passage quoted above) he characterizes the Dionysian or tragic position in different, and contradictory, terms: "Dionysian art, too, wants to convince us of the eternal pleasure of existence; but we are to seek this pleasure not within the appearances, but rather behind the appearances" (*BT*:17).

The "primordial one" seeks pleasure in the appearances rather than behind them, but the primordial one itself does not appear. The Silenian may seem to seek pleasure in appearances, but this pleasure presupposes an escape from appearance, a merging, behind appearances, with the one, a metaphysical absorption. The Dionysian position retains elements of both: like the one, the Dionysian attends to the appearances themselves rather than looking beyond or behind them; but unlike the one, and unlike the Silenian, the Dionysian remains among the appearances, existing as "an erring, striving, suffering individual." As a human being, I can "impel to existence" only by existing, thus, only by appearing. "Be as I am," then, suggests something quite different from "be one with me." First, it suggests a position that makes no commitment to the actual existence of the primordial one—a non-metaphysical position. Moreover, the imperative "be as I am" demands that I live my own life, not the life of the real or imagined one, that I seek my satisfaction within appearances rather than behind appearances, but that the satisfaction I seek indeed be my own, that my artistic activity be not for the sake of the Divine Spectator (Schopenhauerian or Olympian), but rather for the sake of my self, and perhaps for others like me.

A Tragic Culture

In closing this chapter, I return to a question introduced at its beginning: what must happen, according to Nietzsche, if modernity is to become a healthy and flourishing period, like that of his classical Greece, rather than a sickly and declining one, like that of his ancient India? In Nietzsche's lifetime, as in ours, the Socratic illusion predominates. That it has long predominated is not, according to Nietzsche, to be deplored. On the contrary, given the alternative, its reign has been salutary:

> if we imagine that the whole incalculable sum of energy used up for this world tendency had been used not in the service of knowledge but for the practical, i. e., egoistic aims of individuals and peoples, then we realize that in that case universal wars of annihilation and continual migrations of peoples would probably have weakened the instinctive lust for life to such an extent that suicide would have become a general custom and individuals might have experienced the final remnant of a sense of duty when, like the inhabitants of the Fiji islands, as sons they had strangled their parents, as friends, their friends—a *practical pessimism* that might have been able to produce a gruesome ethic of genocide [*Volkermord*] motivated by pity, which, incidentally, is and was present in the world wherever art did not appear in some form, particularly as religion and science, as a remedy and preventive for this breath of pestilence. (*BT*:15)

Art, according to Nietzsche, is the only thing that saves us from bestiality. This "art" can take various forms, including religion and science; what is important is that there be a myth, a story, that is widely accepted and that provides reasons for individuals and peoples—particularly the nobler natures, for whom the "more common illusions" are ineffective—to behave other than "egoistically."

The problem, for Nietzsche and for us, is that the Socratic myth, which deposed the tragic disposition, is dying. The Socratically-minded cannot help seeking to extend science, to make it comprehensive, but in so extending it, they cannot help running into its limits, and seeing from there "what defies illumination" [*das Unaufhellbare*]. At this point, Nietzsche tells us, "the new form of insight breaks through, *tragic insight,* which, merely to be endured, needs art as a protection and remedy" (*BT*:15).

If we abandon the Socratic dream, do we need art, as protection and remedy? The Nietzsche of 1872 thinks so, but that Nietzsche thinks also that we require a "metaphysical consolation." The later Nietzsche disagrees on the latter point. Does he also on the former? From the perspective of the later Nietzsche, as I have sketched it, what "breaks through" following the death of Socraticism is not "tragic insight" but rather "Silenian wisdom." The question becomes, is there available to us, from the "perspective of life," as opposed to the perspective of science, morality, or art, a "tragic disposition" that would allow us to affirm the human condition without relying on illusions? For the most part, *The Birth of Tragedy* suggests that there is not (see esp. *BT*:23). Yet just as *The Birth of Tragedy* provides glimpses of the Dionysian behind the Silenian, it suggests the prospect of a "tragic culture" that would avoid reliance on illusions:

> [the tragic culture] replaces science, as the highest goal, with the wisdom that, undeceived by the seductive distraction of science, turns with unmoved eyes to a comprehensive view of the world, and seeks to grasp, with sympathetic feelings of love, the eternal suffering as its own. (*BT*:18)

Those who "are as the primordial one is"—the Dionysians, as opposed to Silenians—seek, like scientists, a "comprehensive view of the whole," but a more objective one, "undeceived by the seductive distraction of science," i. e., by the technological faith that we come not merely to view but rather to comprehend, not merely to appreciate but rather to fathom, and that, having comprehended, having fathomed, we will be able to correct, able to heal.

Concerning how we are to move toward this "comprehensive view of the whole," which may or may not be "the perspective of life," *The Birth of Tragedy* has little more to say. For development, we must turn to *The Genealogy of Morals.*

4

Genealogies

Locke, in the seventeenth century, postulated (and rejected) an impossible language in which each individual thing, each stone, each bird and each branch, would have its own name; Funes once projected an analogous language, but discarded it because it seemed too general to him, too ambiguous. In fact, Funes remembered not only every leaf of every tree of every wood, but also every one of the times he had perceived or imagined it. . . . Not only was it difficult for him to comprehend that the generic symbol dog embraces so many unlike individuals of diverse size and form; it bothered him that the dog at three fourteen (seen from the side) should have the same name as the dog at three fifteen (seen from the front). His own face in the mirror, his own hands, surprised him every time he saw them.

Jorge Luis Borges

By "lion" I mean only this yellow clump that has sprung forth from a bush in the savannah, this hoarse grunt that exhales an odor of bloody flesh, and the white fur of the belly and the pink of the under-paws and the sharp angle of the retractile claws just as I see them over me now with a mixture of sensations that I call "lion" in order to give it a name though I want to be clear it has nothing to do with the word "lion" nor even with the idea of lion which one might form in other circumstances.

Italo Calvino

Self-Knowledge, Genealogy, Hermeneutics

I turn to *The Genealogy of Morals* in order to examine the "logic" available to the complete nihilist, and the "objectivity" sought by the advocate of Dionysian affirmation. Given these interests, my choice of *The Genealogy* may be initially surprising, for its title seems to announce a treatment not of science and method, but rather of morality. Nevertheless, from the beginning of its Preface it is clear that here, as in *The Birth of Tragedy*, knowledge and wisdom are at issue.

The Christian-moral tradition in Western philosophy begins with Socrates's adoption of the Delphic imperative, "know thyself," and with his contention that the unexamined life is not worth living. That tradition draws toward its end, Nietzsche argues, as it approaches the conclusion that the examined life is not worth living, either. But Nietzsche is not prepared simply to accept either Socrates's contention or the tradition's conclusion; instead, he charges that the tradition has ignored the Delphic imperative rather than obey it. Over two thousand years after Socrates, Nietzsche opens his polemical *Genealogy* by insisting, "we are unknown, we knowers, ourselves to ourselves": we are *unbekannt*, unfamiliar to or even unacquainted with ourselves (*GM*,P:1). And the "we" who exhibit this ignorance are not the a- or anti-philosophical masses, not those who do not seek to examine, but rather, precisely, the progeny of Socrates, the "knowers": *wir Erkennenden*. Busy as bees (Nietzsche's metaphor), we knowers have roamed far afield, gathering the most abstruse bits of knowledge and storing them carefully in our hives—our heads, our libraries, our hard disks—but we have not sought ourselves, because we haven't had the time. We may know something, but we do not know ourselves; we may have examined various things, but we continue to lead unexamined lives.

It is because "we are unknown, we knowers, ourselves to ourselves" that Nietzsche undertakes his genealogical investigation of morality. And because we unknown knowers have been, broadly speaking, scientists, his genealogy proceeds, in words adapted from the "Self-criticism" of *The Birth of Tragedy*, not from the perspective of science, but rather from that of life:

> under what conditions did man devise these value judgments good and evil? and what value do they themselves possess? Have they hitherto hindered or furthered human prosperity? Are they a sign of distress, of impoverishment, of the degeneration of life? Or is there revealed in them, on the contrary, the plenitude, force, and will of life, its courage, certainty, future? (*GM*,P:3)

As this passage suggests, Nietzsche's genealogy is hermeneutical in that it takes moral judgments not as truth claims to be evaluated, but rather—like radical nihilism, like pessimism—as signs to be interpreted. And neither the signs nor the interpretations are to be sought in the "English fashion" of "gazing around haphazardly in the blue." On the contrary,

> it must be obvious which color is a hundred times more vital for a genealogist of morals than blue: namely *gray*, that is, what is documented, what can actually be confirmed and has actually existed, in short the entire long hieroglyphic record, so hard to decipher, of the moral past of mankind! (*GM*,P:7)

In that Nietzsche's hermeneutics requires consideration of "what is documented, what can actually be confirmed and has actually existed," it cannot be metaphysical: its data are given empirically, not a priori. Moreover, because the "document" it considers is a "hieroglyphic record," "hard to decipher," it cannot revert to positivism: the registering of the data is only the first step.

In addition to being non-metaphysical and non-positivistic, Nietzsche's hermeneutics must be genealogical rather than eidetic, archaeological, or teleological. It cannot be eidetic, for the seekers of eternal *eide* or essences are those who merely "gaze around haphazardly in the blue." It cannot be archaeological, for it does not seek foundational origins. On the contrary, Nietzsche insists that "for historiography of all sorts" there is "no more important proposition" than that

> the cause of a thing's origination, and its eventual utility, its factual employment and placement in a system of purposes, lie worlds apart; that something available [*etwas Vorhandenes*], having somehow attained a stability, is again and again reinterpreted for new views [*Ansichten*], confiscated anew, transformed and rearranged for new uses; that everything that happens in the organic world is an overpowering, a mastering, and that, again, all overpowering and mastering is a reinterpreting, an arranging whereby the previous "meaning" and "purpose" must necessarily be obscured or even entirely extinguished. (*GM*,II:12)

Just as Nietzsche's genealogical hermeneutics cannot be archaeological because meanings and uses are not determined by origins, it cannot be teleological because they are no more determined by goals:

> The "development" of a thing, a custom, an organ, is thus nothing like a *progressus* toward a goal, even less a logical *progressus* by the shortest route and with the smallest expenditure of force—but rather the succession of more or less profound, more or less mutually independent processes of subduing that play themselves off on it, plus the resistances they always encounter, the attempts at transformation for the purpose of defense and reaction, and the results of successful counteractions. The form is fluid, but the "meaning" is even more so. (*GM*,II:12)

What this means for philosophy, Nietzsche is convinced, is that static or ahistorical conceptual analysis is impossible, or possible only at the price of misleading, even dangerous, distortion. In *The Wanderer and his Shadow*, he provides an example:

> The word "revenge" is said so quickly, it almost seems as if it could not contain more than one root concept and feeling. And so people are still trying to find this root—just as our economists still have not got tired of smelling such a unity in the word "value" and of looking for the original root concept of value. As if all words were not pockets into which now this and now that has been put, and now many things at once! (*HH*,WS:33)

As a genealogical hermeneuticist, Nietzsche neither begins nor ends his investigations either by registering facts or creating fictions, or by identifying essences, origins, or ends. But this does not mean that he can do nothing more than simply track the developments of concepts and of the practices associated with them. Instead, he attempts also to assess concept-practices from "the perspective of life," seeking first to determine which complexes are life-enhancing, which life-denying, and then to cultivate the former while impairing the latter.

Readers who move quickly through *The Genealogy*—readers who lack, or do not use, "fingers for nuances"—may emerge from it with the conviction that distinguishing the life-enhancing from the life-denying is, for Nietzsche, a relatively simple matter. He first opposes "noble moralities," which encourage self-assertive strength, to "slave moralities," which foster humility and self-abnegation; he may then appear simply to laud the former while castigating the latter. But so too can the Nietzsche of *The Birth of Tragedy* appear simply to condemn Socraticism. In both cases, the simplicity of the appearance is misleading.

In *The Birth of Tragedy,* we have seen, Nietzsche acknowledges that Socraticism has had salutary consequences throughout much of its history: it has been the sole alternative to genocidal wars. Similarly, in *The Genealogy of Morals* he recognizes that the role played in history by the "slave rebellion in morality," which displaced the rule of the blond beasts, has been in many ways a positive one:

> Only on the soil of this *essentially dangerous* form of human existence, the priestly form, has the human being become an *interesting animal,* only here has the human soul acquired *depth* in a higher sense and become evil—and these are the two basic respects in which the human being has hitherto been superior to other beasts! (GM,I:6)

> Human history would be altogether too stupid an affair were it not for the spirit that has entered into it through the powerless. (GM,I:7)

> The existence on earth of an animal soul turned against itself, taking sides against itself, was something so new, profound, unheard of, enigmatic, contradictory, and *pregnant with a future* that the aspect of the earth was essentially altered. (GM,II:16)

Just as the slave valuation is not always and everywhere life-denying, neither is the noble valuation simply life-enhancing. Nietzsche deems a return to the stupid violence of the "blond beast" neither possible nor desirable. On the contrary, the most important question that emerges from *The Genealogy of Morals,* as from *The Birth of Tragedy,* asks what form a renewal of noble morality, a rebirth of the tragic disposition, could take, now that the illusion of Socraticism, with its slave morality, is losing its effectiveness.

This is a question Nietzsche answers, if at all, only in *Zarathustra.* If he answers it there, he does not do so simply or directly. On the contrary, he may appear not even to raise it. I have been arguing, throughout Part One of this book, that Nietzsche's affirmative teachings are historically situated: the completion of nihilism presupposes the movement through religious and radical nihilism, the rebirth of tragedy presupposes the Socratic interlude, and the restoration of noble morality advocated by Nietzsche depends upon the cleverness and sophistication that distinguish us from blond beasts—the intelligence we have developed during the rule of slave morality. History, it seems, is central; yet in *Zarathustra*, history can appear to be irrelevant. *Zarathustra* is set not here and now, but rather on an unfamiliar and only vaguely described landscape, and in an unspecified but technologically primitive time. This setting suggests that Nietzsche aims, in *Zarathustra*, for a kind of universality, or perhaps of objectivity. I believe that he does so aim, but also that his message is carefully targeted for those of us who live in the wake of the death of the Christian God. We can receive the message, however, only if our fingers for nuances are nimble.

In order, in part, further to exercise our fingers for nuances, I do not now take the path that would lead directly to *Zarathustra*. Instead, I examine a few of the chambers contained in *The Genealogy*'s labyrinth. I do so in part because they are fascinating in themselves, and in part because what is to be discovered within them is useful to explorers of *Zarathustra*.

Punishment

The project guiding Michel Foucault's justly respected *Discipline and Punish* is first articulated—as Foucault himself acknowledges—in sections 13 and 14 of *The Genealogy*'s Second Essay, where Nietzsche sketches the task of a hermeneutical genealogy of punishment. "Words are seeming bridges," according to Zarathustra, between things that are "eternally different" (Z,III:13.2; 272.14–15); in *The Genealogy*, he exposes "punishment" as such a bridge.

In considering punishment, Nietzsche distinguishes the relatively enduring sequence of punitive procedures from the specific uses to which the procedures are put; Nietzsche plausibly insists on the historical priority of the former. Currently, imprisonment is one such procedure, and given our economic investment in prisons, the procedure is extremely resistant to change, no matter how much evidence we may have that prisons are not doing what we want them to do, that they are not effective means of punishment. Worse yet, perhaps, no matter how we may change our beliefs concerning what "effective punishment" might require, we will be inclined to continue to use our prisons to apply the punishments, simply because the prisons are available.

Concerning our notion of "effective punishment"—concerning what it is that we want our prisons, our fines, our community service, and our electric chairs to do—Nietzsche insists that it is not only fluid, but also, already in his time, incoherent. A lengthy historical sequence of changes in the uses of procedures (torture, incarceration) has led to a "concept" that has no consistent, logically analyzable complex of meanings:

> the previous history of punishment in general, the history of its employment for the most various purposes, finally crystallizes into a kind of unity that is hard to disentangle, hard to analyze and, as must be emphasized especially, totally indefinable. (Today it is impossible to say for certain why people are really punished: all concepts in which an entire process is semiotically concentrated elude definition; only that which has no history is definable.) (GM,II:13)

Nietzsche provides a list of interpretations of punishment, stressing that despite its length it is far from complete:

> Punishment as a means of rendering harmless, of preventing further harm. Punishment as recompense to the injured party for the harm done, rendered in any form (even in that of a compensating affect). Punishment as the isolation of a disturbance of equilibrium, so as to guard against any further spread of the disturbance. Punishment as a means of inspiring fear of those who determine and execute the punishment. Punishment as a kind of repayment for the advantages the criminal has enjoyed hitherto. . . . Punishment as the expulsion of a degenerate element. . . . Punishment as a festival, namely as the rape and mockery of a finally defeated enemy. Punishment as the making of a memory, whether for him who suffers the punishment—so-called "improvement"—or for those who witness its execution. Punishment as payment of a fee stipulated by the power that protects the wrongdoer from the excesses of revenge. Punishment as a compromise with revenge in its natural state when the latter is still maintained and claimed as a privilege by powerful clans. Punishment as a declaration of war and a war measure against an enemy of peace, of the law, of order, of the authorities, whom, as a danger to the community, as one who has broken the contract that defines the conditions under which it exists, as a rebel, a traitor, and breaker of the peace, one opposes with the means of war. (GM,II:13)

The overdetermination [*Überladung*] of the concept of punishment with "utilities of all sorts" (GM,II:14) explains, in part, why it can be manipulated so effectively by enterprising politicians (or, better, by enterprising media consultants). In the 1988 United States presidential campaign, racist commercials exploited the contradiction between the procedure of granting furloughs to prisoners and the interpretation of punishment as a means of protecting citizens from criminals. To devastating effect, the commercials obscured entirely the empirically supported contention that the furlough policy had played a valuable role in punishment interpreted as rehabilitation. Similarly, whereas opponents of capital punishment emphasize its obvious failure as a procedure for rehabilitation, its supporters rely on its conceptual (if not, perhaps, empirical) defensibility as a means of deterrence.

As Nietzsche stresses, what makes these issues so complicated is, first, that there is not any one specific end we are trying to reach by punishing criminals; and second, that many of the procedures we employ for the sake of one or more of our current ends were originally developed for other purposes entirely. It is already clear to Nietzsche that the last place a criminal is likely to be rehabilitated is in a prison. That has been clear to many others as well, for over a century—and even well before imprisonment replaced torture as the primary means of punishment, as Foucault shows in fascinating detail.

No practical consequences emerge from Nietzsche's brief reflections on punishment: he is no penologist. His reflections do, however, contribute to our knowledge of ourselves, for they reveal a deep confusion that is easily obscured: the simplicity of the word "punishment" tends to blind us to the complexity, indeed, the mutual inconsistency, of the means and ends to which the word can refer. And if some of "us knowers" already know what *The Genealogy* has to teach about punishment, that could well be due, in part, to the dissemination of Nietzsche's teachings over the past hundred years. Powerful evidence that many of us do not yet know has been provided, quite recently, by the political effectiveness of Willie Horton.

The Birth of God

In his examination of "punishment," Nietzsche empties an egregiously overstuffed word-pocket, revealing objectively and logically that and how the word has become indefinable. Such revelation is one important task for genealogical hermeneutics, but not the only one. I turn now to a Nietzschean investigation that concerns origin rather than definition or utility.

Late in *The Genealogy*'s Second Essay, Nietzsche announces, "This should suffice once and for all concerning the origin of the 'holy God' [*Dies genüge ein für alle Mal über die Herkunft des 'heiligen Gottes'*]" (GM,II:23). What "should suffice"? Has Nietzsche disposed of the question by answering it? Yes and no, for he has provided it with at least three distinct answers. First, the invention of the Christian God is presented as an aspect of the "imaginary revenge" of the priests leading the slave rebellion in morality: belief in this God consoles the weak by giving apparent substance to their dreams of watching the strong suffer (GM,I:15), and undermines the self-affirmation of the strong by confronting them with a being stronger than they (GM,I:7–8, II:16). Second, we are told that when, through the development of bad conscience, human beings became "pregnant with a future," "divine spectators were needed to do justice to the spectacle that thus began": once human existence comes to be seen as a historical drama, it appears meaningless unless it has an immortal audience (GM,II:16). Third, Nietzsche argues that as human societies develop, they deem themselves increasingly in debt to their earliest ancestors. As the ancestors recede into the past, they are increasingly and variously deified (*GM*,II:19); the Christian God is "the maximal god attained so far," the one "therefore accompanied by the maximum feeling of guilty indebtedness [*Schuldgefühl*] on earth" (*GM*,II:20). This is the final result of humanity's "will to erect an ideal—that of the 'holy God'— and in the face of the ideal to feel the palpable certainty of its own absolute unworthiness" (*GM*,II:22).

How does this complex of explanations suffice, "once and for all, concerning the origin of the 'holy God' "? Has Nietzsche proved that the idea of God begins simply, always and everywhere, with the desire for revenge, against another (the priest's vengeance on the blond beast) or against oneself (the blond beast convinced by the priest that bestiality is evil)? If so, has he not contradicted himself by providing other explanations as well? Has he not also revealed himself as a dogmatic archaeologist—as one concerned primarily with exposing determinative origins? And has he not, finally, opened himself to a fundamental objection raised by Eugen Fink:

> This method of unmasking can always be increased, overtrumped; one could just as well ask what it signifies, symptomatically, that someone finds in the morality of love of neighbor only desire for revenge, in respect for God only neurosis—is such a psychology of the dregs itself the expression of a stunted life that is blind to value? (Fink, 130).

Has Nietzsche treated the origin of the Christian God sufficiently by answering it? No, for he has given it three answers, each of which undermines the authority of the other two. If his treatment "suffices" for the question of origin, then, it does so by showing that the question has no single or simple answer. The question cannot be answered simply or singly because it can be given indefinitely many plausible answers, and there is no compelling reason for accepting one of the answers as simply true. According to Zarathustra, "When Gods die, they always die many kinds of death" (*Z*,IV:6). Likewise, when they are born, they emerge through many kinds of birth. If that is so, it may be that no answer to the "question of how the 'holy God' originated" is simply false, but it will also be the case that no answer is simply true, precisely because there is no simple, or single, answer.

For some, religious faith may indeed originate in the desire for revenge. But not for all—not necessarily, and not, no doubt, empirically. When Zarathustra first descends from his mountain, he brings with him the gift of the overman, a substitute for the god that has died, a meaning or illusion that will give human beings reason to live. The first person he encounters is a hermit, described as a saint. The two recognize each other; the hermit recalls Zarathustra's ascent to the mountain ten years earlier, and asks why Zarathustra now returns to human society. Zarathustra responds, "I bring humanity a gift," and then asks the saint what he does, alone in his forest.

The saint responds, "I make songs and sing them, and when I make songs, I laugh, cry, and hum: thus do I praise God." He then asks Zarathustra what gift he brings humanity, but Zarathustra declines to answer: "What could I have to give you? Let me get away quickly, before I take something from you." Once he is alone, Zarathustra speaks to his heart: "Can this be possible? This old saint, in his forest, has still heard nothing of this, that God is dead!" (Z,P:2).

The saint believes in God, yet he makes no attempt to induce guilt, in himself or in others; nothing in his words or deeds suggests that his God traces its origin to the desire for revenge. Zarathustra's response to their encounter reveals his consequent recognition of the saint as a figure to be at least accepted, and perhaps even admired, even if not, for Zarathustra himself, to be emulated. Zarathustra's interaction with him thus provides strong, if oblique, support for my contention that Nietzsche's disposal of the question of the holy God's origin is not a matter of his answering it.

If this contention is accepted, then what the later Nietzsche describes as "insight into the falsity of previous interpretations" (N:2[109] / WP:599), including the religious interpretation, would mean *not* that we can know that there is no God, but rather that we can know that the perspective of those who believe that God exists is only one perspective, and one that is not obligatory. What is false is not the perspective itself, but the perspective's denial that it is a perspective. The perspectivist need not insist to the religious dogmatist—as Zarathustra does not insist to the saint—"you cannot know, you cannot be sure that your God exists." Such an assertion would require a supporting epistemological argument. No such argument is required by the observation, "Yours is one way of looking at things; there are others." The dogmatist will insist that the others are wrong or corrupt or misguided, but even the most committed dogmatists must recognize that not all share their beliefs.

Facts and Interpretations

Having considered two genealogical investigations—the analysis of "punishment," and the origin of God—I turn to an example that is more narrowly hermeneutical, that is, a case of interpretation where development plays a less prominent role. I turn to pain and suffering, of which Nietzsche writes:

> It is plain that in this essay I proceed on a presupposition I do not first have to demonstrate to readers of the kind I need: that man's "sinfulness" is not a fact, but merely the interpretation of a fact, namely of physiological depression—the latter viewed in a religio-moral perspective that is no longer binding on us. (GM,III:16)

There are facts, Nietzsche here tells us—"physiological depression" is his
example—but there are also interpretations. Elsewhere, he is more extreme:

> Against positivism, which halts at phenomena—"There are only facts"—I would
> say: No, facts are precisely what there are not, only interpretations [*Interpreta-
> tionen*]. We cannot establish any fact "in itself"—perhaps it is folly to want to
> do such a thing. . . .
>   In so far as the word "knowledge" means anything, the world is knowable;
> but it is interpretable [*deutbar*] otherwise, it has no meaning [*Sinn*] behind it,
> but countless meanings.—"Perspectivism." (N:7[60] / WP:481)

According to the passage from *The Genealogy of Morals,* there are facts;
according to the roughly contemporaneous note, there are only interpretations. Later in *The Genealogy,* Nietzsche provides a formulation that may
resolve the apparent contradiction. He notes a "fact," but immediately adds,
"What does this mean? For this fact has to be interpreted; in itself it just
stands there, stupid to all eternity, like every 'thing-in-itself' "(*GM*,III:7).
There are facts, but the facts are insignificant—"stupid"—until interpreted,
and because facts are always open to multiple interpretations, no "fact"
alone entails a unique, "correct" interpretation. To the introduction of any
"fact," an appropriate response is, "so what?"
   The problem, differently stated, is not that there are no facts, but that
there are too many facts. There are too many in that not all can be registered,
and not all can be interrelated. In one sense, then, there are indeed no facts:
every reporting of a single fact entails the exclusion of indefinitely many
other facts, any one of which may be relevant to the interpretation of the
one reported. Even to register a fact, then, is to interpret, in that the registering involves the singling out of the specific fact. It is a "fact" that the words,
"*Du gehst zu Frauen? Vergiss die Peitsche nicht!* [You go to women? Do
not forget the whip!]" are found in a book usually attributed to Nietzsche
(*Z*,I:18); but the citation of those words, out of their context, is itself an
interpretation in that it involves an exclusionary selection. And even if I were
to cite the entire work in which those words appear, or the entire Nietzschean
corpus, the interpretive moment would remain: why cite *Zarathustra* rather
than *Twilight of the Idols?* why cite Nietzsche rather than Maurice Sendak?
why cite rather than weed the garden?
   If selection is "interpretation," then there are indeed no "facts," but only
"interpretations." Yet it may also be the case that some things I say are true
whereas others are false: "in so far as the word 'knowledge' means anything,
the world is knowable." But if there are truths, if there is knowledge then,
it seems, there must be facts. That I am a Caucasian male is true (exclusion-
arily true, of course, in that I am many other things as well); that I am a
black female is false. But as soon as this truth or fact—or any other—is

selectively registered, the problem of interpretation arises once again: what is the significance of the fact? Its significance in Williamstown, Massachusetts is not what it would be in Johannesburg, or in Harlem. Similarly, it is a fact that one can make a fire by rubbing two sticks together, but the significance of that fact for us is not what it was for our early ancestors.

According to Nietzsche, even a "fact" as apparently primitive as pain is the product of hermeneutical activity: "I consider even 'physiological pain' to be not a fact but only an interpretation—a causal interpretation—of facts that have hitherto defied exact formulation—too vague to be scientifically serious—a fat word replacing a very thin question mark" (GM,III.16). The putative "fact" may be that there is a certain kind of sensation; but whether the sensation means that something is wrong, that something should be done, is a matter of interpretation. If I begin to gasp for breath as I sit quietly in my chair, I may well rush to a doctor; if I do the same as I play basketball, I may instead simply regret the effects of increasing age. Some "pains," no doubt, are to be avoided or regretted, but there are also "pains" that we should welcome: "the pangs of the woman giving birth hallow all pain; all becoming and growing—all that guarantees a future—involves pain" (TI,X:4).

Ascetic Ideals

The hermeneutical and genealogical examples I have considered are, I think, representative of Nietzsche's method, and exemplify his objectivity and his logic. In turning now to a final example from The Genealogy, I turn explicitly in the direction of Zarathustra. The example is ascetic ideals, the topic of The Genealogy's Third Essay; the particular importance of this Essay to readers of Zarathustra is indicated by Nietzsche in The Genealogy's Preface, where he writes,

> An aphorism, properly stamped and molded, has not been "deciphered" when it has simply been read; rather, one has then to begin its exegesis, for which is required an art of exegesis. I have offered in the third essay of the present book an example of what I regard as "exegesis" in such a case—an aphorism is prefixed to this essay, the essay itself is a commentary on it. (GM,P:8)

The aphorism in question, from Zarathustra's "Of Reading and Writing," reads, "Unconcerned, mocking, violent —thus wisdom wants us: she is a woman and always loves only a warrior." If to read is to interpret and interpretation requires an art of exegesis, then Nietzsche's own reading of his aphorism might be expected to instruct us in what he considers to be the appropriate art.

I note at the outset that whereas Nietzsche's chosen aphorism informs us that wisdom loves *only* warriors, it does not assert that she loves *all* warriors, and Nietzsche regularly insists that warriors of most kinds are related to wisdom only through a mutual indifference. *The Genealogy* itself denies that wisdom loves the warlike blond beasts who were overcome by the ascetic priests; if left under the control of the former, "human history would be altogether too dumb an affair" (GM,I:7). Concerning the kind of warrior wisdom might love, Zarathustra provides what may be a valuable qualification in admonishing his "brothers in war": "if you cannot be saints of knowledge [*Erkenntnis*], be for me at least her warriors" (Z,I:10). If Zarathustra is a warrior, then he is certainly of this sort, as is Nietzsche himself: the only war either wages is "war without powder and smoke, without warlike poses, without pathos and strained limbs" (*EH*,VI:1).

Whereas Nietzsche's aphorism speaks of warriors, the title of his "commentary" on it announces an apparently distinct topic, i. e., "the significance of ascetic ideals." It should come as no surprise, at this point, that these ideals have no single or simple meaning. The Essay opens:

What do ascetic ideals signify?—In artists, nothing or too many things; in philosophers and scholars something like an inkling [*Witterung*] and instinct for the most favorable preconditions of a higher spirituality; in women, in the best cases, one more seductive charm, a touch of *morbidezza* on beautiful flesh, the angelic look of a pretty, plump animal; in the physiologically injured and atrophied (the majority of mortals) an attempt to see themselves as "too good" for this world, a saintly form of debauch [*Ausschweifung*], their chief weapon in the struggle against slow pain and boredom; in priests, the authentic priestly faith, their best power tool, as well as the "supreme" license for power; in saints, finally, a pretext for hibernation, their newest lust for glory, their repose in nothingness ("God"), their form of insanity [*Irrsinn*]. (GM,III:1)

Of these six types of ascetic, *The Genealogy*'s Third Essay treats only three, i.e., artists, philosophers-scholars, and priests. To these I now turn.

The asceticism of the artist, Nietzsche tells us, can mean either nothing or too many things. That which "means nothing" is the "healthy" or disciplined sensuality of Goethe and Feuerbach, not a true asceticism. "There is no necessary antithesis between chastity and sensuality [*Sinnlichkeit*]; every good marriage, every genuine affair of the heart [*eigentliche Herzensliebschaft*] transcends this antithesis." And even when there is an opposition, it need not be debilitating; mortals are used to balancing such things:

At least this holds good for all those well-constituted, joyful mortals who are far from regarding their unstable equilibrium between "animal and angel" as necessarily an argument against existence—the subtlest and brightest among them have even found in it, like Goethe and Hafiz, one *more* stimulus to life. It is precisely such "contradictions" that seduce one to existence. (GM,III:2)

On the other hand, the moral stance of the truly ascetic artist, the anti-sensualist, means "too many things" in that it always points beyond the artist toward a different source: artists "do not stand nearly independently enough in the world and *against* the world for their changing valuations to deserve attention *in themselves*"; artists are always "valets of a morality or philosophy or religion" (*GM*,III:5). Nietzsche's paradigmatic example of such an ascetic is Wagner, who, under the influence of Schopenhauer, re-verses his basic aesthetic position: music, which had been a mere means, becomes end. Wagner, as musician, is thereby elevated: he becomes the "mouthpiece of the in-itself," a "telephone to the beyond." Wagner's asceti-cism, then, is the price to be paid for quasi-divine status; this asceticism means "too many things" in that to determine its significance, one must look beyond the valet to the master.

Philosophical asceticism, like its artistic counterpart, is complex:

> As long as there are philosophers on earth, and wherever there have been philosophers (from India to England, to take the antithetical poles of philosophi-cal endowment), there unquestionably exists a peculiar philosophers' irritation at and rancor against sensuality. . . . There also exists a peculiar philosophers' prejudice and affection in favor of the whole ascetic ideal. (*GM*,III:7)

The "irritation and rancor" suggest a devaluation of sensuality, but the devaluation is not always moral. For those whose philosophical inclinations are strongest, the senses are not temptations to be resisted, but distractions to be ignored:

> The three great slogans of the ascetic ideal are familiar: poverty, humility, chastity. Now take a close look at the lives of all the great, fruitful, inventive spirits: you will always encounter all three to a certain degree. *Not*, it goes without saying, as though these constituted their "virtues"—what has this kind of man to do with virtues!—but as the most appropriate and natural conditions of their *best* existence, their *fairest* fruitfulness. . . . There is nothing in this of the chastity that arises from any kind of ascetic scruple or hatred of the senses . . . : it is rather the will of their dominating instinct, at least during their periods of great pregnancy. (*GM*,III:8)

For similar reasons, the philosopher views his asceticism as a form of self-gratification rather than one of self-denial:

> the philosopher sees in [the ascetic ideal] an optimum condition for the highest and boldest spirituality and smiles—he does *not* deny "existence," he rather affirms *his* existence and *only* his existence, and this perhaps to the point at which he is not far from harboring the impious wish: "let the world perish, but let there be philosophy, the philosopher, me!" (*GM*,III:7)

Nietzsche thus sides with Plato, in opposition to Freud, in viewing intellec-tual drives, at least in some, as sexuality transformed, even intensified, rather than as sexuality repressed. Concerning Schopenhauer, Nietzsche writes,

> the sight of the beautiful obviously had upon him the effect of releasing the *chief energy* of his nature (the energy of contemplation and deepened vision), so that this exploded and all at once became the master of his consciousness. This should by no means preclude the possibility that the sweetness and plenitude peculiar to the aesthetic state might be derived precisely from the ingredient of "sensual-ity" . . . —so that sensuality is not overcome by the appearance of the aesthetic condition, as Schopenhauer believed, but only transfigured and no longer enters consciousness as sexual excitement. (*GM*,III:8)

On the whole, then, there is a natural affinity between philosophy and asceticism: energy that is expended intellectually cannot be expended sensu-ally, and the philosopher prefers intellectual expenditure, for reasons that are selfish rather than moral. In addition to this natural relation, however, there is a historically conditioned one—one that requires genealogical analy-sis. For most of human history, according to Nietzsche, philosophy itself has been considered immoral:

> Consider the various drives and virtues of the philosopher one by one—the drive to doubt, the drive to deny, the drive to hesitate (the "ephectic" drive), the analytic drive, the drive to investigate, to seek, to risk, the drive to compare, to balance, the will to neutrality and objectivity, the will to every "without anger or affection"—: has it been recognized that for the longest time all of these went against the first requirements of morality and of conscience? (not to speak of reason in general, which even Luther loved to call "Mrs. Clever the clever whore"). (*GM*,III:9)

Given such a valuation, philosophy must appear, even to the philosopher, as morally corrupt. But this means that if there are to be philosophers, they must not appear as philosophers, even to themselves. Instead, they must be concealed:

> the philosophical spirit always had to disguise and cocoon itself in the previously established types of the contemplative human being, i. e., as priest, sorcerer, soothsayer, in general as religious, in order even to be possible to any degree at all: the ascetic ideal has long served the philosopher as a form of appearance, as a presupposition for existence,—the philosopher had to exhibit it in order to be able to be a philosopher, and had to believe in it in order to be able to exhibit it. The peculiar world-denying, withdrawn attitude of the philosopher, hostile to life, suspicious of the senses, freed from sensuality, which has been maintained down to the most modern times and has become virtually the philosopher's

gesture in itself—it is above all a result of the emergency conditions under which philosophy arose and survived at all. (*GM*,III:10)

Only those in power can break moral laws with impunity; throughout most of human history, philosophers have had to break moral laws in order to be philosophers, but philosophy has provided no power; philosophers have therefore had to pose as religious figures, in order to gain the protection of the gods they were taken to serve or to represent. Further protection is gained by the philosopher's apparent lack of interest in what is most valued by others: what has the farmer, the merchant, the soldier, or the politician to fear from those whose allegiance is to chastity, poverty, and humility?

Philosophers, then, have disguised themselves as ascetic priests. This at least is Nietzsche's story, and although it may have some plausibility, it is also incomplete: it has told us that philosophers have had to exhibit the priestly ascetic ideal in order to survive and that they had to *believe in* the ideal in order to be able to exhibit it, but we do not yet know what Nietzsche takes ascetic ideals to signify in the case of priests.

Priestly asceticism is distinguished from its philosophical counterpart by two distinct but related features. First, the priest embraces the ascetic ideal as such, rather than accepting it for the sake of something else. For the philosopher, the ascetic ideal is either a disguise or a mere consequence of intellectualism; for the priest, however, this ideal is "not only his faith but also his will, his power, his interest. His *right* to exist stands or falls with that ideal" (*GM*,III:11). Second, the priest's valuation of asceticism is reactive, and therefore imperialistic. The self-affirmative perspective of the philosopher leads to an indifference to the sensualism of others; the philosopher judges only, "better, for me, to philosophize." The philosopher may also believe, "I am happier, philosophizing, than these who do otherwise," but even then there is no necessary step to the judgment, "better that all should be philosophers." The reactive perspective of the priest, on the other hand, leads to a condemnation of all sensualism.

In the terms of *The Genealogy*'s First Essay, whereas the philosopher's asceticism can be a feature of a noble morality, the priest's is essential to slave morality, and slave moralities, unlike their noble counterparts, necessarily take themselves to apply to all:

While every noble morality develops from a triumphant affirmation of itself, slave morality from the outset says No to what is "outside," what is "different," what is "not itself"; and *this* No is its creative deed. This inversion of the value-positing eye—this *need* to direct one's view outward instead of back to oneself—is of the essence of *ressentiment:* in order to exist, slave morality always first needs a hostile external world; it needs, physiologically speaking, external stimuli in order to act at all—its action is fundamentally reaction. (*GM*,I:10)

From the perspective of a slave morality, I can affirm my own goodness only indirectly: I am not like these others, these others are evil, therefore I am good. For the argument to succeed, the "evil" must apply in the same way to all: anyone who is like these others is evil, I am not like them, therefore I am good.

No comparable condemnation is presupposed within the perspective of the self-affirmative philosopher, or of the primitive warrior or blond beast, as Nietzsche argues with the support of the "hieroglyphic record" he seeks to decipher:

> One should not overlook the almost benevolent nuances that the Greek nobility, for example, bestows on all the words it employs to distinguish the lower orders from itself; how they are continuously mingled and sweetened with a kind of pity, consideration, and forbearance, so that finally almost all the words referring to the common man have remained as expressions signifying "unhappy," "pitiable" (compare *deilos, deilaios, poneros, mochtheros,* the last two of which properly designate the common man as work-slave and beast of burden). . . . The "well-born" *felt* themselves to be the "happy"; they did not have to establish their happiness artificially by examining their enemies. . . . (*GM*,I:10)

Among their "others," then, there may be some that the nobles pity or even despise, but there will also be some that are honored, even, Nietzsche insists, loved: "How much reverence has a noble man for his enemies!—and such reverence is a bridge to love.—For he desires his enemy for himself, as his mark of distinction; he can endure no other enemy than one in whom there is nothing to despise and *very much* to honor!" For the slave, on the other hand, "others" are to be condemned: "In contrast to this, picture 'the enemy' as the man of *ressentiment* conceives him—and here precisely is his deed, his creation: he has conceived 'the evil enemy,' 'the *Evil One,*' and this in fact is his basic concept, from which he then evolves, as an afterthought and pendant, a 'good one'—himself!" (*GM*,I:10).

That noble warriors or blond beasts fail to condemn their others does not, certainly, mean that they do them no harm. As Nietzsche stresses,

> once they go outside, where the strange, the *stranger* is found, they are not much better than uncaged beasts of prey. . . . They go *back* to the innocent conscience of the beast of prey, as triumphant monsters who perhaps emerge from a disgusting [*scheusslichen*] procession of murder, arson, rape, and torture, exhilarated and undisturbed of soul, as if it were no more than a student's prank . . . . (*GM*,I:11)

I stress again that Nietzsche does not advocate a return to a "noble morality" of this sort. He can therefore assert that in Napoleon, "the problem of the *noble ideal as such* is made flesh—one might well ponder *what* kind of problem it is: Napoleon, this synthesis of the *inhuman and superhuman*" (*GM*,I:16).

I emphasize, because the point is easily missed, that Nietzsche explicitly identifies Napoleon as incarnating the *problem* of the noble ideal, *not* its solution: the solution would be not the synthesis of inhuman and superhuman, but rather the separation of the superhuman from the inhuman. Prior to Nietzsche's "transvaluation," the two have appeared to be necessarily conjoined. Slave moralities have judged, in effect, that the inhuman is too high a price to pay for the superhuman—better to settle for an "all too human" mediocrity. Past noble moralities, on the other hand, have judged that it is better to have both the superhuman and the inhuman than to have neither. From the conflict emerges Nietzsche's genealogical question: is the connection between the inhuman and the superhuman one that can be severed? The two have been together, for millennia, in the same pocket; are they together, Nietzsche asks, because they are inseparable, or because no one has tried to unstuff the pocket?

If the connection can be severed at all, it cannot be severed within the framework of a slave, or universal, morality: any law all *should* obey must be one all *are able* to obey, and thus a law that applies on the level of the lowest common denominator. Even priestly asceticism—the nihilistic, "hypnotic muffling of all sensitivity" [*Gesammtdämpfung der Sensibilität*]—is too strict a law, for it requires an "intellectual Stoicism" of which most are incapable. Priests have therefore found other ways of spreading their teachings, and thus their power. One method, particularly effective on "work-slaves and prisoners," and especially on "women, who are usually both," is habituation in "mechanical activity" [*die machinale Tätigkeit*] and indoctrination in "the blessing of labor" [*den Segen der Arbeit*]. Other effective means to anti-sensualism include "the prescribing of a petty pleasure that is easily attainable and can be made into a regular event"—a prescription immeasurably facilitated by the development of network television—and even training in gaining pleasure by causing pleasure, better known as love of neighbor [*Nächstenliebe*] (*GM*,III:18).

Such have been the end and means of the priests and of their asceticism. Their "slave rebellion in morality" was unrecognized before Nietzsche, he insists, only because it was so successful. The deepest reason for its continued success is that human beings would rather "will *nothingness* than *not* will" (*GM*,III:1,28). A counterideal has been lacking.

Counterideals

Nietzsche is aware, of course, that many of his post-Enlightenment contemporaries would champion modern science as the counterideal to Christianity. In *The Genealogy*, as in *The Birth of Tragedy*, Nietzsche explicitly rejects this thesis: "science today has absolutely no belief in itself, let alone an ideal above it—and where it still inspires passion, love, ardor, and *suffering* at all, it is not the opposite of the ascetic ideal but rather *the latest and noblest form of it*" (*GM*,III:23).

Science emerges, according to Nietzsche, from Christianity. Jesus teaches, "You shall know the truth, and the truth shall make you free." Science attempts, in its own way, to know the truth, but one of the truths it discovers is that, at best, we cannot know whether or not God exists; this truth is made explicit by Kant. Christianity thus undermines its own doctrine; it thereby undermines its own morality. Christian morality is binding, Nietzsche insists, only if we must be moral to avoid being punished. If God is dead, there is no one to punish us for being immoral, so the death of God is to be followed by the death of morality. This death will occupy the two centuries following Nietzsche, the centuries of nihilism's rule (*GM*,III:27).

To say that science emerges from and then undermines Christianity is not to say that science, or the scientist, is simply despicable:

> Today there are plenty of modest and worthy laborers among scholars, too, who are happy in their little nooks; and because they are happy there, they sometimes demand rather immodestly that one ought to be content with things today, generally—especially in the domain of science, where so much that is useful remains to be done. I am not denying that; the last thing I want is to destroy the pleasure these honest workers take in their craft: for I approve of their work. But that one works rigorously in the sciences and that there are contented workers certainly does *not* prove that science as a whole possesses a goal, a will, an ideal, or the passion of a great faith. The opposite is the case, to repeat: where it is not the latest expression of the ascetic ideal—and the exceptions are too rare, noble, and atypical to refute the general proposition—science today is a *hiding place* for every kind of discontent, disbelief, gnawing worm, *despectio sui*, bad conscience—it is the unrest of the *lack* of ideals, the suffering from the *lack* of any great love, the discontent in the face of involuntary contentment. (*GM*,III:23)

To clarify and support this charge against science, Nietzsche cites an argument from *Joyful Science*: the scientist's belief in truth is a metaphysical belief, an "affirmation of a world other than that of life, nature, and history,"—a world, perhaps, of nothing but quarks and quasars—and therewith a denial of "this world, *our* world" (*JS*:344; quoted *GM*,III:24). "We knowers of today," godless and antimetaphysical though we take ourselves to be, remain Platonists in this most important sense.

Scientists may not qualify as opponents of the ascetic ideal, but Nietzsche identifies other candidates. Chief among them are "free spirits," those philosophers and scholars who explicitly oppose the ascetic ideal. This claim, too, Nietzsche rejects, insisting that such counteridealism is itself a form of idealism, a way of looking away from the real, and hence of denying life. The free spirits' faith in their opposition to the ideal is their "last" faith:

These nay-sayers and outsiders of today who are unconditional on one point—their insistence on intellectual cleanliness; these hard, severe, abstinent, heroic spirits who constitute the honor of our age; all these pale atheists, anti-Christians, immoralists, nihilists, these skeptics, ephectics, hectics of spirit (. . .), these last idealists of knowledge, within whom alone intellectual conscience is today alive and well,—they certainly believe they are as completely liberated from the ascetic ideal as possible, these "free, *very* free spirits"; and yet . . . they themselves embody it today and perhaps they alone. . . . They are far from being *free* spirits: *for they still have faith in truth.* (*GM*,III:24)

The free spirits' "faith in truth" is another form of scientific objectivism, and thus another form of dogmatism: it depends on the basic conviction that there is one truth, one way, that is for all. In rejecting this faith, Nietzsche points us in the direction of his own counterideal:

Henceforth, my dear philosophers, let us be on guard against the dangerous old conceptual fiction that posited a "pure, will-less, painless, timeless knowing subject"; let us guard against the snares of such contradictory concepts as "pure reason," "absolute spirituality," "knowledge in itself": these always demand that we should think of an eye that is completely unthinkable, an eye turned in no particular direction, in which the active and interpreting forces, through which alone seeing becomes seeing *something*, are supposed to be lacking; these always demand of the eye an absurdity and a nonsense. There is *only* a perspectival seeing, *only* a perspectival "knowing"; and the *more* affects we allow to speak about one thing, the *more* eyes, different eyes, we can use to observe one thing, the more complete will be our "concept" of this thing, our "objectivity." But to eliminate the will altogether, to suspend each and every affect, supposing we were capable of this—what would that mean but to *castrate* the intellect? (*GM*,III:12)

Priests and other dogmatists, we know, condemn diversity: they insist that theirs is the one way that is the way for all. Blond beasts do not condemn diversity, but neither do they affirm it; they are indifferent to ways that are other than their own way. This indifference provides the opening for the inhuman: the otherness of the others is not to be respected, therefore murder, rape, etc., need not be justified. In the passage I have just cited, Nietzsche suggests a motive for taking a third stance with respect to diversity, i.e., affirming it: if I want to learn about something—life, for example—one important way of learning is seeing other ways it may be seen. For that, other seers are helpful, indeed, necessary:

to see differently in this way for once, to *want* to see differently, is no small discipline and preparation of the intellect for its future "objectivity"—the latter understood not as "contemplation without interest" (which is a nonsensical absurdity), but as the ability to *control* one's Pro and Con and to dispose of them, so that one knows how to employ a *variety* of perspectives and affective interpretations in the service of knowledge. (*GM*,III:12)

This perspectival objectivity is a feature of Nietzsche's counterideal; but can the counterideal succeed? Can it supplant science and modernity? Can philosophy free itself from priestly asceticism? "Is there sufficient pride, daring, courage, self-confidence available today, sufficient will of the spirit, will to responsibility, *freedom of will*, for 'the philosopher' to be henceforth—possible on earth?" (*GM*,III:10).

Measured even by the standards of the ancient Greeks, our entire modern way of life, insofar as it is not weakness but power and consciousness of power, has the appearance of sheer *hybris* and godlessness: for the longest time it was precisely the reverse of those things we hold in honor today that had a good conscience on its side and God for its guardian. Our whole attitude toward nature, the way we violate her with the aid of machines and the heedless inventiveness of our technicians and engineers, is *hybris* . . . our attitude toward *ourselves* is *hybris,* for we experiment with animals and, carried away by curiosity, we cheerfully vivisect our souls. . . . We violate ourselves nowadays, no doubt of it, we nutcrackers of the soul, ever questioning and questionable, as if life were nothing but cracking nuts; and thus we are bound to grow day-by-day more questionable, *worthier* of asking questions [*Fragwürdiger, würdiger zu fragen*]; perhaps also worthier—of living? (*GM*,III:9)

The question that emerges from *The Genealogy* is the question that emerges from *The Birth of Tragedy,* albeit in a different form: what are we to make of, or do with, our recognition that we are always hermeneuticists (both theoretically and practically), confronted never with static, isolated facts or objects that speak simply for themselves, but rather, always, with genealogically conditioned configurations that we must interpret? How can we sever the powerful bonds that have developed, over the centuries, between philosophy and asceticism, decency and morality, science and technology, superhuman and inhuman?

The Genealogy does not answer these questions, but it points us in the direction of Nietzsche's answer. Its Third Essay

offers the answer to the question whence the ascetic ideal, the priests' ideal, derives its tremendous *power* although it is the *harmful* ideal *par excellence,* a will to the end, an ideal of decadence. Answer: not, as people may believe, because God is at work behind the priests but *faute de mieux*—because it was the only ideal so far, because it had no rival. "For man would rather will even nothingness than *not* will."—Above all, a *counterideal* was lacking—*until* Zarathustra. (EH,XII)

II
Eternal Return

Leaving there and proceeding for three days toward the east, you reach Diomira, a city with sixty silver domes, bronze statues of all the gods, streets paved with lead, a crystal theater, a golden cock that crows each morning on a tower. All these beauties will already be familiar to the visitor, who has seen them also in other cities. But the special quality of this city for the man who arrives there on a September evening, when the days are growing shorter and the multicolored lamps are lighted all at once at the doors of the food stalls and from a terrace a woman's voice cries ooh!, is that he feels envy toward those who now believe they have once before lived an evening identical to this and who think they were happy, that time.

Italo Calvino

5

Eternal Return Revisited

If this were a book by Italo Calvino, you might now encounter the following:

You have now read about thirty pages and you're becoming caught up in the story. At a certain point you remark: "This sentence sounds somehow familiar. In fact, this whole passage reads like something I've read before." Of course: there are themes that recur, the text is interwoven with these reprises, which serve to express the fluctuation of time. You are the sort of reader who is sensitive to such refinements; you are quick to catch the author's intentions and nothing escapes you. But, at the same time, you also feel a certain dismay; just when you were beginning to grow truly interested, at this very point the author feels called upon to display one of those virtuoso tricks so customary in modern writing, repeating a paragraph word for word. Did you say paragraph? Why, it's a whole page; you make the comparison, he hasn't changed even a comma. And as you continue, what develops? Nothing: the narration is repeated, identical to the pages you have read!

Wait a minute! Look at the page number. Damn! From page 32 you've gone back to page 17! What you thought was a stylistic subtlety on the author's part is simply a printer's mistake: they have inserted the same pages twice. The mistake occurred as they were binding the volume: a book is made up of sixteen-page signatures; each signature is a large sheet on which sixteen pages are printed, and which is then folded over eight times; when all the signatures are bound together, it can happen that two identical signatures end up in the same copy; it's the sort of accident that happens now and then. You leaf anxiously through the next pages to find page 33, assuming it exists; a repeated signature would be a minor inconvenience, the irreparable damage comes when the proper signature has vanished, landing in another copy where perhaps that one will be doubled and this one will be missing. In any event, you want to pick up the thread of your reading, nothing else matters to you, you had reached a point where you can't skip even one page.

Here is page 31 again, page 32 . . . and then what comes next? Page 17 all over again, a third time! What kind of book did they sell you, anyway? They bound together all these copies of the same signature, not another page in the whole book is any good.

You fling the book on the floor, you would hurl it out of the window, even out of the closed window, through the slats of the Venetian blinds; let them shred its incongruous quires, let sentences, words, morphemes, phonemes gush forth, beyond recomposition into discourse; through the panes, and if they are of unbreakable glass so much the better, hurl the book and reduce it to photons, undulatory vibrations, polarized spectra; through the wall, let the book crumble into molecules and atoms passing between atom and atom of the reinforced concrete, breaking up into electrons, neutrons, neutrinos, elementary particles more and more minute; through the telephone wires, let it be reduced to electronic impulses, into flow of information, shaken by redundancies and noises, and let it be degraded into a swirling entropy. You would like to throw it out of the house, out of the block, beyond the neighborhood, beyond the city limits, beyond the state confines, beyond the regional administration, beyond the national community, beyond the Common Market, beyond Western culture, beyond the continental shelf, beyond the atmosphere, the biosphere, the stratosphere, the field of gravity, the solar system, the galaxy, the cumulus of galaxies, to succeed in hurling it beyond the point the galaxies have reached in their expansion, where space-time has not yet arrived, where it would be received by nonbeing, or, rather, the not-being which has never been and will never be, to be lost in the most absolutely guaranteed undeniable negativity. Merely what it deserves, neither more nor less. (*If On a Winter's Night*, 25–27)

And what our lives deserve, too. After all, I'm not now writing this paragraph for the first time, nor you reading it—or so we seem to be told by Nietzsche and Zarathustra, teachers of the eternal return (Z,III:13.2, 275.29–30; *TI*,X:5). And when I finish writing this paragraph, and you reading it, neither of us will go on to anything truly new, like Calvino's unreachable page 33; instead, we will return, I to something I've written, you to something you've read, not once before, but infinitely many times. And not because of a printer's error.

The thought of eternal return, Nietzsche tells us, is one that can transform us, one that may well crush us: what if we are as we now are and do as we now do not once but rather once more, and not, by far, for the last time?

Well, so what? Who cares? Is this a thought that affects us at all, to say nothing of transforming or crushing us? What if we have all been here before? Certainly, none of us can remember it—and that as a matter of principle, not merely of fact. So why should we care? How could we possibly care? The notion of living the same life over and over again sounds boring, perhaps—but on second thought not even that: how can it be boring to repeat our lives if we have always already forgotten what is going to happen next? What difference could it possibly make? None at all, it seems—it can't possibly make a difference, because it asserts a difference that is really not a difference: if a universe in which everything recurs eternally is absolutely indistinguishable from one in which everything happens only once, then, we may insist with Leibniz, these two universes are not two, but rather one. There seems to be simply no difference between my writing and your reading as one-time events, and as eternally returning ones.

But perhaps there is a difference, after all. Milan Kundera writes:

The idea of eternal return is a mysterious one, and Nietzsche has often perplexed other philosophers with it: to think that everything recurs as we once experienced it, and that the recurrence itself recurs ad infinitum! What does this mad myth signify?

Putting it negatively, the myth of eternal return states that a life which disappears once and for all, which does not return, is like a shadow, without weight, dead in advance, and whether it was horrible, beautiful, or sublime, its horror, sublimity, and beauty mean nothing. We need take no more note of it than of a war between two African kingdoms in the fourteenth century, a war that altered nothing in the destiny of the world, even if a hundred thousand blacks perished in excruciating torment.

Will the war between the two African kingdoms in the fourteenth century itself be altered if it recurs again and again, in eternal return?

It will: it will become a solid mass, permanently protuberant, its inanity irreparable.

If the French Revolution were to recur eternally, French historians would be less proud of Robespierre. But because they deal with something that will not return, the bloody years of the Revolution have turned into mere words, theories, and discussions, have become lighter than feathers, frightening no one. There is an infinite difference between a Robespierre who occurs only once in history and a Robespierre who eternally returns, chopping off French heads.

Let us therefore agree that the idea of eternal return implies a perspective from which things appear other than as we know them: they appear without the mitigating circumstance of their transitory nature. This mitigating circumstance prevents us from coming to a verdict. For how can we condemn something that is ephemeral, in transit? In the sunset of dissolution, everything is illuminated by the aura of nostalgia, even the guillotine.

Not long ago, I caught myself experiencing a most incredible sensation. Leafing through a book on Hitler, I was touched by some of his portraits: they reminded me of my childhood. I grew up during the war; several members of my family perished in Hitler's concentration camps; but what were their deaths compared with the memories of a lost period in my life, a period that would never return?

This reconciliation with Hitler reveals the profound moral perversity of a world that rests essentially on the nonexistence of return, for in this world everything is pardoned in advance and therefore cynically permitted.

If every second of our lives recurs an infinite number of times, we are nailed to eternity as Jesus Christ was nailed to the cross. It is a terrifying prospect. In the world of eternal return the weight of unbearable responsibility lies heavy on every move we make. That is why Nietzsche called the idea of eternal return the heaviest of burdens (*das schwerste Gewicht*). (*Lightness*, 3–5)

If nothing returns, there is no "weight": "everything is pardoned in advance and therefore cynically permitted," or, in the words of Kundera's title, being is unbearably light. But why should unrepeated events be "light"? And how could repetition endow them with "weight"?

At the outset, we must note that Kundera's estimation of eternal return follows Nietzsche in presupposing that there is no God, or that God is dead. If there is a living God who will confront us on judgment day, we can scarcely view our acts as simply ephemeral and insignificant. On the other hand, as Nietzsche and Dostoevsky insist, if God is dead, if nothing is true, then everything is permitted.

Yes, responds Kundera, everything is permitted—*unless* everything returns, eternally. Kundera reads the thought of eternal return as a weighty one, a thought giving to acts and events the moral import they would lack in a godless universe wherein every act or event occurred only once: "There is an infinite difference between a Robespierre who occurs only once in history and a Robespierre who eternally returns, chopping off French heads." So Kundera tells us. But is there a difference? What could it be? "The war between the two African kingdoms in the fourteenth century . . . will become a solid mass, permanently protuberant, its inanity irreparable." How so? Does it escape inanity by occurring only once? Or does the singularity of its occurrence makes its inanity reparable? How is it repaired? How would its return make its protuberance permanent? Wouldn't it continue to be "protuberant" only on those rare occasions when it was remembered? Would eternal return make a difference, or no difference at all? Is Kundera's "infinite difference" not, ultimately, a meaningless identity?

I see no satisfactory answers for these questions. But perhaps they are the wrong questions. Kundera himself seems to acknowledge that it makes no difference whether or not Robespierre *actually* returns eternally. The thought of eternal return, he writes, provides "a *perspective* from which things *appear* other than as we know them": a perspective, a way of looking at things, not a truth, not (necessarily) the way things are.

The perspective of eternal return, Kundera tells us (problematically, he admits—he too is trying to make sense of Nietzsche's "mad myth"), provides our acts with moral weight, but thereby places a weight on us: "the weight of unbearable responsibility lies heavy on every move we make." This, according to Kundera, is why Nietzsche calls the thought "the heaviest burden." But what makes the thought burdensome?

"The Heaviest Burden" [*Das grösste Schwergewicht*] is the title for the section in *Joyful Science* where Nietzsche first introduces the thought of eternal return. The section reads as follows:

What if a demon crept after you one day or night in your loneliest solitude and said to you: "This life, as you live it now and have lived it, you will have to live again and again, times without number; and there will be nothing new in it, but every pain and every joy and every thought and sigh and all unspeakably small and great in your life must return to you, and everything in the same series and sequence—and in the same way this spider and this moonlight among the trees, and in the same way this moment and I myself. The eternal hourglass of existence will be turned again and again—and you with it, you dust grain of dust!"— Would you not throw yourself down and gnash your teeth and curse the demon who thus spoke? Or have you experienced a tremendous moment in which you would have answered him: "You are a god and never did I hear anything more divine!" If this thought gained power over you as you are now, it would transform you and perhaps crush you; the question in all and everything: "do you want this again and again, times without number?" would lie as the heaviest burden upon all your actions. Or how well disposed towards yourself and towards life would you have to become to have no greater desire than for this ultimate eternal sanction and seal? (JS:341)

The thought of eternal return, Nietzsche writes, is one that can "gain power" over me; if it gains power over me, it will certainly transform me, and it may crush me—it may be the heaviest of burdens. But maybe not. It might not be burdensome at all. Whether it is or not depends on "how well disposed" I am—or become—towards myself and towards life; it depends on how I view my life, on the perspective that I take.

Describing a perspective at one extreme—the one from which Nietzsche's thought would indeed be felt as a crushing burden —Schopenhauer writes:

it is really unbelievable how meaninglessly and insignificantly, viewed from the outside, the lives of most human beings flow by, and how dully and stupidly, experienced from within. Such a life is an insipid [mattes] longing and agonizing, a dreamlike staggering [Taumeln] through life's four ages all the way to death, accompanied by a series of trivial thoughts. These lives are like clockworks that are wound up and then go, without knowing why; and every time a human being is conceived and born, the clock of human life is wound up once again, in order now to repeat once again the hurdy-gurdy song [Leierstück] it has already played out numberless times, measure for measure and beat for beat, with insignificant variations. . . . [I]t may be that there has never been a thought-ful [besonnen] and honest man who, at the end of his life, would wish to go through it once again, who would not prefer to that even total nonbeing. (WWR,I:58; order altered)

It may be, Schopenhauer suspects, that there has never been "a thoughtful and honest man" who, given the choice, would not hurl his life into Calvino's "most absolutely guaranteed undeniable negativity" rather than live it again. Merely what it deserves, no more and no less. It may be, as Nietzsche asserts elsewhere, that "concerning life, the wisest of all ages have passed the same judgment: it is no good [es taugt nichts]" (TI,II:1). But the question remains: why should Schopenhauer's "thoughtful and honest man," or Nietzsche's "wisest of all ages," be crushed by the thought of eternal return? Would not the "wisest," like the "thoughtful," come to realize that repetition is irrelevant, even meaningless, unless it is accompanied by recollection? Would not the wisest see that even if recollection without repetition is empty—because we cannot change what we cannot repeat—repetition without recollection is also blind? That if an event occurs only once then, as Kundera suggests, "whether it was horrible, beautiful, or sublime, its horror, sublimity, and beauty mean nothing"; but that its recurrence makes it no more meaningful?

The wise and the thoughtful might indeed "come to realize" that the thought of eternal return makes no difference, just as I seem to have come to that realization, perhaps bringing you along with me. This conclusion is easily drawn as one sits comfortably, objectively and bemusedly contemplating what Nietzsche calls his "most abysmal thought." But Nietzsche is not concerned, at least primarily, with the conclusions we draw from our logical reflections, with what we get by "groping along threads with cowardly hands," timorously "deducing" rather than daringly "guessing" (Z,III:2.1). Nietzsche does not write, "What if, one sunny afternoon, you were to sit comfortably in your favorite chair reading a scholarly treatise wherein a relatively non-threatening academic type raised the question, second hand, 'What if you're not doing this for the first time?' " Would Nietzsche expect you to respond, at that point (which is this point), either by cursing and gnashing your teeth, or by praising me, your humble author, as a god?

In "The Heaviest Burden," Nietzsche is not concerned with a cosmological hypothesis we can consider, calmly and rationally, in warm and well-lit rooms. His concern, instead, is with how we would react *immediately*, rather than upon reflection, *individually*, rather than communally, in our "loneliest solitude," rather than in our familiar everydayness, and if confronted not by a professor or a book or a theory, but rather by a demon. Rejecting a hypothesis is one thing, facing a demon another.

In their moments of loneliest solitude, confronted by the demon, the "wisest of all ages," the "thoughtful and honest," would, Nietzsche tells us, respond to the demon by hurling themselves down, gnashing their teeth and cursing. Those who are dishonest or merely thoughtless, on the other hand, taken in by life's "gaudy paint job" or distracted by utopian, Socratic dreams, might view the demon as an epiphenomenal manifestation of synaptic or intestinal disturbance, easily drowned in wine coolers or Pepto-Bismol.

At the very least, in introducing the thought of eternal return, Nietzsche wants to raise for us the question whether there is a perspective, a way of being disposed towards ourselves and our lives, that would allow us to respond to the demon not with gnashing teeth and cursing lips, and certainly not with anti-flatulents or martinis, but rather with the jubilant exclamation, "You are a god and never did I hear anything more divine." Lacking that perspective, he suggests, our prospects are bleak: either we try to avoid seeing through life's gaudy paint job—we avoid recognizing that our lives are indeed constantly exposed to, even if not always beset by, Schopenhauer's "terrible pains and tortures," preferring to delude ourselves into thinking that life's pains and tortures, such as death and disease, are reserved for others, and certainly not for us or for those we love; and that science, the Socratic panacea, will soon find remedies in any case—either we so deceive ourselves, or we see life as the wisest have always seen it, as no good. But if life is no good, and God, having died, can no longer punish us for committing suicide, the conclusion strengthens that Silenus is right, that the best we can do is to put ourselves out of our misery: I cannot arrange never to have been born, but I can arrange to die soon.

Within this chapter so far, I have been concerned with one question raised by Nietzsche's thought of the eternal return. That question is, *if* the thought means what it appears to mean, if it is intended to lead us to entertain a vision of a cosmic cycle in which all events are repeated, endlessly, in a single sequence—*if* this is Nietzsche's thought, my question has been, why should we care about it? What difference could it make? I have not offered a single, decisive answer to this question, although I have suggested that this eternal return is important, if at all, not as a scientist's hypothesis, inviting rational assessment, but rather as a demon's proclamation, forcing visceral reaction.

How I would react to Nietzsche's demon depends on how I view myself and my life; it depends on my perspective. Many possible perspectives, Nietzsche suggests, focus on phantasms that become transparent when examined closely; many others, thought through to their ends, reveal suicide as the logical consequence of their acceptance. Through the thought of eternal return, as a challenge, Nietzsche seeks to encourage us to seek a different perspective, a way of viewing our lives that is affirmative without being deceptive or dishonest. This seems to suggest that, if we now consider life itself, if we now seek such a perspective, the thought of eternal return will have done its work: it will have redirected our attention. I think indeed that Nietzsche intends that the thought direct our attention toward our earthly lives—but I don't think that this requires our turning away from the thought of eternal return. I suspect, on the contrary, that it leads us back to the thought, but to a different version of the thought.

We (I, at least) have been led toward reflection on life, and on how life may be viewed, through the thought of an endlessly repeated sequence of events. This is one sense of "eternal return" or, better, it governs one constellation of senses: eternal return as hypothesis, as perspective, and as challenge. I now want to introduce some reasons for thinking that there may be another sense of "eternal return," a sense that does not merely point us toward the problem of perspectives, but is itself an essential aspect of Nietzsche's own affirmative perspective. So far, I have presupposed that eternal return means, essentially, endless sequential repetition; I now want to ask whether that is all that it means.

This may appear to be a question not worth asking. After all, "The

Heaviest Burden," cited above, seems quite clear: there is no question concerning what we are being asked to think, the only question is, why bother? No doubt, the content of the thought of eternal return, as the thought is there expressed, is clear: the luminous clarity of the section is one of its most striking features. And if some doubt is raised by the relatively early date of "The Heaviest Burden," that doubt seems to be overcome by *Ecce Homo*'s explicit clarification of *Zarathustra*'s "doctrine of the 'eternal recurrence' " as the teaching "of the unconditional and infinitely repeated circular course of all things" (*EH*,IV:3).

This evidence, no doubt, is powerful; and yet I am not wholly convinced by it. What I am not convinced of is that the notion of an infinite historical repetition expresses the thought in its most important form. Words are pockets, and many meanings have been and still may be stuffed into "eternal" and "return." These meanings may combine in various ways. In the remainder of this chapter I indicate why I suspect that another way of combining "eternal" and "return" develops within Zarathustra; in the following chapter, I attempt to determine what that other way might be.

I begin by suggesting that *if* "eternal return" names (at least) two distinct but related thoughts, that should not surprise us. Not only does Nietzsche recognize words as pockets, he also regularly stuffs the words he uses with multiple meanings, introducing systematic ambiguities into his own works. Frequently, he focuses on a word as used in the philosophical tradition, subjecting it to conceptual and/or genealogical analysis in order to reveal that its use is either arbitrarily speculative or self-destructively incoherent. Once he has thus undermined the traditional use of the word—typically, its "metaphysical" use, its use within the "Christian-moral" tradition—he reappropriates the term itself, providing it with a non-metaphysical signification.

The most conspicuous consequence of this Nietzschean practice is that it has convinced many that Nietzsche constantly contradicts himself. I have introduced passages where Nietzsche castigates truth and logic, for example, but also passages where he claims to tell us the truth, and to proceed logically. In *The Birth of Tragedy*, in passages not cited above, Nietzsche both criticizes morality for being a "deception," and insists that "all life depends on deception" (*BT*,SC:5). At times, Nietzsche seems to contradict himself even within single passages: he first undermines one usage of a term, and then reappropriates the term for his own use. For example:

> The antithesis of a true and an apparent world is lacking: there is only one world, and it is false, cruel, contradictory, seductive, without meaning. . . . A world thus constituted is the true world. (*N*:11[415] / *WP*:853)

In this passage, we are told both that our world is false and that it is true, but the conjunction does not yield the blatant contradiction that may appear to result. Our world is not the "true" world that would gain its truth only through opposition to an "apparent" world; it is not the "true world" of the most vulgar version of Platonistic metaphysics, which Nietzsche takes to have been the predominant form for some twenty-five hundred years. From this Platonistic perspective, our world is not true, but false, for it lacks the features a metaphysically true world would have to exhibit. In a word, our world is temporal—transient and alterable—whereas the metaphysically true world would have to be eternal—permanent and invariable. But to say that our world is "false" in the metaphysical sense is no objection to it or to its truth, if we abandon the metaphysical perspective. On the contrary: if we no longer accept the metaphysical notion of truth, then we are free to recognize our temporal, variable world precisely as the true world, that is, as the world we actually inhabit, the only world with which we need be concerned.

Nietzsche's anti-metaphysical use of words as pockets should make at least plausible my suggestion that "eternal return" may have more than one meaning. In further support of the suggestion, I turn to a different sort of evidence, provided by the way eternal return is treated in *Thus Spoke Zarathustra*.

As I indicate in my opening chapter, in *Ecce Homo* Nietzsche describes *Zarathustra* as "standing alone" among his books as the one in which his "yes-saying teachings" are presented. He also there identifies eternal return as *Zarathustra*'s "fundamental conception" (*EH*,X,1). Yet what is most striking about *Zarathustra*, in light of Nietzsche's retrospective description, is the extraordinarily problematic status of the thought of eternal return within it. I examine its status in the following chapter, but I note now— as an additional fish hook—that although it is the work's "fundamental conception," Zarathustra, rarely short of words, expresses it only in recounting a dream, and then only in a preliminary fashion, before he has directly confronted it. Following his confrontation with the thought, he seems to discuss it not at all; what we hear of it we hear not from him, but from his animals. This bizarre fact requires careful interpretation. The thought itself appears to be simple, and easily expressed—witness "The Heaviest Burden." Yet in *Zarathustra*, where *Ecce Homo* raises the expectation that it should be presented at least as directly and forcefully, it arises, when it arises at all, in ambiguous and perplexing ways. Why should this be so? Only, it seems to me, if the "fundamental thought" of *Zarathustra* is not the thought described in "The Heaviest Burden," or even in *Ecce Homo*.

To see what the "fundamental thought" of *Zarathustra* might be, we must turn, without further ado, to that book itself.

6

The Resurrection of Zarathustra's Soul

Human beings are not born once and for all on the day their mothers give birth to them . . .; life obliges them over and over again to give birth to themselves.

Gabriel García Márquez

Into the Labyrinth

"Only where there are tombs are there resurrections"; thus spoke Zarathustra (Z,II:11; 145.13). "Nietzsche is unconcerned with tombs and resurrections, and certainly with souls"; thus have spoken generations of commentators. Nevertheless, a careful reading of *Thus Spoke Zarathustra* reveals that Zarathustra has a soul, and that it is twice entombed and twice resurrected. My purpose in this chapter is to establish the relevance of those resurrections to Nietzsche's affirmative teachings, and thereby to resurrect Zarathustra's soul yet again, to reverse the fate it has met at the hands of scholars and philosophers who, by simply ignoring it, have subjected it to a third, hermeneutical entombment.

That Zarathustra's soul has often been ignored is perhaps not surprising given that throughout Part I of the book Nietzsche himself scarcely mentions it. Worse yet, Zarathustra can appear, in Part I, to be a champion of the body and an enemy of the soul. In the fourth of his "Speeches," Zarathustra reports that "the awakened one," "the one who knows," says, "I am body purely and simply, and nothing besides; and soul is only a word for something in the body" (Z,I:4; 39.7–9). But thus speaks only the awakened one, and although he may speak thus at all times, Zarathustra quotes him only when speaking to one tempted to despise his body.

Zarathustra says different things to different people; he also says some things to no people, but only to his animals, and some things not even to his animals, but only to himself. To determine the significance of Zarathustra's citation of "the awakened one," or of any other of Zarathustra's utterances, one must consider the audience to whom it is presented; often, one must also consider where Zarathustra stands, in terms of his own development, at the time of the utterance.

In terms of its audience as well as of its subject matter, the speech within which Zarathustra quotes "the awakened one," and which includes his most explicit discussion of body and soul, is complex: Zarathustra twice tells us that he wants to "speak his word to the despisers of the body" (39.2, 40.19), and thrice explicitly addresses "you despisers of the body" (40.25–6, 32, 41.5), but the central exposition (39.12–40.18) is addressed to "my brother" (39.12–13, 40.3), one of Zarathustra's companions. The structure of the section suggests that this particular brother is in danger of becoming a despiser of the body: for "you despisers of the body," Zarathustra's words come "too late" (40.31), whereas for the brother, there may still be time. Zarathustra attempts to use this time; but what he tells this companion about the soul, at this time, is not his last word on the subject.

As for Zarathustra's own soul, in the Prologue it is "unmoved," and there is no indication that it stirs at all before Zarathustra's return to his mountain at the end of Part I. As Part II opens, however, it is "full of impatience and desire" for his companions, and by the time of "The Night Song" (Z,II:9) it has become a "leaping fountain" and "the song of a lover." Nevertheless, it remains silent and unaddressed—in Parts I and II Zarathustra often speaks to his heart, but never to his soul—until, near the end of Part III, Zarathustra uses the form of address "O my soul" twenty-two times in a single section (Z,III:14), one that ends with Zarathustra exhorting his soul to sing. In the final two sections of Part III, the soul sings its songs, thereby providing Nietzsche's deepest elaborations of the thought of the eternal return, the "highest formulation of affirmation that can be attained" (EH,IX:1). What is thereby affirmed, I contend, is not a circular course of history, not a cosmic repetition, but rather the resurrection of the Nietzschean soul, a resurrection not elsewhere or elsewhen or once and for all—not a single, decisive event in some hinterworld or distant future—but rather here and now and repeatedly, a re-creation of the soul and by the soul, on an earth that has regained the "innocence of becoming."

I have noted that previous commentators have failed to recognize the importance of Zarathustra's soul, and I have asserted that they have consequently misinterpreted the doctrine of eternal return. I certainly do not suggest, however, that my predecessors have been unsympathetic or obtuse (some have certainly been both, but many have been neither). If they have failed in the ways I indicate, their failure has been due primarily to insufficient attention to the details of the text. If my attempted resurrection of Zarathustra's soul is to succeed, I must consider minutiae—I must finger nuances— from various sections of the text; I must attend to the order and interrelations of the sections as well as to their individual contents. Readers who have been firmly hooked by my earlier chapters (if such there be), as well as readers of *Zarathustra* who have been puzzled, intrigued, and/or frustrated by the the sections I discuss will, I hope, find my analyses helpful; in any case, such readers will agree with me that Nietzsche is worth the effort. On the other hand, readers who, for example, ask nothing more than to be reminded of

Raskolnikov as they peruse "Of the Pale Criminal"—readers for whom such associations count as insights into the text—are likely to be bored by my details. Any such readers who may have persevered to this point have now been forewarned.

In insisting on the importance of attention to details, I do not mean to suggest that I have attended to all of *Zarathustra*'s details. According to the Nietzschean position sketched in the previous chapter, a position I share, all human activity is "interpretive" in that it involves selection. In the terms of my title's metaphor, to act is to move within a labyrinth. The labyrinthine nature of Nietzsche's *Zarathustra* is apparent to all who have struggled with it; this book "for everyone and no one" contains a wealth of details, presented in an order that often seems simply chaotic. In this chapter, I follow one path within the labyrinth; I attempt, for the most part, to confine to endnotes my forays onto other paths.

I attempt to follow the path through *Zarathustra* traced by references to souls, and particularly to Zarathustra's soul, in part because (as I have suggested) it is a path other wanderers have left unexplored. This, of course, is far from sufficient reason; according to the general hermeneutical position I have sketched, there are countless untraced paths within any work. I follow my path, again, because I seek Nietzsche's affirmative teachings, which Nietzsche himself tells us are to be found in Zarathustra's doctrine of eternal return, and that doctrine emerges most fully, I am convinced, within the sections recounting Zarathustra's interactions with his soul.

All texts may be labyrinthine, but some are more confusing than others. Hoping to minimize confusion, I now provide first the briefest of descriptions of the labyrinth of *Zarathustra* itself, and then a map (not the only possible one, no doubt) for the labyrinth that is this chapter.

The first of *Zarathustra*'s four Parts begins with Zarathustra's descent from his mountain; the Prologue presents his encounter with the masses in a marketplace, and "Zarathustra's Speeches," his exchanges with the young men who become his companions. He departs for his mountain at the end of Part I, only to return to his companions at the beginning of Part II. He remains with them until the beginning of Part III, when he begins a second return journey to his mountain. Part III describes that journey, and then presents Zarathustra alone save for the occasional company of his two animals, a snake and an eagle. He remains on the mountain throughout Part IV, meeting a series of "higher men" who come in search of him. The book ends as it begins, as Zarathustra leaves his cave, "glowing and strong as a morning sun emerging from dark mountains," in order once again to return to "his work" below.

In this chapter, I follow not Zarathustra's own path, but rather the path traced by the book's references to his soul. I begin with souls in general: on the basis of several sections in Part I, I argue in "Wild Dogs and High Hopes" that the proper function of the soul in the economy of the individual is to invest the body's passions with a "highest goal," and then to "hold holy this highest hope." In "Zarathustra's Highest Hope" I turn to Zarathustra's soul, charting its development in Parts I–III from its initial, tranquil embracing of the overman as goal to the abandonment of any such exclusively futural hope, and consequently to a doubt and despair that can be overcome only through reconciliation with the thought of the eternal return. "Dwarves, Buffoons, and Barrel-Organs" examines Nietzsche's most direct discussions of eternal return, in "Of the Vision and the Riddle" (Z,III:2) and "The Convalescent" (Z,III:13), arguing that neither offers a reliable formulation of the thought. The attention paid to Zarathustra's soul leads instead, in "The Resurrection of Zarathustra's Soul," to the three closing sections of Part III where, I argue, eternal return is given a new sense that binds it to soul and to resurrection. Finally, in "Resurrection and Self-Creation" I describe the essential features of the earthly resurrection dramatized by Zarathustra's own transformations.

Wild Dogs and High Hopes

Zarathustra discusses the relation of body and soul most directly in "Of the Despisers of the Body." The account he gives there is complicated not only by the plurality of its audiences (described above), but also by the introduction of such additional elements as reason, spirit, I, and self. Yet the polemical intent seems clear: in opposition to what Nietzsche generally calls the "Christian-moral" or "metaphysical" interpretation of the relation, according to which the soul should rule the body, Zarathustra elevates the body over the soul. This seems clear, however, only if the abstract analysis is taken in isolation, only if the commentary provided by the concrete examples of the two immediately following sections is ignored. The examples reveal that the soul plays a role both more complex and more important than the abstract account indicates, a role that is often decisive and potentially salutary.

"Of the Despisers of the Body" opens by distinguishing between two accounts of the relation of body and soul:

> "Body am I and soul"—so says the child. And why should one not say what children say?
> But the awakened one, the one who knows, says: "Body am I purely and simply [ganz und gar], and soul is only a word for something in [an] the body." (Z,I:4; 39.5–9)

These options are exclusive but not exhaustive; some human beings are neither children nor awakened. A third view is espoused by the despisers of the body, who, like the hinterworldly of the previous section—those who attempt to see through the mere appearances of our world in order to glimpse a true world behind it—long to be souls, purely and simply, to be free from the bodies that bind them to the earth. The body "is a sickly thing to them, and they would dearly like to get out of their skins. That is why they hearken to the preachers of death, and why they themselves preach hinterworlds" (Z,I:3; 38.4–6).

The hinterworldly perspective—the religious nihilists' perspective—has been powerful yet, Zarathustra suggests, it depends upon an illusion: the soul the hinterworldly seek to affirm, the soul whose proper dwelling place would be behind our world, is nothing positive, but rather an indeterminate negation. The hinterworldly begin not by affirming the soul, but rather by denying the body: "Verily, they believe most strongly not in hinterworlds and redeeming drops of blood, but rather in the body, and their own body is, for them, their thing in itself" (Z,I:3; 38.1–3). They must therefore be termed "despisers of the body"; they are not lovers of the soul.

Because it is merely the negation of the body, the soul dreamed of by the hinterworldly and the despisers of the body is an empty dream; the "awakened one" knows better, and therefore speaks of the soul as "something in the body." This soul, like "spirit" and "sense," is a "small tool and plaything" of the body; spirit is the "small reason" that both serves and amuses the "great reason" of the body (38.12–14, 21). The true self of the individual thus resides not in soul, sense, or spirit, but rather in the body: "Behind your thoughts and feelings, my brother, stands a powerful commander, an unknown sage—he is called the self. He resides in your body, he is your body" (Z,I:4; 40.3–5).

The self, the body "commands," it seems, in that it determines ends: the "leaps and flights" of the I are detours to the goals of the self (40.10–11); "the creative body created spirit for itself as the hand of its willing" (40.23–24). Yet what the self, the body wills—all that it truly wills—is "to create beyond itself" (40.28–39); such creation is its "total fervor" (40.29–30), its sole desire. When it can no longer create beyond itself—as in the despisers of the body—then it longs only for death (40.26–27).

The "brother" addressed in the middle section of "Of the Despisers of the Body" is admonished to attend to the "great reason" of the body, just as the "brothers" addressed in "Of the Hinterworldly" (Z,I:3) are told to heed "the voice of the healthy body, the complete and foursquare body," a voice that speaks of the "meaning of the earth" (38.7–10), the overman (e. g., Z,P:3; 14.29–30). The bodies of the despisers are not healthy, they can no longer create beyond themselves, and thus speak no longer of the meaning of the earth; they speak only of death (even if they term death "afterlife").

From "Of the Despisers of the Body," we learn to distinguish healthy bodies from sickly ones, and we learn that the voice of the healthy body should be heeded. To see *how* it may be heeded, we must turn to "Of Joys and Passions" (Z,I:5), and to see what results when it is *not* heeded, we must look to "Of the Pale Criminal" (Z,I:6).

The pale criminal has heeded not the voice of the body, but rather that of the soul: "Behold this poor body! What it suffered and desired was interpreted by this poor soul,—it was interpreted as murderous lust and greed for the joy of the knife" (Z,I:6; 46.33–47.2). The voice of the pale criminal's body spoke, and his soul heard. But what it heard, it then had to interpret. The soul's interpretation of what the body suffered and desired led to the deed the pale criminal cannot bear, a senseless murder. The murder was desired, it seems, neither by the body nor by the soul; nevertheless, it became deed. The deed resulted from the soul's interpretation of what the body itself "suffered and desired"; but what did the body itself "suffer and desire"?

> What is this man? A heap of diseases that reach out through spirit into the world: there they want to find their prey.
> What is this man? A knot of wild snakes that are seldom at peace among one another,—that is why they go forth for themselves and seek prey in the world. (Z,I:6; 46.27–32)

At the time of the deed the pale criminal's body, reaching out through his spirit into the world, was diseased rather than healthy; but what made it diseased? What made of the body's will to create beyond itself, its will to overcome itself, a "knot of wild snakes," a "heap of diseases"? The cause was not, as with the despisers of body, an impotence or inability to create; the "heap of diseases," the "knot of wild snakes" do in some sense create beyond themselves, they "go forth for themselves to seek prey in the world." What then is the source of the pale criminal's disease, a disease clearly distinct from that of the despisers of the body? An answer to this question is suggested in the immediately preceding section, "Of Joys and Passions." There, Zarathustra tells his "brother," "Once you suffered passions [*hattest du Leidenschaften*] and called them evil" (43.1); "once you had wild dogs in your cellar" (43.11).

The brother, like the pale criminal, once suffered passions; the brother's passions became "wild dogs," the pale criminal's, "wild snakes." The brother's passions became "wild dogs," we are told, when they were called evil. To call the passions evil—or good, or bad, or whatever—is to interpret them. The voice of the body speaks in the passions; interpretation of what the voice says, we know from "Of the Pale Criminal," is the work of the soul. The pale criminal's soul interpreted what his body "suffered and desired" as "murderous lust and greed for the joy of the knife." Yet before it had made this interpretation, his body was already a "heap of diseases," his desires, a "knot of wild snakes." From "Of Joys and Passions," we learn that the desires become wild animals when they are interpreted as evil. We thereby learn that the interpretation imposed on the pale criminal's body by his soul is twofold: his soul first determined his passions as evil, and thus as "wild snakes"; it then judged that the passions must desire what wild snakes desire, that is, "murderous lust and the greed of the knife."

Once the passions are determined as evil, it follows that if they escape the control of the soul, they will act evilly; this is one of two central aspects of the motivation for the murder. The second aspect indicates why murder is the specific evil: the deed occurs only when the soul has failed in its struggle to suppress the body and its desires. The revenge it takes for its failure is revenge against another body and that body's desires; the best revenge requires the spilling of the body's vital force.

The pale criminal is the victim of his soul. His soul damns his body's desires as evil, and represses them for as long as it can. When it can do so no longer, it releases them as savages, to commit a senseless murder. The pale criminal's "poor reason" cannot comprehend the "madness before the deed" (46.12), the madness of the savage snakes; it therefore adds its interpretation, and with it the deed of robbery, intended to disguise the true motive (46.17–19).

The pale criminal's story is completed with his "madness after the deed" (46.9): "He then saw himself always as the doer of one deed. Madness I call this: the exception inverted itself, becoming the essence" (46.6–7). In his madness after the deed the pale criminal concludes, in effect, "Murderer am I purely and simply, and nothing besides," murderer once and for all, murderer in essence. But who or what is this murderer? Does the pale criminal take himself to be murderer in body, or in soul? He takes himself to be murderer once and for all, yet the body is nothing once and for all. The body grows, develops, and decays, the body eats and excretes, the body wakes and sleeps. The soul, according to the Christian-moral tradition from which the pale criminal cannot escape, is permanent and unchanging; the soul, and the soul alone, can be "once and for all"; that is why it can be immortal. The pale criminal cannot view himself as murderer merely in his body, he can be murderer only in the depth of his soul. Given this self-determination, there is no more hope, no more future for the pale criminal than for the despisers of the body: "For one who suffers so much from himself, there is no redemption save a speedy death" (45.10–11).

So interpreted, the example of the pale criminal seems to contradict the results of the analysis given "Of the Despisers of the Body." According to that analysis, the body rules the soul, yet I have argued that the downfall of the pale criminal is caused by the soul rather than by the body. At the very least, the case of the pale criminal clearly shows that even if the soul is merely something "in the body," it is something that can undermine the body: it can be the source of the body's destruction. From the preceding section, "Of

Joys and Passions," we learn that it can, and perhaps even must, also mediate the body's creation.

Like the pale criminal, the "brother" addressed in "Of Joys and Passions" once suffered from himself; he, too, once "suffered passions and called them evil" (43.1). Unlike the pale criminal, however, the brother was able to overcome himself, he was able to transform his passions: "now you have only your virtues: they grew out of your passions" (43.2–3). Once, the brother had "wild dogs" in his cellar, but the wild dogs were not released as savages, to seek prey in the world; instead, "in the end they were transformed into birds and dear singers" (43.11–12). The pale criminal's desires underwent no such transformation; how did the "brother" avoid the criminal's fate? According to Zarathustra, "You laid your highest goal to the heart of these passions: they then became your virtues and your joys" (43.4–5).

Who accomplished the transformation? Zarathustra says, "you" did. The brother himself caused the transformation; the brother him*self*, but through which "self," or which aspect of the self? There is no direct indication, and that itself is surprising, given the distinctions among body, soul, spirit, self, etc., introduced in the preceding section. Yet those distinctions, in conjunction with the description of the pale criminal, enable us to answer the question. How are the pale criminal's desires transformed? Not through the body, certainly: the body does not transform the passions, the body *is* the passions. The task of *interpreting* the passions, we know from "Of the Pale Criminal," is the task of the soul. The brother's soul, then, transformed his passions; it did so by "laying its highest goal to their heart."

What is this highest goal? We do not know, for it is not named. Indeed, Zarathustra tells the brother that it is better left unnamed, because better pursued in solitude and for its own sake rather than among the many, in order to impress (42.3–10). But even if it is unnamed, it is not left wholly undetermined. What is necessary, if the soul's aim is to transform the passions, is that the soul not pursue an end that requires the denial of the body— that hinders the body's drive to "create beyond itself." This is necessary because, as we learn from the example of the pale criminal, the healthy body is not to be denied. The soul must invest its end in the heart of the body's passions, it must embrace an end the body may share, and must view that end as so shared. Rather than naming his virtue, the solitary brother would do better by saying, " 'inexpressible and nameless is that which gives my soul agony [*Qual*] and sweetness *and is also still the hunger of my entrails*' " (42.8–10; my emphasis).

The solitary brother, like the pale criminal, determines himself. But whereas the pale criminal's self-identification is with a past deed, the solitary brother's is with a future goal; the pale criminal's determination leads through self-denial to destruction, ultimately self-destruction, the brother's, through self-expression to creation. In encouraging the solitary brother to retain his love for his "earthly virtue," Zarathustra heralds the advice he will give to the noble youth by the tree on the mountainside: "do not cast aside the hero in your soul! Hold holy your highest hope" (Z,I:8; 54.4–6).

The soul, says the awakened one, is something "in the body"; this soul is not the soul sought by the hinterworldly, not something apart from the body, something that would survive the body's death, that would attain its satisfaction only through the body's frustration, its salvation only through the body's destruction. It is "something" in the body, but it is a decisive something. The body has its desires and its passions, it even "commands" those desires and passions, but its commands are not always authoritative— witness the pale criminal—and even when they are, they remain directionless. The body desires, vaguely, to "create beyond itself"; but only the soul can invest the body's passions with a "highest goal," and only the soul can then "hold holy its highest hope."

Zarathustra's Highest Hope

In Part I, Zarathustra has a hope that he holds holy; because he holds it holy he can report twice, in the Prologue, that his soul is "unmoved." Following the end of his first speech to the masses in the marketplace, Zarathustra says to his heart: "Unmoved is my soul and bright, like the mountains in the morning. But [these people] think I am cold, a mocker [Spötter] with fearsome jokes" (Z,P:5; 21.1–3).

Zarathustra denies being a "mocker with fearsome jokes," but later stresses that the danger that threatens to undermine anyone who is noble is that of becoming "one who is impudent, who derides, who annihilates [ein Frecher, ein Höhnender, ein Vernichter]" (Z,I:8; 53.28–29). The mocker is such an annihilator, a mere destroyer who does not create, a lion who cannot become child (see Z,I:1)—a radical nihilist. Speaking to a potentially noble youth, Zarathustra warns: "Ah, I knew noble ones who lost their highest hopes. And then they slandered all high hopes" (53.30–31). The noble one's highest hope is a "hero in [the] soul" (54.5); when it is abandoned, nothing is left save pleasures of the body:

> Then they lived impudently in brief pleasures (Lüsten), and they scarcely cast goals beyond the day.
> . . . Once they thought to become heroes: now they are voluptuaries [Lüst-linge]. To them, the hero is an affliction and a terror [ein Gram und ein Grauen]. (Z,I:8; 53.32–33, 54.2–3).

Throughout Part I, Zarathustra's hero is not an affliction and a terror, it is rather the secure hope that keeps his soul unmoved. He bears this hope with him as he descends to the valley following a ten-year sojourn on his mountain: his hope is the promise of the overman, a replacement for the god who is dead. This hope is the gift he attempts to give to the masses in the marketplace; their indifference confronts it with its first test. The first test is passed: the pettiness of the masses leaves Zarathustra's soul unmoved. The masses do, however, change his mind. After discovering that they are not drawn to the gift by talk of the overman as meaning of the earth, Zarathustra tries speaking instead of the alternative to the overman, the last humans, who announce, "we have invented happiness," as they "hop and blink" on an earth become small (Z,P:5). This brings no more success, and Zarathustra concludes that he is "not the mouth for these ears" (Z,P:5; 20.29–30). Yet his soul remains unmoved (Z,P:8; 25.12) in that his goal, his highest hope, remains unchanged. Rather than casting aside the hero in his soul, he casts aside the masses; he turns to the search for companions who will come to embrace his hero, who will share his highest hope.

After the Prologue, there are no further references to Zarathustra's soul until Part II. Part I closes as Zarathustra voluntarily leaves his companions, returning to his mountain, but at the beginning of Part II—following the passage of "moons and years" (Z,II:1; 105.9)—we are told that his soul "became full of impatience and desire to see those whom he loved" (Z,II:1; 105.5–6). He nevertheless waits, "like a sower who has planted his seeds" (105.4–5); he has told his followers that they must lose him and find themselves, and that only when all have denied him will he return (Z,I:22.3; 101.28–29). Yet he returns before his seeds have ripened; his return is motivated by a dream that suggests to him that his teachings are being distorted. Following the dream, he repeatedly insists that he now *may* [*darf*] return to his companions, that something that had been prohibited is now permitted (Z,II:1; 106.18,19; 107.10,16). Zarathustra must justify his return because his desire to see those he loves is in conflict with his "highest hope": if his companions have not ceased to follow him and begun to follow themselves (Z,I:22.3; 101.11–102.2), then his return will not hasten the coming of the overman.

Zarathustra's dream, then, allows him to rationalize his return to his companions: he continues to act for the sake of the overman. Moreover, he reveals to them, more fully than before, just what originally led him to embrace the hope of the overman: "Life is a fountain [*Born*] of joy [*Lust*]; but where the rabble also drink, there all wells [*Brunnen*] are poisoned. . . . The bite on which I gagged the most is not the knowledge that life itself requires hostility and death and torture-crosses—but once I asked, and I was almost choked by the question: What? does life require even the rabble?" (Z,II:6; 124.1–2, 125.1–5).

Zarathustra's earlier disgust with the rabble was at the same time a problem with history: "holding my nose, I walked disgruntled through all of yesterday and today: verily, all of yesterday and today smells foul of the writing rabble" (125.17–19). Denying yesterday and today, Zarathustra looked to tomorrow: "On the tree, future, we build our nest; and in our solitude eagles shall bring us nourishment in their beaks" (126.19–20).

Zarathustra's longing for the overman of the future has its origin in disgust with the rabble of the past and present; the affirmation is grounded in a negation, a denial. Just as the hinterworldly affirmation of the soul is a mere consequence of the denial of the body, Zarathustra's affirmation of the overman is nothing more than a consequence of his denial of the all-too-human. The affirmation can last only as long as Zarathustra can retain his hope that the overman will someday hatch from the egg laid in the nest built on the tree "future." As long as he retains that hope, his disgust with yesterday and today does not extend to life itself: his hope remains holy and his soul unmoved.

In "The Child with the Mirror," Zarathustra's soul is moved but his hope unchanged; in "The Night Song," his soul moves itself as his hope falters. His soul is "a leaping fountain" (136.3, 138.10), the "song of a lover" (136.5, 138.12): "Something unstilled, unstillable is within me; it wants to be voiced. A desire for love is within me; it speaks the language of love" (136.6–8).

Zarathustra does not love, he has a desire for love. Yet his first reported words to a human being—the saint he encounters as he first descends from his mountain—are, "I love humanity" (Z,P:2; 13.1). When the saint brings that love into question by insisting, "love for humanity would do me in" (13.5–6), Zarathustra acknowledges that he had misspoken: "Did I speak of love? I bring humanity a gift" (13.7–8). Nevertheless, in his Prologue he lists eighteen types of human beings that he loves (Z,P:4; 17.3–18.20). This may be mere rhetoric, an attempt to convince the masses to accept his gift. In any case, however, if Zarathustra's relation to other human beings is one of mere giving, if he receives nothing, then he cannot "love" them in the way that, in "The Night Song," he desires to love. He complains there: "I do not know the happiness of those who receive. . . . This is my poverty, that my hand never rests from giving" (136.18, 20–21).

One might readily acknowledge that humanity has nothing to give to Zarathustra; but what about the overman? Does Zarathustra not love the overman? Does he not receive something from the overman, i. e., a "meaning" for life? If there were no such meaning, he has said, he would accept the soporific teachings of the "chair of virtue," i.e., "wake in order to sleep well" (Z,I:2; 34.19): "Verily, if life had no sense [Sinn] and I had to choose nonsense [Unsinn], this would be for me, too, the nonsense most worthy of being chosen" (34.20–21). His sense, his meaning, can only have been the overman. Yet in "The Night Song," when he seeks something to love, he does not even mention the overman. Nor, unless I am mistaken, does he ever, anywhere in the book, directly tell us that he loves the overman. In any case, the overman does not satisfy his need for love; that is why his soul has become a "leaping fountain": he is beginning to recognize that his highest hope will not suffice.

In "The Night Song," Zarathustra announces that he longs to love; he does not love either man or overman. In the following section, "The Dancing Song," he identifies an object, perhaps *the* object, of his love: "Deeply I love only life—and verily, most of all when I hate life" (140.26–28). This love may be deep, but it too is insufficient:

"The sun has set long ago," he said at last; "the meadow is moist, a chill comes from the woods.

"Something unknown [*Ein Unbekanntes*] is around me and looks thoughtful. What? Are you still alive, Zarathustra?

"Why? What for? By what? Whither? Where? How? Is it not folly still to be alive?" (141.22–27)

Why? and What for? The Zarathustra of Part I would answer, for sake of the overman! By what? By will to the overman! Whither? Toward the overman! That these questions arise reveals that the overman is no longer a satisfactory answer. But if the overman has been Zarathustra's highest hope, and it is now cast aside with nothing to replace it, either he can no longer love life, or that love cannot sustain him: "Is it not folly still to be alive?"

In "The Dancing Song," we learn that Zarathustra's love of life gives him nothing to live for, no basis for affirmation of the future; in the immediately following section, "The Tomb Song," we learn that the past is as deeply problematic. Heretofore, the absence of what is past has not been a source of discontent; the past has appeared either as something to be condemned (e. g., Z,II:6, 125.17–19), or as something to be affirmed merely as a way, and not as what it was (Z,I:3; 37.4–7). In "The Tomb Song," however, Zarathustra looks back on his own past as something of great value, whose loss is to be deeply mourned: "Verily, you died too soon for me, you fugitives" (143.3); the "visions and dearest wonders" (143.20–21) of Zarathustra's youth were murdered, and they cannot be brought back. This past—Zarathustra's individual past—is not something impoverished whose existence must be justified, but rather something rich whose loss forces the question: "How can a life that so robs us be worth living?" "Is it not folly still to be alive?"

Zarathustra now indicates that this is a question he has asked, and answered, before, but also that from the time the question is raised until the time it is answered, the questioner's soul is entombed. The answering of the question is thus tantamount to a resurrection of the soul:

How did I get over and overcome such wounds? How did my soul rise again out of these tombs?

Indeed, in me there is something invulnerable and unburiable, something that explodes rock: that is *my will*. Silent and unchanged it strides through the years
. . .

Indeed, for me, you are still the shatterer of all tombs. Hail to thee, my will! And only where there are tombs are there resurrections. (144.33–145.3, 145.12–13)

In the following section, "Of Self-Overcoming," Zarathustra generalizes the conclusion of "The Tomb Song": not only has his will kept him going, will is what keeps everything that lives going. "And life itself confided this secret to me: 'Behold,' it said, 'I am *that which must always overcome itself.*
. . . Whatever I create and however much I love it—soon I must oppose it and my love; thus my will wills it' " (148.16–18, 28–29).

Zarathustra's soul is first entombed when he recognizes, following the loss of his youth, that all that exists is doomed to be overcome, that to come into being is to be doomed to pass away; following this recognition he draws the conclusion attributed in "Of Redemption" to the "spirit of revenge": " 'Everything passes away, so everything deserves to pass away' " (Z,II:20; 180.31–32). If to be is to be doomed to be overcome, then to say "My youth should not have been overcome, should not have passed away" is to say "My youth should not have been," and consequently, "I should not have been." This conclusion reiterates the wisdom of Silenus: the best thing for a human being is never to be born, the second best is to die soon. The spirit of revenge, with its "ill-will against time and its 'it was' " (180.17–18), teaches that life robs us not only of youth, but of all that is of value; such a thieving life is not worth living.

The spirit of revenge draws its life-denying conclusion from the argument, "everything passes away, so everything deserves to pass away." The doctrine of the will to power likewise teaches that everything passes away, yet Zarathustra presents it as the basis of the will to life, thus, as a basis for the affirmation of life. It can be this basis only in that, unlike the spirit of revenge, it insists that life, with its continual self-overcoming, also brings us not only youth, but all that is of value. Life indeed takes away, but only life can give.

Life giveth, and life taketh away; blessed be the name of life? A life that gives may be better than one that merely takes, but one in which every giving is always a taking is not easily affirmed. Nevertheless, Zarathustra admonishes, "Let us speak of this, you who are wisest, even if it be bad. Silence is worse; all truths that are kept silent become poisonous" (149.22–24).

"All truths that are kept silent become poisonous"; if I suppress the teaching of the will to power—the teaching of the ubiquity, even necessity, of transience—then must I not condemn life for robbing me of my youth? Must I not then reason: if I affirm life, I affirm the passing away of my youth, and I thereby deny or condemn my youth; I affirm the passing away of myself and of those I love, and I therefore deny or condemn myself and those I love? If I accept the teaching of the will to power, I reason quite differently: if I affirm my youth, I thereby affirm its passing, and I thereby affirm life. In opposition to the will to revenge, the will to power insists: "everything passes away, so everything deserves to exist." That everything passes away may be "bad," but it is true, and it may not be impossible both to accept its truth and to affirm life as worth living. The danger is greater, Zarathustra insists, if its truth is denied, if it is kept silent, for it then becomes poisonous, and poisons life itself.

Everything passes away, so everything deserves to exist. If this is the teaching of the will to power, is it a teaching Zarathustra can embrace? Does everything deserve to exist? Even the rabble? If Zarathustra abandons the overman, turning away from the future, he can turn only to present or past; he must then once again confront his disgust with the rabble. Only when that disgust has been overcome will his soul be fully resurrected.

Dwarves, Buffoons, and Barrel-organs

The problem of the rabble becomes, or merges with, the problem of the eternal return: in "The Convalescent," Zarathustra retrospectively announces, "eternal recurrence even for the smallest! That was my satiety with all existence" (274.33–34). Zarathustra overcomes his life-denying satiety only by facing the thought of the eternal return, but it is not easy to determine either what the thought is, or what results from Zarathustra's confrontation with it.

The first extended account of the return is given in "Of the Vision and the Riddle"; Zarathustra presents the account to his fellow travelers on a ship voyaging from the Blessed Isles to the mainland. On the evening of the second day out, Zarathustra describes to the others the "riddle" that he saw in the "vision of the most solitary." In his vision, Zarathustra encounters for the first time his "devil and arch-enemy," the spirit of gravity, half dwarf and half mole—the minotaur of his labyrinth and of Nietzsche's, mole and dwarf rather than bull and man, a combination that makes this minotaur no less dangerous than Theseus's, but considerably more devious. In his vision, Zarathustra climbs a mountain in a "corpse-colored twilight," bearing the mole-dwarf on his shoulder. The dwarf drips leaden thoughts into Zarathustra's ear: all climbing is in vain, for whatever rises must fall (198.16–24).

After much climbing, dreaming, and thinking, Zarathustra's courage ultimately brings him to a stand. He challenges: "Dwarf! You! Or I!" (198.34).

Zarathustra then digresses, praising courage to his fellow voyagers. Courage, he tells them, deals the most deadly blows; the courage that is a "chiming play" overcomes every pain, and strikes dead not only the dizziness that threatens all who see abysses, but also pity, and even death itself. This courage ultimately attacks, announcing, "Was that life? Well then! Once more!" (199.13–14), affirming a doctrine of eternal return.

Following his digression, Zarathustra repeats his challenge to the dwarf, now adding an assertion of his own superiority: "I am the stronger of us two: you do not know my most abysmal thought! *It*—you could not bear" (199.18–20). At this, the dwarf leaps down from Zarathustra's shoulder and squats on a stone. Zarathustra then provides his only direct, extended account of the doctrine of eternal return:

> "Behold this gateway! Dwarf!" I spoke further: "it has two faces. Two pathways come together here: no one has ever reached the end of either.
>
> This long alley back: it goes on for an eternity. And that long alley ahead— that is another eternity.
>
> They contradict each other, these pathways; they collide:—and it is here, in this gateway, that they come together. The name of the gateway is written above: 'Moment.'
>
> But whoever goes further along either one of them—and further and further: do you believe, dwarf, that the pathways contradict each other eternally?" (199.25–200.6)

The dwarf does not answer Zarathustra's question; instead, he transforms Zarathustra's intratemporal, linear image into an extratemporal, circular one: " 'Everything that is straight lies,' murmured the dwarf contemptuously. 'All truth is crooked, time itself is a circle' " (200.7–8).

Zarathustra forcefully rejects the new image as being a simplification, an amelioration, precisely in that it substitutes for the perspective of the moment—a radically temporal perspective—a perspective outside of time, one from which the shape of time as a whole may be viewed:

> "You spirit of gravity!" I said angrily, "don't make it too easy for yourself, or I will let you squat where you squat, lamefoot—and I have carried you *high!*
>
> "Behold," I spoke further, "this moment! From this gateway, Moment, runs a long, eternal alley *backwards:* behind us lies an eternity.
>
> "Must not whatever of all things *can* run already *have* run, once, in this alley? Must not whatever of all things *can* happen already have happened once, have been done, have gone by once?
>
> "And if everything has already been: what do you think, dwarf, about this moment? Must not this gateway too already have been there?
>
> "And are not all things firmly knotted in such a way that this moment draws *all* things to come after it? *Therefore*—even itself?

"For whatever of all things *can* run: in this long alley *ahead*, they *must* run once again!—
"And this slow spider that crawls in the moonlight, and this moonlight itself, and I and you in the gateway, whispering together, whispering of eternal things— must not all of us already have been there?
"—and must we not return and run in that other alley, ahead, before us, in this long, terrible alley—must we not eternally return?—" (200.9–33)

These questions, like the earlier one, go unanswered; but here there is no response at all from the dwarf, for this vision fades, only to be replaced by another vision, the one containing the riddle. Yet the unanswered questions pose riddles of their own: Why are they asked? What do they suggest? What is Zarathustra's most abysmal thought, and what of it does he think the dwarf will be unable to bear? The obvious answer is that the dwarf cannot bear the thought that he will return eternally. The answer seems obvious in that Zarathustra's questions seem rhetorical: Zarathustra clearly anticipates that the dwarf could answer only in the affirmative. By why could the dwarf not bear the thought of returning? He himself has said that time is a circle; if time is a circle, must it not run continually through all its points? Does not the dwarf himself teach that everything returns?

These considerations suggest that the obvious answer to the question what the dwarf cannot bear may not be the correct answer. Fortunately, there is another option, suggested already by the specific interchange between Zarathustra and the dwarf: the dwarf cannot bear the thought of the eternity of the moment, the thought that he never escapes from the moment, that he can never stand outside time, that he is rather trapped between the two pathways. Wherever he has been, in the past, he has been within the moment; wherever he will be, in the future, he will be within the moment.

To say that the dwarf is trapped within the moment is to say something about the *form* of time, something about temporality; to say that the encounter between Zarathustra and the dwarf will return or recur endlessly is to say something about the *content* of time, something about events or, more broadly, about history. In relating his "most abysmal thought" to the dwarf, Zarathustra includes both aspects; yet there is no necessary connection between the two. I may affirm that as long as I live I will live within the moment, without affirming that after I die I will live again.

Is Zarathustra's most abysmal thought a thought of temporal form, or of temporal content, or of both at once? What returns eternally, the structure of the moment as gateway, with its two colliding pathways; or specific events, including such details as spiders and moonlight; or both? "Of the Vision and the Riddle" provides no answer to this question; instead, it supplies another riddle.

As he asks the dwarf, "must we not return eternally?" Zarathustra's courage falters: "Thus I spoke, ever more softly: for I was afraid of my own thoughts and hinterthoughts" (200.34–201.1). Zarathustra then hears the howling of a dog, and finds himself in a transformed landscape:

> Where had the dwarf gone? And the gateway? And the spider? And all the whispering? Had I been dreaming? Had I awakened? All at once I was standing between wild cliffs, alone, desolate, in the most desolate moonlight. (201.15–18)

Zarathustra sees the dog, leaping and whining, and beside it a young shepherd choking on a "black, heavy snake" that has crawled into his throat as he slept. Zarathustra cries out, urging the shepherd to bite. The shepherd does bite, then spits out the snake's head and leaps up, "no longer shepherd, no longer human,—one transformed, surrounded by light, who laughed! Never yet on earth any human being laughed as *he* laughed!" (202.17–19). Zarathustra yearns for such laughter: "now a thirst is gnawing at me, a longing that is never stilled" (202.21–22). Yet he wonders, and asks his fellow voyagers to help him to solve the riddle:

> *what* did I then see in a metaphor [*im Gleichnisse*]? And *who* is it that must come one day?
> *Who* is the shepherd into whose throat the snake thus crawled? *Who* is this person into whose throat everything that is heaviest and blackest thus crawled? (202.8–13)

These questions, like the earlier ones, receive no answers in "Of the Vision of the Riddle," but they arise again in the next extended account of the eternal return, in "The Convalescent."

In "Of the Vision and the Riddle," Zarathustra describes his most abysmal thought, but he does not confront it; in "The Convalescent," he explicitly summons it: "Arise, abysmal thought, out of my depths! . . . And once you are awake, you shall stay awake eternally for me" (270.13,22). This summons itself contains an indication that the contentual form of the doctrine, according to which all individuals and events recur identically, has been abandoned: the thought can "stay awake eternally" for Zarathustra only if he does not forget it, that is, only if he does not, "returning eternally," return as one who has not yet thought his most abysmal thought.

As the thought comes close enough for Zarathustra to take its hand, he shrieks, "Disgust, disgust, disgust—woe is me!" and collapses as though dead. His snake remains with him, and his eagle leaves only to fetch food (271.15–18). After seven days, Zarathustra sits up and takes a quince [*Rosenapfel*], smells it, and finds the odor pleasing. His animals take this action as a sign that "the time had come to talk to him" (271.25–26). The animals

attempt to distract Zarathustra from his "sour, heavy" thought; they seek
to lure him out of his cave into the world, which for them is a garden. Rather
than take this advice, Zarathustra requests that the animals keep up their
"jabbering," which refreshes him:

> "How lovely it is that there are words and tones [*Töne*]! Are not words and
> tones rainbows and seeming bridges between things which are eternally apart?
> "To every soul belongs another world; for every soul, every other soul is a
> hinterworld.
> "The semblance falsifies most beautifully between things that are most similar;
> for the smallest gap is the hardest to bridge.
> "For me—how should there be any outside-myself? There is no outside. But
> all sounds make us forget this; how lovely it is that we forget.
> "Have not names and tones been given to things that man might find things
> refreshing? Speaking is a beautiful folly: with it man dances over all things.
> "How lovely is all talking, and all the deception of tones! With tones our love
> dances on many-hued rainbows." (272.13–27)

Instead of taking the animals' advice, instead of leaving his cave, Zarathustra offers these perplexing remarks on language. Words, he asserts, are
"rainbows and seeming bridges between things that are eternally apart"; the
"smallest gap" between such things is the "hardest to bridge." Where does
one find the smallest gap? One place suggested by Zarathustra is in the word
"hinterworld." Earlier, Zarathustra rebuked believers in "hinterworlds" for
denying life; he now suggests that every soul somehow contains its own
"hinterworlds." The "hinterworld" Zarathustra here acknowledges is not,
of course, the Christian-moral hinterworld; neither is his "eternity" the
Christian-moral eternity, nor his soul the Christian-moral soul. In all these
cases, and others besides, words bridge gaps; the thought of eternal return
had appeared abysmal, perhaps, chiefly because Zarathustra had not seen
the gaps the words had concealed.

More broadly, directly, and simply: the "things which are eternally apart"
are *The Genealogy*'s uninterpreted "facts," of which there are so many
that no account can adequately treat them all. The "words and tones" are
interpretations that make it possible for souls to inhabit worlds. Any two
dogs (or fire-dogs), for example, are "eternally apart"; we happen to have
the word "dog," which "falsifies" their differences by masking them; in a
different scheme of classification, chihuahuas might not be associated with
St. Bernards, and Nietzsche not with Hitler. Because of this arbitrariness,
speaking is "folly": we can't give "things" the names that are simply
"right"—as the wisdom opposed to Nietzsche's "folly" would require—
because there are no names that are simply right.

On the one hand, speech as folly, speaking as dancing, makes life possible,
for it transforms the "things eternally apart," incorporating them into a

habitable world. The animals' speech reflects one such transformative incor-
poration; a prosaic version of Zarathustra's lengthy response to them might
read, "Indeed, that is one of many ways to look at things—and how nice it
is that there are many ways." The animals' way of "looking at things" is
important to Zarathustra not because it is the "right" way, or because it is
to become his way, but rather, precisely, because it reminds him that there
are many ways. Before returning to his mountain, Zarathustra was "transformed" (Z,II:19; 172.23) by the prospect of one way of looking at things,
that of the Soothsayer: "Everything is empty, everything is the same, everything has already been. . . . Verily, we are already too tired even to die; now
we are still awake and we live on—in sepulchers" (172.4–5, 20–21). The
animals inadvertently aid Zarathustra's recognition that the Soothsayer's
perspective is not inescapable, even if it is neither false nor incorrect in the
ordinary sense.

On the other hand, speech as folly can make life impossible, for speeches
can become calcified, and when they do we tend to forget that they are not
true, i.e., not absolutely binding, not free from alternatives. Such calcifica-
tion, we know, is what makes genealogical investigation necessary. Adapting
terms Nietzsche uses in the passage under discussion: the "gaps" between
things are bridged by words, not abolished, and since they are merely
bridged, they may always be bridged differently. The danger arises when
we forget the gaps altogether. Nietzschean enlightenment often requires
precisely that a forgotten gap—such as, perhaps, that between philosophy
and priestly asceticism, or that between science and technology—be remembered.

Zarathustra's animals have no interest in words or in gaps; rather than
respond directly to his musings on language, they seek to distract his attention from dancing words to dancing things:

> "Zarathustra," responded the animals, "to those who think as we do, all things
> themselves dance: they come and offer their hands and laugh and flee—and
> come back.
>
> "Everything goes, everything comes back; eternally rolls the wheel of being.
> Everything dies, everything blooms again, eternally runs the year of being.
>
> "Everything breaks, everything is put back together [neu gefügt]; the same
> house of being eternally builds itself. Everything parts [scheidet], everything
> greets again; the ring of being remains eternally true to itself.
>
> "In every instant [Nu], being begins; around every here rolls the ball there.
> The center [Mitte] is everywhere [überall]. The path of eternity is crooked
> [krumm]." (272.28–273.5)

The opening of the animals' speech is wholly consistent with the position
I have attributed to Zarathustra: in that we know things only insofar as we

bespeak them, it is as appropriate to say that things dance as that words do. As the animals continue, however, they develop this position by suggesting that the dance of things is rigidly predetermined.

As they continue, the animals speak both of temporal form and of temporal content but, as Heidegger has noted, the terms in which they speak are reminiscent of the dwarf, who murmurs, "All truth is crooked [*krumm*], time itself is a circle" (200.7–8). That this doctrine is life-denying is also suggested by a yet earlier passage: "God is a thought that makes everything straight crooked [*krumm*] and everything that stands wobble [*drehend*]. What? Time would be gone, and everything transitory only a lie?" (Z,II:2; 110.18–20). Yet despite these similarities, Zarathustra does not directly accuse his animals of trivializing the thought of the return:

> "Oh you buffoons [*Schalks-Narren*] and barrel-organs [*Drehorgeln*]!" answered Zarathustra and smiled again, "how well you know what had to fulfill itself within seven days:—
> "—and how that monster [*Untier*] crept into my throat [*Schlund*] and choked me! But I bit off its head and spat it away from me.
> "And you—you have already made of this a hurdy-gurdy [*Leier-Lied*] song?" (273.6–12)

Although this accusation is less direct, Zarathustra clearly implies that his animals, like the dwarf, take things too lightly; their "hurdy-gurdy song" cannot be the appropriate form for expressing the thought of the eternal return. Moreover, the inappropriateness of the animals' reaction next leads Zarathustra to express his surprise that his animals watched his suffering at all; he takes their behavior to reveal a joy in cruelty he had thought limited to human beings. The expression of surprise leads into a tirade against forms of human cruelty and *ressentiment*, and then to a recollection of his disgust and his "sickness," concluding with the identification of the "eternal return of the smallest" as the cause of his "satiety with all existence" (274.33–34).

Zarathustra's recollection is interrupted by his animals, who "did not allow him to speak further" (275.3). As before, they seek to distract him, to draw him out into their world, to "the roses and the bees and the swarms of doves" (275.7–8). Again, Zarathustra ignores their advice, addressing them again as "buffoons and barrel-organs" (275.13), and asking now whether they want to make a "hurdy-gurdy song" of his convalescence as well (275.18–19). For the second time, the animals interrupt; they then develop *Thus Spoke Zarathustra*'s most complete and coherent account of the doctrine of eternal return, a clear cosmological vision of eternal repetition, culminating with their anticipation of what Zarathustra will say at the time of his death.

The animals' final account of the eternal return is generally taken to express Nietzsche's own deepest thoughts; even Heidegger, who stresses the unreliability of the animals' first account, accepts the second as authoritative. Heidegger stresses that Zarathustra himself provides no account of the eternal return in "The Convalescent," but rather than looking to the succeeding sections, where Zarathustra does speak, Heidegger seeks to derive the correct doctrine "mediately," from the animals' speech (*Nietzsche*, I:310; ET, 55–56). Thomas Altizer sees no need for the mediation: "Nowhere did Nietzsche more triumphantly reach his goal of speaking volumes in a few words than in this passage of *Zarathustra*" ("Eternal Recurrence and the Kingdom of God," 242–43). The reason the animals' speech seems definitive is, I assume, that the account says what we may well expect Zarathustra to say at this point. The expectation can be so strong as to lead readers who are usually both careful and acute to take the death speech, recounted in the first person singular, to be Zarathustra's own; this error is made by both Harold Alderman (101) and J. P. Stern (165).

Stern recognizes that the animals' view continues to be the view of the dwarf, and takes this identity to be a sign of Nietzsche's failure: "Zarathustra can only elaborate what the dwarf has said, he can only bring out the annihilating, nihilistic aspect of the Janus-faced myth" (165); "[Nietzsche] decrees that the process shall be infinite, circular and intolerable: an infinite repetition of the same" (162). Stern's evaluation would be forceful if the words of the death speech were Zarathustra's words—but they are not.

The words of the death speech are the animals' words, not Zarathustra's; but perhaps the animals speak for Zarathustra. That they are capable of doing so is the view of Alderman, according to whom the animals are "Zarathustra's Socratic *daimon*" (101), and of Heidegger, who stresses, "after all, they are *his* animals" (*Nietzsche*, I:313; ET, 58). They are indeed his animals: although they are his, they are also animals. They are indeed "true to the earth" (Alderman, 101), as Zarathustra seeks to be, but—to adapt a Heideggerian phrase—the animals are not yet false to the earth, whereas Zarathustra strives to be no longer false to the earth. The animals' world has always been a garden, but that is because it is not the human world; they have seen the human world only from a great distance (Z,P:10; 27.11–15), and have never encountered rabble or preachers of death or reverse cripples. Of course the animals say "yes" to life—they have no cause to say no. For just this reason, their affirmation cannot be adequate for those who have been led to deny.

Advocates of Zarathustra's animals might respond by suggesting that Zarathustra's failure to object to the "death speech" must be taken as an indication of his acceptance of it. Indeed, he does not object, but his silence is not presented as evidence of agreement:

> After the animals had spoken these words they were silent, expecting that
> Zarathustra would say something to them: but *Zarathustra did not hear that*

they were silent. Instead, he lay still, with closed eyes, like one asleep, although he did not sleep: for he was then conversing with his soul. But the snake and the eagle, when they found that he was silent in this way, respected the great stillness around him and carefully withdrew. (277.6–13; my emphasis)

Zarathustra "did not hear" that his animals were silent; why not? Perhaps he was so absorbed by what they had said, by his own reflections on their words, that he was beyond them entirely. But perhaps, after their earlier jabbering, he had not bothered to listen to them; perhaps he did not hear their silence because he had not heard their speech. Which hermeneutical option are we to choose? The former—that Zarathustra is absorbed by what his animals have said—has no support beyond the passage in question. The latter—that Zarathustra has paid no attention to his dictated "death speech"—is supported both by what Zarathustra himself says in the closing sections of Part III, and by what we learn about the animals in Part IV.

Following their withdrawal at the end of "The Convalescent," we hear no more of Zarathustra's animals until the opening section of Part IV. There, they appear not as ones who can speak for Zarathustra, but rather as ones with whom he cannot speak. He addresses them again as "buffoons" (Z,IV:1; 295.14–15), and then intentionally eludes them by announcing that he goes to offer a sacrifice. The animals simply accept this nonsense, not even wondering to what or whom Zarathustra could possibly be making the sacrifice: "That I spoke of sacrifices and honey sacrifices was merely a ruse and, truly, a useful bit of foolishness! Up here I can speak more freely than before hermits' caves and hermits' pets [*Hausthieren*]" (296.16–19).

Zarathustra's animals do not speak for him, and he does not speak his own deepest thoughts to them; in their "pre-theoretical innocence" (Alderman, 116), they would not understand. As the closing lines of "The Convalescent" suggest, the time has come for Zarathustra to speak with his soul.

The Resurrection of Zarathustra's Soul

As "The Convalescent" closes, Zarathustra converses with his soul; in the following section, "Of the Great Longing," he directly addresses his soul twenty-two times. At the close of the section, Zarathustra begs his soul to sing; the titles of the next two sections, the final ones in Part III, indicate that both are songs, presumably songs sung by Zarathustra's resurrected soul.

The first twelve sentences in "Of the Great Longing," each of which constitutes a single paragraph, all have "I" as the subject, and are all in the past tense; in them, Zarathustra tells his soul what he has done for it, and thus why it may owe him thanks. His first service to his soul was to bring it into time and motion, to free it from its Christian-moral stability and stagnation. "O my soul, I taught you to say 'today' as well as 'once' [*Einst*] and 'formerly' [*Ehemals*] and to dance your leaping circle dance [*Reigen*] over every here and there and yonder" (278.2–4). The Christian-moral soul, locked in its timeless eternity, can say only "now," and cannot dance. In freeing his soul from these Christian-moral limitations, Zarathustra has freed it from others as well: from shame (278.7), sin (278.12), obeying, knee-bending, and obsequiousness (279.3–4).

The nature of Zarathustra's second service to his soul is less clear: "O my soul, I redeemed you from all corners, I brushed dust, spiders, and twilight [*Zwielicht*] from you" (278.5–6). The spiders and twilight are reminiscent of "The Vision and the Riddle": in the dream reported there, Zarathustra climbs through a "corpse-colored twilight [*Dämmerung*]" (Z,III:2.1; 198.1), and a "slow spider" is among the seemingly trivial items listed as returning eternally (200.27). The twilight is also reminiscent of "The Soothsayer," where Zarathustra is "transformed" (Z,II:19; 172.23) by the "long twilight" [*Dämmerung*]) (173.4, 175.11) of a life described by the words of the Soothsayer: "Everything is empty, everything is the same, everything has already been. . . . Verily, we are already too tired even to die; now we are still awake and we live on—in sepulchers" (172.4–5, 20–21). As Zarathustra then dreams about being surrounded by sepulchers, he smells "dust-covered eternities" (173.28). Indeed, his soul itself is "dust-covered" (173.29); he has not yet brushed the dust from it (278.5–6).

Zarathustra's first service to his soul, we know, was to temporalize it, to free it from God; but the soul can be freed from God only if God is dead. God is dead for Zarathustra, but also for the Soothsayer; because the Soothsayer's God is dead, for him "everything is empty, everything is the same, everything has already been." The cosmological version of eternal return introduced by Zarathustra in "Of the Vision and the Riddle," and reasserted by his animals in "The Convalescent," likewise teaches that "everything is the same, everything has already been," and thus, perhaps, that "everything is empty." If God is dead, it may appear, life is not worth living. Yet for Zarathustra life is—or can be—worth living. That it can be clarifies the second service he has performed for his soul: he has redeemed it from the death of God.

Zarathustra has shown his soul that, despite the death of God, not all things are "the same." On the contrary, some things are to be denied, others affirmed: "O my soul, I gave you the right to say no as the storm says no and yes as the open sky says yes" (278.13–14). Nor has everything "already been": "O my soul, I gave you back your freedom over created and uncreated things: and who knows as you know the delight of things to come?" (278.17–19; cf. 279). Nor is it the case that "everything is empty"; there is no kingdom of heaven, but there is a worthy replacement: "O my soul, I gave your earthly kingdom all wisdom to drink, all new wines and also all immemorially old, strong wines of wisdom" (279.9–11).

For Zarathustra as for the Soothsayer, God is dead; but only for the Soothsayer does God's death continue to be a cause for despair. Zarathustra speaks not of being "too tired even to die," but rather of a great longing, the longing first aroused in him by the vision of the laughing shepherd (Z,III:2.2; 202.23). The nature of the longing becomes clearer in the second part of the song where, having recounted what he has done for his soul, Zarathustra describes his soul's current condition. The fruit of Zarathustra's soul is ripe, yet his soul is waiting, longing for the "golden marvel," the "boat [Nachen] of free will" (280.23; cf. 280.17–18) and for its master, the "vintner who waits with his diamond vintner's knife" (280.24–25; cf. 280.10–11), the "great redeemer . . . the nameless one—for whom only songs of the future will find the name" (280.26–27). The wait should not be long, however, for the breath of Zarathustra's soul is "already fragrant" with these songs (280.28): "already your melancholy rests in the blessedness of songs of the future" (280.30–31). The section closes with Zarathustra fervently urging his soul to sing its songs (280.33–34, 281.1–3).

Zarathustra's soul's first song is presented in the only section in the book whose title explicitly alludes to a previous section: "The Other Dancing Song" announces itself in contrast to Part II's "The Dancing Song." Appropriately, the songs themselves contain marked similarities that serve to emphasize their differences. Both begin, "Lately I gazed into your eyes, O life" (140.6, 282.3), but whereas in "The Dancing Song" the gaze is a sinking into the unfathomable [in's Unergründliche] (140.6–7), in "The Other Dancing Song" it is a glimpsing of the vintner's boat, of "a golden bark [Kahn] glittering upon nightly waters, a sinking, drinking, and once again beckoning golden, tossing bark" (282.6–8). In "The Dancing Song," Zarathustra speaks both to life and to his wisdom, but finds himself, at the end, seeming "again to sink into the unfathomable" (141.18–19). The section closes with the despairing questions discussed above: "Why? What for? By what? Whither? Where? How? Is it not folly still to be alive?" (141.26–27). In "The Other Dancing Song," Zarathustra's soul speaks to life, and of his wisdom, but the section ends on the triumphant note of the song "Once More," as joy wills "deep, deep eternity."

For the earlier Zarathustra of "The Dancing Song," life, to be bearable, must be fathomable. It must be ergründlich, it must be such that he can probe its depths, "fathom" it by getting to the bottom of it, its ground [Grund]. Addressed by Zarathustra as "the unfathomable," however, life responds with mocking laughter: "what you cannot fathom, is unfathomable." Life then denies that she is unfathomable, insisting that she is, instead, "only alterable and wild and in all ways a woman [Weib], and not a virtuous one" (140.10–13). At this point, life's conjunction baffles Zarathustra: if she is essentially alterable, how can she be fathomable? How can one come to grips with what is constantly changing?

Shortly after "The Dancing Song's" report of his initial confrontation with life, Zarathustra reports another, in which the answer to his questions begins to take shape. Addressing those who are wisest (as opposed to those famous for wisdom, to whom he speaks in Z,II:8), Zarathustra first unmasks what they take to be their "will to truth" as a form of the will to power, the will to make all things thinkable; "for you doubt with a good mistrust that being is already thinkable" (Z,II:12; 146.6–7). The ultimate goal of the wisest is technological mastery: they seek to make all beings "yield and bend" [*fügen und biegen*] to them. In the terms of *The Birth of Tragedy*, "the wisest" are Socratics, who seek, by fathoming being, to heal it.

Zarathustra attempts to convince the wisest that existence cannot be healed, in their sense; this is one aspect of the "truth" that, if kept silent, becomes poisonous. Much of his evidence comes from a discussion with life herself, wherein life reveals to him her secret: " 'Behold, I am that *which must always overcome itself* ' " (148.16–18). In discovering this secret Zarathustra has, in a sense, "fathomed" life: he has grasped her essential nature, he understands what she is. But he has not thereby gotten to the bottom of things in the sense of reaching a stable foundation upon which he can then build, a knowledge that would provide him with the means of "healing" existence. On the contrary, he has discovered that the "essence" of life is precisely her variability, her inexhaustibility.

Once he has "fathomed" life as inexhaustible, Zarathustra no longer dives from his boat, risking drowning as he seeks to get to the bottom of things. Nor does he join the priests in seeking to escape the sea altogether. He knows, as they do not, that what appear to be islands on our sea are instead sleeping monsters (Z,II:4; 117.23–24): "False values and delusive words: these are the worst of monsters for mortals,—long does calamity sleep and wait within them. But finally it comes and awakes and devours and entraps whatever has built huts upon it" (Z,II:4; 117.25–118.2). Instead of seeking either to fathom or to land, Zarathustra accepts that life is, in effect, life at sea; hence, his affinity with sailors (see Z,III:2.1). With this acceptance, the doubt and despair that end "The Dancing Song" are banished, to be replaced, in "The Other Dancing Song," with words of affirmation and joy.

"The Other Dancing Song" ends affirmatively, but it, too, contains a strong suggestion of life-denial. Life confronts Zarathustra with an accusation:

"O Zarathustra, you are not faithful enough to me!

"You do not love me nearly as much as you say; I know that you are thinking of leaving me soon.

"There is an old, heavy, heavy, booming bell; it booms out at night even up to your cave:

"when you hear this bell beat the hour at midnight, then you think between one and twelve—

"you think, O Zarathustra, I know it, you think of leaving me soon!" (284.27–285.8)

Zarathustra responds with an admission, but adds a qualification that leaves life in perplexity:

"Yes," I answered hesitantly, "but you also know . . ." And I said something into her ear, in the midst of her tangled, yellow, foolish locks. "You *know* that, O Zarathustra? No one knows that." (285.9–13)

Zarathustra knows; but what does he know? The obvious answer is, he knows that he will return: "I'll leave you soon, but I'll be back!" But how could he know that? And even if he thinks he knows it, would he be the only one? Do not Zarathustra's animals "know" that everything returns? Does not the dwarf "know" it?

What does it mean for Zarathustra to leave, abandon, or forsake life? What does or might one forsake life for? The obvious answer might be: for death. This obvious answer seems to be supported by Zarathustra's animals, who were led to dictate Zarathustra's death speech by their fear that Zarathustra was ready to die (276.14). But why should Zarathustra want to die, even if he does know that he will return?

The first place one must look in seeking answers for these questions is the third and final part of "The Other Dancing Song": life has said that Zarathustra's thoughts of "leaving her soon" are midnight thoughts, thoughts he has between the first and twelfth strokes of the clock's bell. In that the third part of the song intersperses its lines with the strokes of the midnight bell, it tells us explicitly, if poetically, what Zarathustra then thinks. Those thoughts close with the triumphal affirmation, "All joy wills eternity—wills deep, deep eternity" (286.14–16).

Life fears that Zarathustra will soon forsake her; the closing song suggests that he would forsake life only for "deep, deep eternity." Zarathustra's animals suspect that Zarathustra is ready to die; but is death a deep eternity? How would Zarathustra's death be a joyful attainment of eternity rather than a woeful, or indifferent, passing away into oblivion, even if a temporary oblivion? In his song, Zarathustra announces, "From a deep dream I have been awakened" (286.2); certainly, death would be no awakening—according to the animals, Zarathustra's soul is as mortal as his body (276.21–22). His literal death would be not an emergence into wakefulness, but rather a sinking into dreamlessness—into nothingness—until the return of the "knot of causes" in which Zarathustra is enmeshed, until the repetition of the same stupid drama. Finally, the song tells us that "all joy wills eternity"; woe, on the other hand, "implores, 'pass away' [*vergeh*]" (286.12).

These considerations suggest that Zarathustra is not contemplating suicide, that he is not on the verge of forsaking his "life," in the most literal sense. What then may he forsake? And what does he know? One thing at least is clear: what he wants is "deep, deep eternity," which may well be distinct from the "shallow" eternities of the Christian-moral tradition on the one hand, and of the dwarf and animals on the other. But what is this "deep, deep eternity"? The question is answered, if at all, in Part III's final section, "The Seven Seals."

"The Seven Seals," subtitled "The Yes and Amen song," consists of seven numbered sections. Each begins with a series of rhetorical hypotheticals describing Zarathustra—"If I am . . . ," "If ever I . . . ," etc.—and each ends with a refrain:

> how should I not lust for eternity and for the wedding ring of rings—the ring of return!
> Never yet did I find the woman by whom I wanted children, unless it be this woman, whom I love: for I love you, O eternity! *For I love you, O eternity!*

Throughout Zarathustra, even before explicit reference to the doctrine of eternal return is made, the ring serves as a symbol for that doctrine (see, e.g., Z,P:10; 27.11–13); it remains a symbol in "The Seven Seals." Yet, as we know, words are seeming bridges between things eternally apart, and the smallest gaps—those disguised by words—are the hardest to bridge, because the words conceal the need for bridging. As Heidegger stresses in a related context, "one man's circle is not another man's circle" (*Nietzsche* I:307; ET, 53). Similarly, one ring may not be another ring, and some rings may only happen to be circles. There are rings that roll; such rings are symbolic of the eternal return as understood by the dwarf and by Zarathustra's animals. But the ring of return praised in "The Seven Seals" is not a ring that rolls; it is a ring not of repetition, but rather of unification. It is the "wedding ring of rings," the *hochzeitliche Ring der Ringe*, the ring of *Hochzeit:* of the wedding or, literally, of "high [*hoch*] time [*Zeit*]."

"High time," like the ring, is closely associated with the doctrine of return. Long before Zarathustra confronts the thought of the return, he knows that it is "high time" for him to do so (see Z,II:18; 167.15–16, 171.9–10; Z,III:3; 204.32–34, 205.18–20). At his "highest time," Zarathustra affirms the "ring of return" as the "wedding ring of rings," the ring that binds future to past, joy to pain, and even noble to base. The fourth of the Seven Seals—titled "Of the Ring of Rings" in Nietzsche's fair copy of the manuscript (*KSA*,14:325)—clearly reveals that the function of the "ring of rings" is the conjoining of opposites:

> If ever I drank a full draft from the foaming seasoning and mixing bowl [*Würz- und Mischkruge*] in which all things are well mixed:

If ever my hand melded the farthest to the nearest and fire to spirit and joy to
pain and the worst to the most goodly:
If I myself am a grain of the dissolving [erlösenden] salt that insures that all
things in the mixing bowl are well mixed:—
Oh how should I not lust for eternity and for the wedding ring of rings . . .
(289.11–21)

The ring of return is a ring of reconciliation, not a ring that rolls; and the
reconciliation is not a reconciliation through death, but rather a reconciliation with life. The third of the Seven Seals decisively severs Zarathustra's
"deep, deep eternity" from any state of mindless oblivion or mindless repetition:

If ever a breath of the creative breath has come to me, a breath of that heavenly
need that compels even accidents to dance in stars' circle dances:
If ever I laughed with the laughter of the creative lightning-bolt that is followed
by thunder, growling but obedient:
If ever I played dice with gods on the godly table of the earth, so that the earth
quaked and broke and rivers of fire snorted forth:—
For the earth is a table of the gods and trembling with creative new worlds
and the dice throws of the gods:—
Oh how should I not lust for eternity . . . (288.22–289.3)

In Nietzsche's fair copy of the manuscript, this third seal is subtitled
"Dionysus" (14:325); it appears as the counterpart to "Of the Great Longing," which there bears the subtitle "Ariadne" (14:324). Just as Ariadne on
Naxos longs unknowingly for Dionysus, the Zarathustra of "Of the Great
Longing" yearns for the vintner with his golden knife. As the creative god
of the third seal, Zarathustra—a "harvester" already in the Prologue (Z,P:9;
26.15)—takes from his soul the ripe fruits that long for the vintner's knife;
rather than hold on to fruits from the past, he subjects his soul, himself, to
the pain that is required if further growth is to be possible. The ripened
grapes must be cut from the vine rather than allowed to rot on it; they must
die so that others may live.
The first seal presents Zarathustra as enemy "of all that is tired and can
neither die nor live" (287.7–8), but also as pregnant with affirmative bolts
of lightning (287.9–11). The second seal presents him as affirmatively surviv-
ing the destruction of old tablets (288.2) and old gods (288.7), the third, as
himself a god among gods. In the fourth, he praises the whole as whole, with
all its conflicting, contradictory parts. In the fifth he sets sail, in the sixth he
dances, in the seventh he flies. Nowhere does he long for his death, and
nowhere does he anticipate his return. The eternity he loves is not an eternity
he seeks, but rather an eternity he has. But what kind of eternity is this?

Resurrection as Self-Creation

If eternity is neither the negation of my earthly life—not Christian-moral eternity—nor the infinite repetition of my earthly life—not the eternity of dwarves, barrel-organs, and buffoons—what then is eternity? Zarathustra's answer, most baldly stated, is that eternity is the omnipresence, the ubiquity of the moment within my earthly life, which is my only life. At every moment in my life, I stand at the intersection of two paths, one leading from the past, one leading toward the future. The moment is not separable from these paths, but neither is it swallowed up by them—it is not the instantaneous *Nu* of the animals.

The moment is bound to the future in that every moment is one from which I must take a single path forward, and in that any moment can be a moment of decision, a point where I change the direction of my development. It might appear that, in one sense, many paths into the future are open, in that I deem myself free to choose. Yet the fact remains that any specific choice is also a limiting choice, every selection an exclusion: I have only one life to live, only one path to follow.

I can choose, perhaps, either to teach my scheduled class tomorrow, or to abandon job and family in order to lead a life of dissolution. But even if this is a fact, it requires interpretation: what is its significance? Am I to view my life, as it continues, as the continual diminution of possibilities, or as the continual expansion of my actuality? I cannot, perhaps, become both brain surgeon and concert pianist; if I become one, I do so at the exclusion of the other. But it is not as though I would first have been both, only to have become but one.

The moment is bound not only to the future, but also to the past. It is bound to the past in that I have reached the moment, at any moment, by following a specific path. If I were now to seek a Zarathustrian cave in order to commune with thoughts and animals for the next ten years, I would commune as one who had abandoned job and family in order to do so; I cannot now decide never to have had job and family in the first place. In addition, I may well have developed ties of affection, comfort, habit, and/or neurosis binding me so strongly to my current way of living that radical changes, at least of certain sorts, would prove impossible. For reasons of a different sort, it would be impossible for me now to become a concert pianist.

The point where I now am, within any moment, is the point from which I must proceed into the future, and I cannot now choose to have followed a different path to take me to the point where I now am. I cannot, for two distinct reasons: first, and obviously, my past is behind me; I have no chance to live through it again, doing things differently. The second reason, less obvious but equally important, is that the only path through the past that leads to my present is precisely the path I have followed: had "I" done differently in the past, I would not now be I, as I am; "I" would be someone else.

This life, with its single and determinate past and its single but not yet determined future, is my eternal life, the only life I can ever have. In this my eternal life, I always return, and the structure of the moment always returns, with its unknowable but singular future, as well as its inescapable past. To will the eternal return is to will this life, with its ineluctable temporality, both formal and contentual. It is to will that, in one sense, my soul be constantly resurrected, within each new moment, but that requires that it constantly die, within each new moment. My soul dies in that it is not simply determined by its past; I can attempt to act differently, I can seek to embrace a different "highest hope." Yet such a death is also a resurrection, for even if I undergo a transformation, I do not create a wholly new soul: I retain my past, in all its concreteness.

In one sense, perhaps, my soul is "resurrected" within every moment; but this is not Zarathustra's sense of resurrection. "Only where there are tombs," he insists, "are there resurrections" (Z,II:11; 145.13). Our souls are entombed when we lose our highest hopes, but that presupposes that we have had highest hopes. Some of us, many of us, have perhaps never found anything that would both "give our souls agony and sweetness and be the hunger of our entrails" (42.9–10). Resurrection in Zarathustra's stricter sense takes place only when one, having lost such a hope, embraces a new one.

Zarathustra thinks of "leaving life soon," in "The Other Dancing Song," not because he thinks simply of dying; for him, "leaving life" can be more complicated than that. As he convalesces, as he overcomes the despair induced by rabble and Soothsayer, he departs from his old life in that he takes a new direction; but the life he leads continues to be his. In willing to live as he henceforth will live, Zarathustra also wills the return of the life he has led; that life, he knows, will be with him throughout his eternity, it will be with him as long as he is at all.

To will the eternal return of this sameness is to will oneself, one's life, in the deepest and most comprehensive sense. Only when I have affirmed my life, under these conditions, have I become one who can will, in the deepest and most comprehensive sense. Hence the admonition, "By all means do what you will, but first be such that you can will" (Z,III:5.3; 216.26–27). Before I become one who can will, I cannot look back on my past and say, "thus did I will it" (Z,II:20; 181.1–18). Nevertheless, on becoming one who can will, I can look back and will this way I have blindly walked (Z,I:3; 37.4–5). I have walked it blindly in that I did not will it—as I walked, I was not yet able to will—but I can now will it as having brought me to where I now am. Following my transformative affirmation of the eternal return, I can will; if I then succeed in willing—if I am strong enough to hold my insight firmly in my grasp, rather than allowing it to be obscured by new gods or hinterworlds, or by weary eyelids, or by a fresh coat of paint—then I live henceforth in such a way that I will later be able to look back and say, "thus did I will it," for I will have been one who willed.

From the perspective of one who can will, I see in addition that no aspect of my past is simply fixed and dead, that my past is not a rock that my will cannot move (Z,II:20; 180.10–11). It is not, for it is growing with every moment, and transformed with every moment. The transformative aspect is what the pale criminal fails to see: "He then saw himself always as the doer of one deed. Madness I call this: the exception inverted itself, becoming the essence" (Z,I:6; 46.6–7). If there is one thing no human being can ever be, it is "the doer of one deed": unavoidably, we are doers of many deeds. "If only he could shake his head, his burden would roll off; but who is to shake this head?" (46.25–26). No one can shake it for him; he must shake it himself.

To shake one's head, to put the past deed into the past, is to respond as Zarathustra responds when he recognizes his compassion for the higher men as his "last sin": "Well then [Wohlan]! That—had its time!" (Z,IV:20; 408.14). "That had its time": the pale criminal's deed had its time, and will always—"eternally," for the pale criminal—have its time, but the significance of the deed is not determined by the deed—the fact—itself; rather, its significance will be determined by the pale criminal's later acts and reflections. The deed could, in principle, have become one from which the pale criminal had learned, or one whose lesson he had ignored. Only because the pale criminal views the deed as his *one* deed does it assume its fatal significance for him. At the extreme opposite to the one the pale criminal takes, it might even be possible for him to forget the deed entirely; even then, however, he would determine himself as having forgotten it. What he can never forget—what even the amnesiac can never forget—is that he has a past. Having a past is a feature of any human being's eternally returning life.

This eternally returning life not only re-creates the past by continually providing it with a new context, and thus with a reinterpretation; it is also creative of the future, in that within every moment I act into a future I do not yet know. I throw the dice, as do others, and no one throw can ever be wholly determinative. The central product of this creative life is my soul; to the extent to which I find what gives *my* soul agony and sweetness and is also the hunger of *my* entrails, I will succeed, in creating my soul, in becoming who I am (Z,IV:1; 297.17). Because in acting I create my soul, it makes perfect sense for the friend I have wronged to respond, "I forgive you for what you did to me; but that you did it to *yourself*—how could I forgive that" (Z,II:3; 115.17–19). In wronging my friend, I determine myself, and the self-determination is something only I can overcome, not something my friend can overcome for me. I overcome it, if at all, through the future deeds that determine its significance.

In that my self-creation is a continual self-overcoming, this creation is never *ex nihilo*, nor is it ever once-and-for-all. I begin where I already am, within a culture, under historical and linguistic circumstances, having developed habits and acquired opinions, having done and said what I have done and said. If I abandon family and homeland, I will always—for my eternity, for as long as I am at all—have abandoned them, I cannot make myself into someone who never had either. I will have abandoned them even if I later return to them; I could not then make myself into someone who never left home. As creator, at any moment, I am thus far from omnipotent; this makes my self-creative decisions the more important, in that all "return eternally": none is simply once-and-for-all, all contribute continually to making me who I am.

This doctrine of eternal return is selective: a doctrine that denies gods, afterlives, and even radically different futures (Marxist or technological utopias, or Kantian indefinite progress)—a doctrine that insists that life is as it is, now, that it will never be anything else—is not for everyone. The doctrine is selective, but it is self-selective. The basis of its acceptance is, to put it one way, phenomenological rather than logical: Zarathustra does not provide arguments, he rather reveals types, leaving it to the individual to choose which type he or she will attempt to become.

The choice is given to the masses in the marketplace: Zarathustra presents all with portraits of the overman and of the last man. When the masses fail to choose the overman, Zarathustra's only recourse is silence: "I am not the mouth for these ears" (Z,P:5; 18.26–27). Similarly, Zarathustra does not seek to convince anyone that God is dead; when he discovers that the old saint does know that God is dead, he declines to give the saint his "gift"— the doctrine of the overman, the substitute for the dead God—saying rather, "What could I have to give you? Let me get away quickly, before I take something from you" (Z,P:2; 13.34–14.1).

As Zarathustra learns to distinguish those to whom he can give from those from whom he would take, and from those who cannot take from him, he becomes increasingly able to apply the principle, "where one can no longer love, there one should *pass by*" (Z,III.7; 225.13–15). The principle is explicitly put into practice early in Part II, where Zarathustra admonishes his disciples, "Here are priests, and even if they are my enemies, pass by them quietly, for me, and with sleeping swords! . . . Evil enemies they are. . . . But my blood is related to theirs, and I want to know my blood honored even in theirs" (Z,II.4; 117.4–5, 8, 10–11).

After embracing the thought of the eternal return, Zarathustra can pass by even the rabble; his confrontation with the thought reveals to him that what he must affirm is not all life, but rather his life. If the rabble are not absent from that life, then it is up to him not to allow his well to be poisoned by them. The disgust (*Ekel*) that dominates the second half of Part II and almost all of Part III is simply absent from Part IV, where Zarathustra uses the word *Ekel* only in clearly retrospective contexts. To be sure, he is not blithely accepting: having given his soul "the right to say no as the storm says no" as well as "yes as the open sky says yes" (278.13–14), he continues to say no—usually, "No! No! Three times no!" (see, perhaps among others, Z,IV:2; 302.32–33 / Z,IV:11; 351.15 / Z,IV:13.6; 359.19). Zarathustra never succumbs to stupid, indiscriminate yea-saying, but neither does he succumb, again, to disgust.

One who moves beyond disgust in this manner—one who advocates the eternal return of his or her life, as it is becoming—becomes true to the earth, and recognizes that "all life is the will to power," that we constantly overcome ourselves, even if we do so by reaffirming ourselves as we have been. The advocate of this eternal return is, perhaps, an "overman," although Zarathustra does not stuff his new meaning into that pocket—he does not, I suspect, precisely in order to avoid seeming to bridge, and thereby concealing, the gap between the purely futural ideality he initially projects and the concretely temporal reality he ultimately affirms. The advocate of this eternal return lives dangerously, of necessity: to continue to live is to continue to throw the dice, and to continue to be exposed to Schopenhauer's pains and torments. The advocate of this eternal return, unlike dwarf or animal, affirms the life Zarathustra recognizes as the human life, the only life that is open to us.

Interpreted as I have interpreted it, the doctrine of eternal return is neither bad physics nor bad metaphysics, but rather, it seems to me, accurate anthropology: it illuminates the nature of human existence. This doctrine is anthropological, but it is not moral; it tells me how I must exist, but not how I should exist. I may be convinced by Nietzsche that living, for human beings, is soul-making, but after recognizing that I am the creator of my soul I must still decide what soul I will struggle to create, given the material and talent available to me, and how that soul will relate to other souls also in the making. This indicates that if I accept Nietzsche's gift, I must go beyond Nietzsche. This suggestion is in no way anti-Nietzschean; it is perfectly fitting that Nietzsche's gift should be not so much an answer as a challenge. The challenge to me is to create—not *ex nihilo,* and not once and for all, but rather on the basis of what it already is, and as it continues to develop—a soul I will be proud of creating, a soul whose existence I can affirm. Nietzsche's gift teaches me that I am creating my soul in any case, whether I know it or not; but it does not teach me, nor does it want to teach me, what kind of soul to create: " 'This is now my way; where is yours?' Thus did I answer those who asked me for 'the way.' *The* way, namely—there is no such thing" (Z,III:11.2; 245.14–16 / cf. Z,I:22.2; 100.27–29).

III
Within the Labyrinth

The Reader is beset by mysterious coincidences. He told me that, for some time, and for the most disparate reasons, he has had to interrupt his reading of novels after a few pages.

"Perhaps they bore you," I said, with my usual tendency toward pessimism. "On the contrary, I am forced to stop reading just when they become most gripping. I can't wait to resume, but when I think I am reopening the book I began, I find a completely different book before me . . ."

"Which instead is terribly boring," I suggest.

"No, even more gripping. But I can't manage to finish this one, either. And so on."

"Your case gives me new hope," I said to him. "With me, more and more often I happen to pick up a novel that has just appeared and I find myself reading the same book I have read a hundred times."

Italo Calvino

7

Art Without Artifact

A person's life consists of a collection of events, the last of which could also change the meaning of the whole, not because it counts more than the previous ones but because once they are included in a life, events are arranged in an order that is not chronological but, rather, corresponds to an inner architecture.

Italo Calvino

I have sketched what I take to be the outlines of Nietzsche's affirmative teachings. The more convincing I have been, the more compelling will appear the need for further explorations within Nietzsche's labyrinth, which is our labyrinth. From the perspective of my reading of *Zarathustra*, I turn in the following chapters to the consideration of some puzzles—particularly ethical and political ones—that emerge from that reading, but that also develop within other explorations within our labyrinth. References to such explorations have been sprinkled through the notes to my earlier chapters, but I deem two recent explorers sufficiently interesting, illuminating, and important to warrant more direct treatment: "philosopher" Alexander Nehamas and "poet" Milan Kundera. Nehamas has recently published an intriguing book on Nietzsche, and although Kundera has not, he has often encountered Nietzsche in his own wanderings through life's labyrinth, wanderings he continues to recount both eloquently and provocatively.

Life as Literature

The central thesis of Alexander Nehamas's admirable *Nietzsche: Life as Literature* elaborates its title: "Nietzsche's view . . . assimilates the ideal person to an ideal literary character and the ideal life to an ideal story" (Nehamas, 166). Nehamas attempts to reveal this assimilation, which also provides the basis for his interpretation of eternal return, by identifying two features of the literary character he takes to apply to the human being as well.

The first feature shared by character and person can be described negatively as a lack of essence, or positively as a holism. Both character and person lack essence, in that for neither is there a core hidden behind or revealed by experiences, words, and deeds. Thus, "literary characters are exhausted by the statements that concern them in the narratives in which they occur: they are in fact nothing more than is said of them, just as they are also nothing less" (165). The same holds for the human being: "no person remains beyond the totality of its experiences and actions" (155).

If every detail concerning the character is "essential," then the character has no "essence" in that it has no core that could be exposed by the stripping away of the merely apparent or accidental. But this means, positively, that "every detail concerning a character has, at least in principle, a point; it is to that extent essential to that character" (165). For the well-constructed character,

> to change even one action on the part of a character is to cause both that character and the story to which it belongs to fall apart. In order to maintain the coherence of the story (and assuming this idea is itself coherent), we would have to make corresponding changes throughout, and we would thus produce an entirely different story; if anything were different, indeed everything would have to be different. (165)

Similarly, for the human being, if any of its "experiences and actions" were different, "then their subject, which is simply their sum total, would also have to be different" (155).

For the human being, then—as, I have argued, for the world—dyadic categories such as substance-accident or essence-appearance are inappropriate, and therefore misleading. If there is no substantial or essential self behind the words and deeds, thoughts and experiences of a human being, then there is no basis for classifying any of these words, deeds, thoughts, and experiences as merely accidental or apparent.

The holism Nehamas attributes to the human being provides the basis for his interpretation of eternal return. Because none of our words, deeds, or experiences are merely accidental, because all contribute to making us who we are,

> the opportunity to live again would necessarily involve the exact repetition of the very same events that constitute my present life. The question therefore is not whether I would or would not do the same things again; in this matter there is no room for choice. The question is only whether I would *want* to do the same things all over again. This is simply the question whether I am glad to have done whatever I have done already, and therefore the question whether I would be willing to acknowledge all my doings as my own. (190)

This question leads me to the second feature Nehamas ascribes to character and person, in addition to holism. The second feature enables us to distinguish the characters and persons whose eternal return can be willed from those whom all, including themselves, would be happy to have seen the last of. In life as in literature, Nehamas asserts, what Nietzsche values is stylish coherence, i.e., consistency of character resulting not from "weakness, mediocrity, and one-dimensionality," but rather from "a large number of powerful and conflicting tendencies that are controlled and harmonized" (7)—in my earlier terms, from investing the body's passions with a "highest goal," a goal that will both give the soul "agony and sweetness" and be "the hunger of the entrails." The couch potato may be consistent, but his consistency does not count for Nehamas as stylish; he lacks anything Nietzsche would recognize as a "highest goal." Of the literary character, Nehamas writes: "Because organization is the most crucial feature of literary characters, the quality of their actions is secondary: the significance and nature of a character's action is inseparable from its place in that organization" (193).

Similarly, "a person worthy of admiration, a person who has (or is) a self, is one whose thoughts, desires, and actions are not haphazard but are instead connected to one another in the intimate way that indicates in all cases the presence of style" (7). "Nietzsche came to see perfect self-sufficiency as a proper test for the perfect life at least partly because his thinking so often concerned literary models" (193–94).

Nehamas presents a powerful and intriguing reading of Nietzsche, one from which I have learned much, and from which I accept much. Nevertheless, Nehamas's zeal in defending his thesis that "life is literature" leads him, occasionally, into problematic formulations. Most important, in my view, is that the potentially transformative aspects of Nietzsche's thought are insufficiently emphasized, and indeed occasionally obscured.

This difficulty is implicit in the passage just quoted. What if, having read and been convinced by Nehamas or Nietzsche, I reflect (to the extent possible) on my thoughts, desires, and actions, past and present, and discover not an appealing and intriguing coherence, but rather a stupid and repellent muddle? Confronted with Nehamas's version of the thought of eternal return, I then ask myself *only* "whether I would *want* to do the same things all over again." My answer, if I have accepted the evaluative perspective Nehamas attributes to Nietzsche, would have to be be "no"—perhaps even, "No! No! Three times no!" But where could I go from here? The thought might well crush me, but how could it transform me?

If I were a literary character, the thought could not transform me. It could not, because I would then be "exhausted" by the statements concerning me within the literary work within which I appeared. But I am not a literary character. According to Nehamas, "no person remains behind the totality of its experiences and actions"; but in what sense are my experiences and actions a "totality," either coherent or muddled? My experiences and actions form a "totality," if at all, only after I am dead; but after I am dead, I can no longer be confronted with the thought of eternal return. As long as I can ask questions, I remain incomplete; but that means, positively, that I have a future.

Of the future, Nehamas writes:

> The unity Nietzsche has in mind can become apparent and truly exist only over time. Though if it is achieved, it is achieved at some time, what is achieved at that time is the unification of one's past with one's present. The future is, therefore, always a danger to it: any new event may prove impossible to unify, at least without further effort, with the self into which one has developed. (185)

The future, Nehamas tells us, is "always a danger" to those who have attained the Nietzschean ideal of stylish coherence. But what about those who have failed? As I have stressed above, and as Nehamas also notes, "the significance and nature of a character's action is inseparable from its place in [that character's] organization" (193). My "organization," unlike the literary character's, is incomplete; but for just this reason, the "significance and nature" of my past words and deeds, thoughts and desires, remain indeterminate. And this indeterminacy adds a crucial clause to the question posed by the thought of eternal return: given that the significance of what I have done is conditioned by what I shall henceforth do, I ask not whether I would now will to repeat my life exactly as it has been up to now; I ask instead, how shall I henceforth act so that I will be able to affirm my being the person I will have become?

For Nehamas, the thought of eternal return is merely a test for my past; in the altered form I suggest, it becomes a challenge for my future. This challenge makes of the future a danger, perhaps, for those who have acted with style in the past, but this is a danger that would be welcomed rather than feared by all whom Nietzsche would admire. Perhaps more important, however, it also makes of the future an opportunity for those who judge their pasts more harshly, whether because they have been cruel or base, or because they have been simply weak or inconsistent.

I would not be surprised if Nehamas were to agree that the thought of eternal return is challenge as well as test, and that it has a transformative function as well as an evaluative one. Indeed, Nehamas might well respond, "yes, but I note that as well." Indeed, he does note what I have been stressing, and eloquently:

> The events of the past are necessarily located through and within a narrative, and different narratives can generate quite different events. . . . By creating, on the basis of the past, an acceptable future, we justify and redeem everything that made this future possible; and that is everything. . . . To accept the present is then to accept all that has led to it. It is in this sense that one can now say of what has already happened, "Thus I willed it." The significance and nature of the past, like the significance and nature of everything else according to Nietz-

sche, lies in its relationships. In particular, the significance of the past lies in its relationship to the future. And since the future is yet to come, neither the significance of the past nor its nature is yet settled. (160–61)

My agreement with this formulation is almost complete, yet even here, it seems to me, transformation is underemphasized. Nehamas describes a present willing of the past, but such a willing is not appropriately described by the phrase, "Thus I willed it"; one in the situation described by Nehamas would say, more appropriately, "Thus I now will it to have been." Only one who has been transformed by the thought of eternal return, that is, by affirmation of the human condition, has become one who can will, and thus, potentially, one who will later be able to say, "thus I willed it."

As I have indicated, my reservations about Nehamas's reading arise less from the details of that reading than from Nehamas's attempt to fit those details under the rubric "life as literature." I move toward a more appropriate rubric by way of one of Nehamas's literary examples:

> Could Anna Karenina, for example, not have fallen in love with Vronsky? Could she not have left her husband? Could she have loved her son less than she did? Could she have been ultimately less conventional than in fact she was? Could she not have been Oblonsky's sister? In regard to literary characters, such questions are at least very difficult, if not impossible, to answer. It is just this feature of the literary situation that underlies and motivates Nietzsche's view of the ideal person and the ideal life. (165)

Anna Karenina, Nehamas suggests, could not not have left her husband. Why not? Is it because, to use a Nehamasian formulation cited above, her remaining with him would be a "new event" that would "prove impossible to unify, at least without further effort, with the self" into which she had developed (185)? Certainly, the suggestion that the course Anna takes minimizes her future efforts is problematic; having left her husband, Anna hardly leads a life that is carefree. But what if Anna had not left her husband? Can we exclude the possibility that she might nevertheless have become an interesting and admirable character? I certainly cannot. If we say that Anna Karenina could not not have left her husband, the reason we give must be not that her life would then have been incoherent, but rather that she would not then have become the character we know as Anna Karenina. She would have become another character, but that character, too, might have attained Nehamas's Nietzschean ideal.

Living as Dancing

Like Nehamas, Milan Kundera invokes Anna Karenina as a literary character exemplifying deep, and therefore often unrecognized, features of the human condition. And although Kundera does not explicitly refer, in this connection, to Nietzsche, his discussion utilizes a second Nietzschean metaphor, one that is, in my view, more appropriate to Nietzsche's affirmative position than is Nehamas's "life as literature":

> Early in the novel that Tereza clutched under her arm when she went to visit Tomas, Anna meets Vronsky in curious circumstances: they are at the railway station when someone is run over by a train. At the end of the novel, Anna throws herself under a train. This symmetrical composition—the same motif appears at the beginning and at the end—may seem quite "novelistic" to you, and I am willing to agree, but only on condition that you refrain from reading such notions as "fictive," "fabricated," and "untrue to life" into the word "novelistic." Because human lives are composed in precisely such a fashion.
>
> They are composed like music. Guided by his sense of beauty, an individual transforms a fortuitous occurrence (Beethoven's music, death under a train) into a motif, which then assumes a permanent place in the composition of the individual's life. Anna could have chosen another way to take her life. But the motif of death and the railway station, unforgettably bound to the birth of love, enticed her in her hour of despair with its dark beauty. Without realizing it, the individual composes his life according to the laws of beauty even in times of greatest distress.
>
> It is wrong, then, to chide the novel for being fascinated by mysterious coincidences (like the meeting of Anna, Vronsky, the railway station, and death or the meeting of Beethoven, Tomas, Tereza, and the cognac), but it is right to chide man for being blind to such coincidences in his daily life. For he thereby deprives his life of a dimension of beauty. (*Lightness*, 52)

Whereas Nehamas emphasizes the constraints placed on Anna—she had to leave her husband, had to love her son as she did, etc.—Kundera acknowledges the variety of the paths open to her. Whereas Nehamas gives us a series of rhetorical questions—"could Anna have done other than she did?"—Kundera asserts flatly, "Anna could have chosen another way to take her life."

Our lives are composed, Kundera tells us, not like literature but rather like music. A literary work is an artifact: it outlives not only the act of its production, but also the life of its producer. It provides, thereby, a semblance of immortality. Not surprisingly, I think, the literary work has precisely this status for Marcel, the fictional narrator of Proust's *Remembrance of Things Past*—a character whose narrative, according to Nehamas, "is the best possible model for the eternal recurrence" (168; see also 188). As Marcel begins, at the end of his narrative of his life, to recognize the form that must be taken by the narrative he is to write—the narrative the reader is near completing—Marcel remarks, "the cruel law of art is that people die and we ourselves die after exhausting every form of suffering, so that over our heads may grow the grass not of oblivion but of eternal life, the vigorous and luxuriant growth of a true work of art, and so that thither, gaily and without a thought for those who are sleeping beneath them, future generations may come to enjoy their *déjeuner sur l'herbe*" (*Remembrance,* III:1095). This passage echoes an earlier reflection, from the occasion of the death of the author Bergotte: "they buried him, but all through the night of mourning, in the lighted shop-windows, his books, arranged three by three, kept vigil like angels with outspread wings and seemed, for him who was no more, the symbol of his resurrection" (*Remembrance,* III:186).

Marcel, in writing, seeks a vicarious permanence in the memory of others—an eternal life not for himself as artist, but rather for his "true work of art." Kundera speaks of a different sort of permanence, the permanence of a "place in the composition of the individual's life." Kundera's permanence is a permanence in memory, perhaps, but the relevant memory is, in the first instance, that of the individual. The "dimension of beauty" present in the "mysterious coincidences" that enter into the compositions of our lives is a dimension open to us if we avoid "being blind to such coincidences"; we need not write about them.

According to Nehamas, "Writing . . . always remains both the main model and the main object of Nietzsche's thinking" (32). Yet at the very least Nietzsche, like Kundera, invokes musical metaphors in addition to literary ones. At times, he intertwines them: "perhaps the whole of *Zarathustra* may be reckoned as music; certainly a rebirth of the art of *hearing* was among its preconditions" (*EH,*IX:1). And it is wholly to the point to note that Zarathustra, the ideal character Nietzsche himself creates, never writes. He never writes, but he speaks, he walks, he laughs, he sings, and he dances. We learn from the sixth of his Seven Seals that his virtue is "a dancer's virtue," that he often leaps "with both feet in golden-emerald rapture" and that his "alpha and omega" is, in part, "that every body shall become a dancer" (*Z,*III:16.6; 290.18–26).

Speeches, like dances, are instances of art without artifact: within the speech or the dance, creator coincides with creation—both with creative act and with created product. The dance is created, but it does not outlive the act of its creation, save perhaps in memory. One dances in order to dance, and perhaps in order to be seen dancing; similarly, according to the perspective I have been developing, which I have presented as Nietzschean, it is possible for us to live in order to live, and perhaps in order to be seen living. One writes, on the other hand, in order to be read.

It is possible to view life as literature, but it is also possible to view living as dancing. Viewed as a dance, my life may be clumsy, or it may be graceful; it may be coherent, or it may be chaotic. It may influence others, and it may do so by inspiring them or appalling them or boring them. But the influence is, necessarily, reciprocal: those who witness my dance are themselves dancers, and our shared steps and missteps are among the occurrences, fortuitous or intentional, that compose our distinct but connected dances (see *HH*,I:27).

Our dances, if they are beautiful, exhibit an eternal return; they are circle dances, not because they repeat the same steps, but rather because, in Kundera's words, they transform fortuitous occurrences into motifs that then assume permanent places in the compositions of our lives. To be sure, for occurrences to be transformed they must first be remembered; but as they are remembered, they are also transformed.

In an age of film and videotape, some dance, perhaps, in order to be recorded; before this age, perhaps, some have danced in order to be paid. Many have lived, and continue to live, for just these reasons: I may view my life as a job, as a curse, as a duty, or as a punishment. Like Nehamas, I find in Nietzsche an insistence that it is also possible for me to view my life as my work of art; but the artwork that is my life is, it seems to me, more a dance inseparable from its dancing than a novel for others to read. And I deem it important, as I take Nietzsche to deem it important, that we recognize that just as some may dance simply in order to dance, it is possible to live simply in order to live—not in order to produce, to repay, to expiate, or to earn. If there is a Nietzschean imperative, an appropriate formulation for it might be, "you have but one life to dance; dance it beautifully."

A beautiful dance, in the terms I have elaborated as Nietzschean, is one that is affirmed by its dancer; to suggest that there are strict criteria all beautiful dances must meet is to revert to the dogmatic perspective of slave moralities. Zarathustra's minotaur, the spirit of gravity, insists, "Good for all, evil for all" (*Z*,III:11.2; 243.26–27); in response to my Nietzschean imperative, he would no doubt proclaim, "beautiful for all," and would seek to force all our dances into the uniform strides of a goose-step. What is not good for all, this minotaur contends, cannot be good for any; what is not beautiful for all cannot be beautiful for any. The minotaur is silenced—never slain—by those who insist, "Good for me, evil for me" (243.25–27), and also, I suggest, "beautiful for me."

Many of us, often, judge ourselves ugly; many of us, often, wish we were otherwise. "If only I had been born rich (or poor), female (or male), if only I had gone to Harvard (or to Southwest Schenectady State), then . . ." Then what, Nietzsche asks? Then I'd be happy? Then I'd be successful? Then my life would be worth living? So I might think; Nietzsche wants to convince me that I would be wrong. I would be wrong not because the course my life has followed has been better, in some absolute sense, than one of the alternative courses I might imagine having followed, or having been able to follow if circumstances had been otherwise. I would be wrong, instead, because if "my" life had followed a different course, it would not be mine. "I" would not, in that case, be someone else; I would not be at all.

Nietzsche encourages us to focus our attention not on the past, but on the future. Not that I should forget my past—on the contrary, he insists, I *am* my past. But my past is, in one Nietzschean formulation, a brute fact that remains meaningless until it is interpreted. And the way I interpret my past is by placing it the context of my future.

In encouraging us to view our pasts within the contexts of our futures, to view our lives as wholes, Nietzsche places a weight on our individual acts and decisions; in our epoch, the weight may not be a burden. Things were different in the epoch preceding the death of God; then, the weight of individual acts and decisions could be crushing, because any one act could, in principle, doom its agent to eternal damnation. Following the death of God, acts and decisions have lost that weight; the danger has arisen that they take on what Kundera calls an "unbearable lightness." Why should I think about what I am to do? Why care about it? One hundred years from now, I'll certainly be dead, the entire planet may well be a nuclear waste dump. Why should I try to produce or to create, why should I be decent, or even polite?

Instead of answering these questions, Nietzsche transforms them. Given that the life I am now living is my eternal life—the only one I will ever live, the one I will live as long as I live—given that what makes me me are my words and deeds and experiences, and not some immutable soul, given that even if what I do may make no difference to the course of the universe for the next few millennia or even for the next few years, it nevertheless makes all the difference to me, because it makes me. Given that this is how life is, I ask not, which way through my life am I obliged to follow? I ask instead, which way am I to make my own? How am I to make *my* life beautiful, that is, a life I can deem worth living, as I continue to live it?

Beauty and Goodness

Nietzsche exhorts us to live beautifully; on this point, Nehamas and I agree. A second point of our agreement is in attributing to Nietzsche an insistence that the assessment of a specific life's beauty is a matter, primarily, for the individual living that life. From these teachings a serious problem emerges: if beauty is the criterion for goodness, and if there are no universal criteria for beauty, is there anything to prevent the mass murderer and the child molester on the one hand, or the couch potato on the other, from viewing their lives as beautiful, and thus as good—even as ideal? This question leads me to one of Nehamas's central concerns: "Nietzsche is clearly much more concerned with the question of how one's actions are to fit together into a coherent, self-sustaining, well-motivated whole than he is with the quality of those actions themselves" (166); for this reason, "the uncomfortable feeling persists that someone might achieve Nietzsche's ideal life and still be nothing short of repugnant" (167).

This uncomfortable feeling arises, for Nehamas, from the teaching that life is literature. According to Nehamas's Nietzsche, "one should not take one's misdeeds seriously for long, [because] virtue does not depend on *what* one does but on *whether* what one does is an expression of one's whole self, of one's 'own will.' " This position makes sense, Nehamas adds, because "these are exactly the considerations that are relevant to the evaluation of literary characters" (166).

Literature, many of us would agree, would be much the poorer if it contained none of what my children refer to as "bad guys"; evil literary characters are often intriguing and fascinating characters, and thus, we might agree, "good" characters; works of literature containing evil, corrupt, and malicious characters are often good literary works. Evil lives often make good literature; what then if life is literature?

A version of the same question arises for Proust's Marcel, who sees the possibility only of a Platonistic answer. Reflecting on Bergotte's death, he writes:

> He was dead. Dead forever? Who can say? Certainly, experiments in spiritualism offer us no more proof than the dogmas of religion that the soul survives death. All that we can say is that everything is arranged in this life as though we entered it carrying a burden of obligations contracted in a former life; there is no reason inherent in the conditions of life on this earth that can make us consider ourselves obliged to do good, to be kind and thoughtful, even to be polite, nor for an atheist artist to consider himself obliged to begin over again a score of times a piece of work the admiration aroused by which will matter little to his worm-eaten body, like the patch of yellow wall painted with so much skill and refinement by an artist destined to be forever unknown and barely identified under the name Vermeer. All these obligations, which have no sanction in our present life, seem to belong to a different world, a world based on kindness, scrupulousness, self-sacrifice, a world entirely different from this one and which we leave in order to be born on this earth, before perhaps returning there to live once again beneath the sway of those unknown laws which we obeyed because we bore their precepts in our hearts, not knowing whose hand had traced them there—those laws to which every profound work of the intellect brings us nearer and which are invisible only—if then!—to fools. So that the idea that Bergotte was not permanently dead is by no means improbable. (*Remembrance*, III:186)

Why should we "do good," why should "be kind and thoughtful," why should we be even polite? Why should we strive to create, knowing as we do that the admiration aroused by our creations will matter little to our worm-eaten bodies? In a manner typical of the Platonistic current in the Western philosophical tradition, Marcel answers: human obligations to be thoughtful and kind could derive only from a different world, one "entirely different from this one."

Nietzsche rejects the notion that there are human obligations deriving from a different world; yet he is not one of Marcel's fools. Nehamas stresses, and I stress, that Nietzsche does not want to take the position of encouraging sadists and egotists. Unbridled egotism, he insists, would lead only to "universal wars of annihilation" (BT:15). His position is made yet more explicit in a passage quoted above, but worth repeating:

> I deny morality as I deny alchemy, that is, I deny their premises: but I do *not* deny that there have been alchemists who believed in these premises and acted in accordance with them.—I also deny immorality: *not* that countless people *feel* themselves to be immoral, but that there is any *true* reason so to feel. It goes without saying that I do not deny—unless I am a fool—that many actions called immoral ought to be avoided and resisted, or that many called moral ought to be done and encouraged—but I think the one should be encouraged and the other avoided *for other reasons than hitherto*. (D:103)

Nietzsche does not want to deny "that many actions called immoral ought to be avoided and resisted, and that many called moral ought to be done and encouraged"; he agrees with Marcel that only fools could think otherwise. Yet he rejects otherworldly sources of obligation; how then can he answer Marcel's questions? What is to be said, or done, to the mass murderer and the child molester, or to the couch potato?

Nehamas responds to this question on Nietzsche's behalf, but his response strikes me as in part inaccurate and in part dangerous, and thus, on the whole, unacceptable. In responding, Nehamas first suggests that Nietzsche severely restricts the audience to whom he addresses his transvaluative teachings:

> Exemplifying the very attitude that prompts him to reject unconditional codes, Nietzsche does not reject them unconditionally. His demand is only that philosophers, and not all people, "take their stand *beyond* good and evil and leave the illusion of moral judgment *beneath* them." (224)

Here, Nehamas suggests that only philosophers—who, he seems to assume, are not "fools" of the sort Marcel and Nietzsche are worried about—are to recognize that moral judgment is illusory. In this central respect, Nehamas's Nietzsche seems to remain a Platonist: he tells noble lies to the masses in order to keep them in line, reserving the truth for the intellectually privileged few.

No doubt, Nietzsche does restrict the scope of some of his teachings; he has Zarathustra announce, for example, "It is a disgrace [*Schmach*] to pray! Not for everyone, but for *you* and me and whoever else has his conscience in his head. For you it is a disgrace to pray" (Z,III:8.2; 227.27–29). I grant in addition that Nietzsche points philosophers beyond dogmatic morality;

he agrees with Marcel that nothing on this earth *obliges* us to be thoughtful or kind. Yet even in the passage Nehamas cites (*TI*,VII:1), Nietzsche does not present his teachings to philosophers alone. And if we distinguish more generally between esoteric and exoteric strains in Nietzsche's teachings, then his immoralism, his apparent advocacy of violence and oppression, must certainly be included among his teachings for the many.

Pace Nehamas, it seems to me that Nietzsche views the retention, by the many, of the illusion of moral judgment not only as undesirable, but even as impossible. It is impossible because, he insists, God is dead, and word of his death is getting around. Christian morality was maintained only by the fear of hell and the promise of heaven—Christian morality works, on a broad scale, only for those who live in order to be paid ("great will be your reward in heaven"); it collapses with the demise of the celestial paymaster. If God is dead, morality dies with him, although only following a lengthier decline.

For this reason, I reject Nehamas's assertion that "Nietzsche . . . does not advocate and does not even foresee a radical change in the lives of most people," although I accept a version of the sentence that follows it immediately: "The last thing he is is a social reformer or revolutionary" (225). Nietzsche is not a "social reformer or revolutionary" in the usual sense in that he does not provide society with an external impetus for reform or revolution, and in that he provides no blueprint for a post-Christian social world. He provides society with no external impetus because there is no need for one; whether we like it or not, society continues to transform itself—as, history shows us, it has done cataclysmically over the century since Nietzsche stopped writing. For this reason, Nietzsche does foresee "radical change in the lives of most people," albeit not so much radical change within the life of the single individual as radical change, over the coming centuries, in the ways the majority of people live. Such change, Nietzsche is convinced, is inevitable: he need not cause it, and he cannot stop it. But he can and does attempt to influence its direction.

Nietzsche's question, more directly, is not whether the Christian form of moral dogmatism can be preserved; Nietzsche is convinced that it cannot be. The question is, what will replace it? A new form of dogmatism? A European Buddhism, perhaps? The idiocy of the last man? Or, perhaps, a world within which at least some human beings will continue to strive both to be kind and thoughtful, and to exhibit the perseverance in the quest for beauty Proust lauds in Vermeer, but "for other reasons than hitherto"—*not* for the sake of moral obligation?

As long as the illusion of moral judgment holds sway, Nietzsche's question cannot be my guiding question, for as long as that illusion holds, Zarathustra's minotaur rules: good for all, evil for all. A post-moral world, one wherein the minotaur was silenced, would be one in which each of us could determine his or her own good; that would have to be a world within which diversity would be encouraged rather than inhibited. But that, it might seem, would entail a new form of moral dogmatism, one with the paradoxical form, "the good for all is that there be no 'good for all' "? How could Nietzsche defend such a perspective, or such affirmation, as one appropriate for everyone? How could Nietzsche defend any general position at all?

With this question, I turn to what I take to be the dangerous part of Nehamas's response to the problem of immoralism. The problem emerges, for Nehamas, through the question, what is a bad life, if life is literature? Must we not respond, the only bad life is a boring life, a life that doesn't make a good story? Are we then to denounce or condemn the couch potato, but not the mass murderer or the child molester? At times, Nehamas seems to point us in this direction. Insisting that Nietzsche's perspectivism "forbids any general evaluation [of life], positive or negative," Nehamas argues:

> What Nietzsche eventually comes to attack directly is not any particular judgment but the very tendency to make general judgments about the value of life in itself, as if there were such a single thing with a character of its own, capable of being praised or blamed by some uniform standard. . . . Life itself has no value, but the life of an individual or a group has as great a value as that individual or group can give it. Some lives are mean or horrible, others magnificent. Life's value depends on what one makes of it, and this is a further sense in which Nietzsche believes that value is created and not discovered. (135)

This conclusion, which follows from the forbidding of any general evaluation of life, is, it seems to me, as dangerous in its implications as any of Nietzsche's "words of war," any of his "thunder and fireworks." If "life itself has no value," and if "some lives are mean and horrible," then those who strive to live beautifully need take no account of those whose lives they deem, on whatever basis, to be ugly.

"Some lives," Nehamas tells us, "are mean or horrible." I agree, but only if we read Nehamas as asserting that some lives *have been* mean or horrible. This correction is vital, for no life can be simply "mean or horrible" until it is over. The life that appears, as it develops, to be simply "mean or horrible" may be a life whose beauty has not yet emerged. As Nietzsche notes in what he calls "a parable," "Not every end is a goal. A melody's end is not its goal; nevertheless, so long as the melody has not reached its end, it also has not reached its goal" (*HH,WS:*204).

Perhaps Nehamas is right in asserting that Nietzsche's perspectivism "forbids any general evaluation [of life], positive or negative"; yet, I have argued, Nietzsche attempts to develop a "general" perspective of life, he attempts to see life as it really is. The lenses of art are not the only lenses we need; Nietzsche exhorts us to view art through the lenses of life. One of the things we see through the lenses of life is that no final evaluation of a life can be made until, at least, the life is over. To say that a life still underway is simply "mean and horrible" is not to express a justifiable opinion, it is to judge prematurely.

Nietzsche's parable, which presents life as melody rather than as literature, provides a basis for rejecting the inhumanity seemingly licensed by the simple classification of some lives as "mean or horrible"; yet it may intensify the problem that led to that classification, for it may also seem to provide further support for the claim that the life of the child molester or serial murderer can be a life that is beautiful. Even if we agree that child molestation is simply ugly, does it follow that a life that has included child molestation must be ugly? That there can be no objection to the execution of the child molester?

A different way to put the question is this: can suicide be noble? Would the life of the pale criminal attain its highest beauty if the pale criminal were to kill himself? Granting that nothing the pale criminal may do following his crime will suffice to make his life, as a whole, one to be emulated—one cannot, I think, will to commit a crime for the sole purpose of then being able to overcome that crime—we must also recognize that the question that faces the pale criminal himself is not, "would I want others to act as I have acted?" Nor is his question the one posed by Nehamas, i.e., "would I want to do the same things all over again?" His question is, rather, what now? What is to be the significance of this murder, which I myself deem repellent, within my life as it continues to develop? Is this calamity to destroy me, or rather, perhaps, to be the basis for my transformation? We approximate the situation the pale criminal is in if we ask ourselves whether we might think better of him, perhaps even be inspired by him, if, instead of committing suicide, he were to seek to help others to learn from his example.

Phrasing the question in terms of suicide indicates that the earlier formulation is too simple. Just as accounts are neither simply true nor simply false, lives are neither simply beautiful or noble nor simply ugly or base. Lives are more or less beautiful, and as long as any life continues, it can, in principle, continue to transform the initial ugliness, if there be such, of its past. This is a general truth about human life, and even a "general judgment about the value of life in itself," although not of the sort Nehamas rightly takes Nietzsche to exclude.

What, then, about child molesters and serial murderers? One might conclude, from what I have said, that we should not kill them—that, to speak more idiomatically and less bluntly, we should abolish capital punishment. But I have said nothing that would support the conclusion that we should not, for example, imprison them.

Zarathustra expresses the principle, "Where one can no longer love, there one should just pass by" (Z,III.7; 225.13–15). This principle may guide us reliably in dealing with couch potatoes we happen not to love; the child molester and the serial murderer, however, provide us with problems of a different sort. It is not possible, always,—and perhaps not desirable, generally—merely to "pass by" a Hitler, a Stalin, or a Charles Manson. What is to be done with them?

Can we exclude the possibility that the life of a Hitler or a Charles Manson might satisfy Nietzsche's criterion for beauty, that is, that a Hitler or a Manson might deem his life beautiful, might will to continue it along the lines it has followed in the past? I cannot exclude that possibility. Does it follow that, if we view them from the "Nietzschean" perspective I have been describing, we are obliged to allow them to do as they will? It does not. If, through the lenses of life, I see my life as mine to dance, then I might well resist those who want to force me to take only the steps they prescribe. I might also choose to resist the one who wants to force others to take only the steps he prescribes, whether those steps involve the obeying of his laws or the satisfying of his desires.

I might choose to resist those who attempt to oppress others but, it seems, I might not. Is this a matter of indifference, as far as Nietzsche is concerned, a matter of individual and arbitrary taste? This question emerges as pressing from my presentation of living as dancing, my suggestion that our lives may be viewed as artworks that are not artifacts. I pursue the question in the following chapter, after approaching it from a different direction.

8

Nobility and Nobilities

Circle Dances

Kundera writes:

A weekly news magazine once ran a picture of a row of uniformed men shoulder-
ing guns and sporting helmets with Plexiglas visors. They are looking in the
direction of a group of young people wearing T-shirts and jeans and holding
hands and dancing in a circle before their eyes.

It is obviously the period immediately preceding a clash with the police, who
are guarding a nuclear power plant, a military training camp, the headquarters
of a political party, or the windows of an embassy. The young people have taken
advantage of this dead time to make a circle and take two steps in place, one
step forward, lift first one leg and then the other—all to a simple folk melody.

I think I understand them. They feel that the circle they describe on the ground
is a magic circle bonding them into a ring. Their hearts are overflowing with an
intense feeling of innocence: they are not united by a *march*, like soldiers or
fascist commandos; they are united by a *dance*, like children. And they can't
wait to spit their innocence in the cops' faces.

That is the way the photographer saw them too, and he highlighted his view
with eloquent contrasts: on the one side the police in the false (imposed, decreed)
unity of their ranks, on the other side the young people in the real (sincere and
organic) unity of their circle; on the one side the police in the *gloom* of their
ambush, on the other the young people in the *joy* of their play.

Circle dancing is magic. It speaks to us through the millennia from the depths
of human memory. Madame Raphael had cut the picture out of the magazine
and would stare at it and dream. She too longed to dance in a ring. All her life
she had looked for a group of people she could hold hands with and dance with
in a ring. First she looked for them in the Methodist Church (her father was a
religious fanatic), then in the Communist Party, then among the Trotskyites,
then in the anti-abortion movement (A child has a right to life!), then in the pro-
abortion movement (A woman has a right to her body!); she looked for them
among the Marxists, the psychoanalysts, and the structuralists; she looked
for them in Lenin, Zen Buddhism, Mao Tse-tung, yogis, the *nouveau roman*,
Brechtian theater, theater of panic; and finally she hoped she could at least
become one with her students, which meant she always forced them to think
and say exactly what she thought and said, and together they formed a single
body and a single soul, a single ring and a single dance. (*Laughter*, 63)

As Kundera reminds us, Nietzsche's words, too, are pockets: praise for child and dance, praise for joy and play become, all too easily, praise for anything that can be called by those names. The animalian innocence of Kundera's circle dancers may be "beyond good and evil," like that of Zarathustra's ass; but such innocence, in human beings, is idiotic. The playful, childish circle dance has indeed its "magic qualities," but these are not the qualities of Nietzschean dance or Nietzschean play:

> Leave a row and you can always go back to it. The row is an open formation. But once a circle closes, there is no return. It is no accident that the planets move in a circle and when a stone breaks loose from one of them it is drawn inexorably away by centrifugal force. Like a meteorite broken loose from a planet, I too fell from the circle and have been falling ever since. Some people remain in the circle until they die, others smash to pieces at the end of a long fall. The latter (my group) always retain a muted nostalgia for the circle dance. After all, we are every one of us inhabitants of a universe where everything turns in circles. (*Laughter*, 65–66)

In Kundera's novel, the most devoted circle dancers break all contact with the earth, the "eternal ground" on which Zarathustra takes his stand, the "hard, primordial rock upon the highest, hardest primordial mountain, to which all winds come as their weathershed, asking where? and whence? and whither?" (Z,IV:1; 298.20–23). Kundera's circle dancers are beyond rock and mountain, beyond storm and question; he reports that he has watched as one

> laughed and stamped the ground a little harder and rose a few inches above the pavement, pulling the others along with her, and before long not one of them was touching the ground, they were taking two steps in place and one step forward without touching the ground, yes, they were rising up over Wenceslaus Square, their ring the very image of a giant wreath taking flight, and I ran off after them down on the ground . . . in the hope of keeping up with that wonderful wreath of bodies rising above the city, and I realized with anguish in my heart that they were flying like birds and I was falling like a stone, that they had wings and I would never have any. (*Laughter*, 67–68)

Kundera's circle dancers, as they rise, are "archangels" (*Laughter*, 74), their laughter the laughter of angels. Angelic laughter is reactive, it is a counterattack against the original laughter of the Devil, the laughter caused by "things deprived suddenly of their putative meaning, the place assigned them in the ostensible order of things" (*Laughter*, 61). Nietzsche's laughter is diabolical in that it follows from his insistence that all meanings are putative, all orders merely ostensible (on the associated laughter, see HH,I:213). But this does not mean that Nietzsche's laughter is simply destructive—Nietzsche's is not what I, following Kundera obliquely, shall term idiotic laughter. The radical nihilist might laugh idiotically, concluding that because meanings are putative and orders ostensible, meaning and order should be destroyed; the complete nihilist concludes, instead, that meanings and orders should be examined. From the observation that an order is alterable it does not follow that it should be altered.

Like all diabolical laughter, Nietzsche's "has a certain malice to it (things have turned out differently from the way they tried to seem), but a certain beneficent relief as well (things are looser than they seemed, we have greater latitude in living with them, their gravity does not oppress us)" (*Laughter*, 61). The angel's reaction to diabolical laughter is less complicated:

> The first time an angel heard the Devil's laughter, he was horrified. It was in the middle of a feast with a lot of people around, and one after the other they joined in the Devil's laughter. It was terribly contagious. The angel was all too aware the laughter was aimed against God and the wonder of His works. He knew he had to act fast, but felt weak and defenseless. And unable to fabricate anything of his own, he simply turned his enemy's tactics against him. He opened his mouth and let out a wobbly, breathy sound in the upper reaches of his vocal register (. . .) and endowed it with the opposite meaning. Whereas the Devil's laughter pointed up the meaninglessness of things, the angel's shout rejoiced in how rationally organized, well conceived, beautiful, good, and sensible everything on earth was.
>
> There they stood, Devil and angel, face to face, mouths open, both making more or less the same sound, but each expressing himself in a unique timbre— absolute opposites. And seeing the laughing angel, the Devil laughed all the harder, all the louder, all the more openly, because the laughing angel was infinitely laughable.
>
> Laughable laughter is cataclysmic. And even so, the angels have gained something by it. They have tricked us all with their semantic hoax. Their imitation laughter and its original (the Devil's) have the same name. People nowadays do not even realize that one and the same external phenomenon embraces two completely contradictory internal attitudes. There are two kinds of laughter, and we lack the words to distinguish them. (*Laughter*, 61–62)

We lack the words, and we are often the victims of semantic hoaxes—as when, to take Nietzsche's most famous example, we confuse the "good" that is opposed to "bad" with the "good" that is opposed to "evil" (*GM*,I). Prudence therefore demands that we proceed with care—which means, for Kundera as for Nietzsche, proceeding as genealogists, scrutinizing the "hieroglyphic record, so hard to decipher, of the moral past of mankind." Kundera's scrutiny leads him to conclude that only according to "the demagogy of the angels" is the Devil a "partisan of Evil" and angels "warriors for Good." In fact,

Angels are partisans not of Good, but of divine creation. The Devil, on the other hand, denies all rational meaning to God's world.
World domination, as everyone knows, is divided between demons and angels. But the good of the world does not require the latter to gain precedence over the former (as I thought when I was young); all it needs is a certain equilibrium of power. If there is too much uncontested meaning on earth (the reign of the angels), man collapses under the burden; if the world loses all meaning (the reign of the demons), life is every bit as impossible. (*Laughter*, 61)

So concludes Kundera, and so concludes Nietzsche:

Verily, it is a blessing and not a blasphemy when I teach: "over all things stands the heaven contingency, the heaven innocence, the heaven chance, the heaven bravado."
"Lord Chance" [*Von Ohngefähr*]—that is the oldest nobility in the world, one that I gave back to all things when I redeemed them from servitude to purpose.
This freedom and heavenly equanimity I placed like an azure bell over all things when I taught that no "eternal will" wills over them and through them.
This bravado and this folly I put in the place of that will when I taught "with everything one thing is impossible—rationality!"
A *little* reason, to be sure, a seed of wisdom sprinkled from star to star—this leaven is mixed in with all things: for the sake of folly wisdom is mixed into all things.
A little wisdom is certainly possible; but this blessed assurance I found in all things: that they would rather *dance,* on the feet of contingency. (Z,III:4; 209.12–30)

As Laurence Lampert has stressed, Zarathustra's restoration of Lord Chance provides for the apparently nihilistic conclusion, "everything is permitted," a deeper significance, "one free of the horror evoked from the good and the just by the destruction of the ground of their virtue, one far beyond the exaltation evoked from the free spirit by the death of the rational spider, a meaning that takes literally 'everything is permitted' by allowing each thing the freedom to be the thing that it is" (Lampert, 178).
Lampert's freedom is the freedom denied by the dogmatic slave morality of the circle dance, with its unearthly aspiration to what Kundera describes as

an idyll, a garden where nightingales sing, a realm of harmony where the world does not rise up as a stranger against man nor man against other men, where the world and all its people are molded from a single stock and the fire lighting up the heavens is the fire burning in the hearts of men, where every man is a note in a magnificent Bach fugue and anyone who refuses his note is a mere black dot, useless and meaningless, easily caught and squashed between the fingers like an insect. (*Laughter*, 8)

Nietzsche, according to Lampert, rejects catching and squashing; instead, he advocates "letting being be." Yet, I have argued, Nietzsche does not—or, at least, need not—advocate letting Mansons and Stalins be. Moreover, much would support the contention that he seeks on the whole not to allow but rather to force. Early on, Zarathustra seems to advocate a single goal for all humanity: "There have been up to now a thousand goals, for there have been a thousand peoples. Only the yoke for the thousand necks is missing, what is missing is the One Goal. Humanity still has no goal" (Z,I:15; 76.15–17). Much later, Zarathustra anticipates the coming of "the Zarathustra-*reich* of a thousand years" (Z,IV:1; 298.15–16), and at the close of the book, Zarathustra descends from his mountain for the third time, in order to resume his "work" [*Werke*] (Z,IV:20; 408.16). What can this work be other than the forging of the yoke for the thousand necks, the yoke that will force all humanity into the circle dance of the Zarathustra-*reich*? Does not Zarathustra, like Kundera's Madame Raphael, seek to force all into "a single body and a single soul, a single ring and a single dance"?

What is Zarathustra's "yoke for the thousand necks"? This question is not easily answered. First, it is a yoke mentioned only once, and only in Part I, when Zarathustra still champions the overman. Even if the yoke were one of political bondage, Zarathustra's invocation of it at this point in his development would not stamp him simply as a despot. But even at this point, he makes clear that his yoke is not a tool of oppression:

> The first creators were peoples; only late do individuals create; verily the individual itself is the most recent creation.
>
> Once peoples hung over themselves tablets of the good. Together, love that wants to rule and love that wants to obey created for themselves such tablets.
>
> Older than joy in the I is joy in the herd: and as long as the good conscience is called "herd," only the bad conscience says "I."
>
> Verily, the devious I, the loveless I who seeks its profit [*Nutzen*] by using [*Nutzen*] the many: that is not the origin of the herd, but its going under.
>
> It has always been lovers and creators who have created good and evil. The fire of love glows in the names of all virtues, and the fire of anger.
>
> Many lands Zarathustra has seen and many peoples: no greater power has Zarathustra found on earth than the works of lovers: "good" and "evil" is their name. (Z,I:15; 75.28–76.11)

Whatever the "Zarathustra-*reich*" may be, it cannot be the result simply of the individual Zarathustra's desire to exert his will to power by enchaining or exploiting the rest of humanity; in the terms of this passage, such an act might be "sly" or "devious," but it would not be creative, and would not be the act of a lover. Nevertheless, Zarathustra's *Reich*, like the enchainment of humanity, would be a result of *Herrschsucht*, the desire to rule.

Weighing the World

The desire to rule is one of the three evils weighed by Zarathustra, in a dream, on the first morning following his final return to his mountain (Z,III:10). In his dream, Zarathustra weighs the world, but not from a transcendent or metaphysical perspective; he stands "beyond the world," but "on a foothill" (235.3–4). He remains on the earth, persevering in his attempt to remain true to the earth.

Beginning in the Prologue, Zarathustra distinguishes, if often only implicitly, not only between earth and heaven but also between earth and world. The distinction is visible in the contrast between the English adjectives "earthy" and "worldly," and in the fact that "earth," unlike "world," names both our planet and the matter of which that planet is composed. One can stand on the earth and one can grasp earth; one can do neither with the world.

The etymological contrast between the two words further clarifies Zarathustra's distinction. "*Welt*" and "world" are both rooted in *wer,* "man," and *ald,* "old." The world is made by old men; the world is constituted by custom or tradition. "*Erde*" and "earth," on the other hand, are both rooted in the Greek *eraze,* "to the ground." They also translate the Greek *ge,* meaning "earth" in the sense of ground or soil.

"The world," for Zarathustra, is the flatland; not only his mountain, but also the foothills [*Vorgebirge*] are beyond the world while remaining on the earth. Some worlds are true to the earth, others are not; those human beings who view worlds from the earth view them through the lenses of life, whereas those who believe themselves able to view from heaven assume access to other lenses. Though we dwell on one and the same earth, we can be worlds apart.

Standing on his foothill, Zarathustra weighs the world not in divine or superhuman fashion, but rather in a "humanly good way" (236.16, 22–23). Through his weighing, Zarathustra seeks to determine the value of the world, "about which so much evil is spoken" (236.10); he finds that the world is a "humanly good thing" (236.9), as is his dream (236.12–13). The balance that makes the world a humanly good thing is between angelic and diabolic laughter, or between wisdom and folly: the world is "not riddle enough to scare [*scheuchen*] away human love, not solution enough to put human wisdom to sleep" (236.7–9).

More specifically, Zarathustra weighs the three aspects of the world considered to be its most evil (236.20–22). The evils are neither acts (murder, theft, etc.) nor institutions (religion, government), but rather drives or character traits that are generally discouraged or suppressed within systems of slave morality. The three are sex [*Wollust*], the desire to rule [*Herrschsucht*], and selfishness [*Selbstsucht*]. Each, Zarathustra acknowledges, can indeed be base; but he insists that each can also be noble.

In naming the second evil *Herrschsucht*, Nietzsche exploits an ambiguity in a manner that should, by now, be familiar. *Herrsch*– is, relatively straightforwardly, "rule" or "master"; *Sucht* is more problematic. "*Sucht*" generally names an addition or uncontrollable need: alcoholism is *Trunksucht*, drug addiction, *Rauschgiftsucht*. This meaning is based in the word's etymology: *Sucht* is from *seuka*, which is related to the English "sick." But, here as often elsewhere, etymology does not determine meaning—origin does not determine significance. The *Sucht* of *Herrschsucht* is related popularly to *Suche*, *suchen*, cognate with the English "seek"; hence, the German idiom *Sucht nach etwas* means seeking or searching for something, without implying that the seeking is in any way a sickness.

The ambiguity of *Herrschsucht* is reminiscent of that of nihilism: the desire to rule can be symptomatic of health and strength, or of sickness and weakness. Nietzsche does not make the contrast explicit; rather, in describing one kind of lust to rule as *not* "diseased and sickly [*Sieches und Süchtiges*]," Nietzsche clearly suggests that other forms *are*. For the healthy alternative, Zarathustra provides the following description:

> *Herrschsucht*: the earthquake that breaks and bursts open all that is decayed and hollow; the rolling, growling, punitive destroyer of whitewashed tombs; the flashing question mark beside premature answers. . . .
>
> *Herrschsucht*: which, however, also ascends luringly to the pure and lonely and up to self-sufficient heights, glowing like a love that luringly paints crimson fulfillments on the earthly heaven.
>
> *Herrschsucht*: but who would call it *Sucht* when what is high lusts [*gelüstet*] down [*hinab*] for power! . . .
>   That the lonely heights should not remain lonely and self-sufficient eternally: that the mountain come to the valley and the wind of the height to the lowlands:—
>   Oh who could find the right name with which to christen the virtue that is this longing [*Sehnsucht*]? "The gift-giving virtue"—thus did Zarathustra once name the unnamable. (Z,III:10.2; 237.30–238.22)

The first requirement for healthy ruling is that the ruler be self-sufficient, that is, that the ruler *need* not rule, that the ruler act from surfeit rather than from lack, from love rather than from greed, that ruling be a giving rather than a taking. The healthy ruler's self-sufficiency first requires, then, the healthy form of Zarathustra's third evil, *Selbstsucht* or selfishness.

Selbstsucht can be a sickness of self disguised as altruism, a sickness that can leads to self-denial or even to "selflessness," the attempt to avoid being a self altogether: " 'selfless'—so, with good reason, have all these world-weary cowards and cross-marked spiders wished themselves to be" (240.1–3). But *Selbstsucht* can also be a virtue rather than a vice: it is noble and healthy when it is a seeking to be a self, a seeking to make oneself a self. The noble individual avoids self-denial, to be sure, but in order to be self-seeking or self-affirming, not in order to be self-serving.

And how does one seek oneself? Zarathustra pursues this question in the immediately following section, whose title, "The Spirit of Gravity," announces its importance:

> One must learn to love oneself—thus I teach—with a wholesome and healthy love, so that one can bear to be with oneself and need not roam. Such roaming baptizes itself "love of the neighbor": with this phrase the best lies and hypocrisies have been perpetrated so far, and especially by such as were a grave burden for all the world.
>
> And verily, that is no command [*Gebot*] for today and tomorrow, to learn to love oneself. No, this is of all arts the subtlest [*feinste*] and most cunning, the ultimate and most patient. For whatever is his own is well concealed from the owner; and of all treasures, it is our own that we dig up last: thus the spirit of gravity orders it. (Z,III:11.2; 242.15–26)

The spirit of gravity imposes its order, we know, through the teaching, "Good for all, evil for all" (243.27). One silences the spirit of gravity by announcing, instead, "That is *my* good and evil"; those who make this announcement have succeeded in discovering themselves (243.25–26), in becoming ones who can will. But this announcement marks a culmination (even if, necessarily, a provisional one); if it marks the final step along the way toward becoming one who can will, toward embarking on the way that is one's own way, then the first step is to deny that there is a way that is the way for all.

Having taken the first step, how does one proceed? Zarathustra's suggestions are general: one must observe—"Many lands Zarathustra has seen and many peoples" (Z,I:15; 74.2, 76.9)—and one must experiment:

> In many ways and manners came I to my truth; not on one ladder did I climb to the height where my eye roams over my distance.
>
> And I did not want to ask about ways,—that was always against my taste! I preferred to ask and to try the ways myself.
>
> A trying and asking was all my going:—and verily, one must also learn to answer such questions! But that—is my taste:
>
> —not good, not bad, but my taste, of which I am no longer ashamed, and which I no longer conceal. (Z,III:11.2; 245.3–13)

Zarathustra's way, I have argued, is not a way of exploitation; my argument is based both on his words and on his deeds. But—and here I move toward the question with which the previous chapter closes—Zarathustra's way is therefore, necessarily, his way alone, it is not a way for all; if it were, it seems, it would be despotic, and Zarathustra rejects despotism. But to say that despotism is wrong for Zarathustra is not to say that it is wrong for others. Might not despotism be the way that was Hitler's way, or Pol Pot's? Might Hitler's have been a life Hitler could affirm? And if it was, is there any basis for Nietzschean objection to it?

Nietzsche may believe, as Plato and Aristotle seem to believe, that the way of the despot is not a way that can be taken thoughtfully or honestly, that no one who views "through the lenses of life," rather than other, arbitrary lenses, would choose the life of the tyrant. The problem may seem more pressing for Nietzsche, given his perspectivism, than for Plato or for Aristotle, but I am not convinced that it is. Aristotle and Plato agree that the philosophical life is the best life for those capable of leading it, and also that philosophical lives will be the happiest of lives. Even if these arguments are accepted, they do not entail the conclusion that every individual human being will attain his or her highest happiness by attempting to live the life of contemplation.

I deem it probable, for example, that the way of the basketball player is a better way for Michael Jordan than would be the way of the philosopher—not only that he thinks it is better for him, but that it really is better for him, in the Nietzschean sense: if he throws his dice on the basketball court, the odds are better that he will live a life he will continue to be able to affirm. Similarly, Mother Theresa's way—the way that is hers—may take her through hospitals rather than into libraries or onto mountaintops. Even if we were to grant to Aristotle and Plato that Mother Theresa or Michael Jordan will not be as happy as the happy philosopher—a suggestion many might deem dubious—it does not follow that Michael should hang up his sneakers, or Mother Theresa abandon her wards, in order to enroll in PhD programs.

Let us be as charitable to Nietzsche as to Aristotle: let us grant that those who are most noble, admirable, and self-affirming will not attempt to exploit others. I have argued, in addition, that the Nietzschean recognizes no moral obligation to allow those who do attempt to oppress others to proceed without obstruction. But even if this is granted, even if Nietzschean "morality" leaves open the possibility of the choice to aid others, Nietzschean taste may seem to close it off.

Nietzschean taste may seem to exclude attempts to aid others, given Zarathustra's castigation of love of neighbor, which disguises "lies and hypocrisies," and is nothing more than "a bad love for oneself" (Z,I:16; 77.3–4). So it may seem, yet there are other other passages clearly denying such an exclusion: as an alternative to love of neighbor, love of those who

are near, Zarathustra advocates not egotism or isolation, but rather love of
those who are far away (77.11), and love of the friend (78.18–21). As he
later admonishes:

> Ah, if only you understood my word: "by all means do what you will—but first
> be such that you *can will!*"
>   "By all means love your neighbor as yourself—but first be for me such that
> *you love yourself*—" (Z,III:5.3; 216.26–29)

Perhaps, then, Zarathustra advocates at least concern for others; but we
must ask again, is this anything more than an arbitrary preference? Does
healthy love of self entail love of others? Might a healthy love for self be
accompanied by hatred, or indifference, for others? For Plato and for Aristotle, arguably, it could: according to the *Republic,* philosophers will rule
only if compelled to do so, and according to the *Nichomachean Ethics,* the
life of isolated contemplation is superior to the life of political activity.

I have arrived at a question that may seem extraordinarily peculiar. Plato
and Aristotle, pillars of Western philosophy, are often taken as pillars of
Western morality as well, and that morality, Nietzsche insists, is based in
some sort of love of neighbor. Nietzsche presents himself as the great opponent of traditional morality, yet I have gotten, somehow, to the question
whether he might not provide us with better reasons for respecting other
human beings.

The question seems peculiar; nevertheless, I pursue it. It might be that
traditional "love of neighbor" is a concern that precludes, rather than presupposes, respect for the other's otherness—just as, according to Nietzsche,
traditional morality has concealed from us the demands of goodness, and
traditional science, those of truth. If I am convinced that my way is the way
for all human beings, whether or not any specific human being recognizes
that it is his or her "true" way, then "love" for the other may entail convert-
ing the other. If I am convinced that all non-Christians, or non-Muslims, or
non-whatevers are doomed to rot in hell for eternity, or even merely to live
unfulfilled for the duration, then am I not obliged, if I love others, to attempt
to alter them? And does that not entail attempting to convince them, by any
means possible, that the ways they have taken to be their own are wrong
ways? Am I not obliged so to proceed, if I both love others and know the
one way that is the way for all? (see *HH*,I:102, 630–34).

On the other hand, if I deny, with Nietzsche, that there is one way for all
then, at the very least, concern for others will not lead me to force a way
upon them. But that is consistent with indifference, and with exploitation.
Here I collide again with the question that closes the preceding chapter: do
I have reasons, if I am a Nietzschean, for respecting or encouraging the ways

of others, and thus for opposing those who would seek to close ways off? Zarathustra insists that I do, although his reasons are not simple. I approach them somewhat obliquely, through a passage I take to be of great importance.

Dangers to History

My compassion for all that is past is that I see: it has been given away [*preisgegeben*],—
Given away to the favor, the spirit, the madness of every generation that comes and reinterprets [*umdeutet*] everything that has been as its own bridge!
A great master of violence [*Gewalt-Herr;* despot] could come, a shrewd monster [*gewitzter Unhold*], who with his favor and disfavor could compel and constrain all that is past until it became the bridge leading to him, his prophecy and herald and cock-crow.
But this is the other danger and my other compassion: whoever is of the mob remembers back only as far as his grandfather—with his grandfather time stops.
Thus is all that is past given away: for it could some day come to pass that the mob would be master and all time be drowned in shallow waters.
Therefore, oh my brothers, a *new nobility* is needed, one for which the mob and all mastery through violence [*Gewalt-Herrischen*] is the opponent, one that writes the word "noble" anew, on new tablets.
For many nobles are needed and many kinds of nobility, *for there to be nobility.* Or, as I once spoke in a parable: "Precisely this is godliness, that there are gods, but no God!" (Z,III:12.11, entire)

We know, from *The Birth of Tragedy* and from *The Genealogy of Morals,* that Nietzsche is deeply concerned with recollecting and interpreting the past: he advocates a transvaluation that would take us not back to the inhumanity of the blond beasts, but rather beyond the necessity of inhumanity. His transvaluative step presupposes a proper recollection of, and thus a proper respect for, the past.

In the passage I have just quoted, Zarathustra elaborates on the importance of the past: he identifies two specific dangers. Here as often elsewhere, Kundera provides valuable commentary: "the struggle of man against power," he writes, "is the struggle of memory against forgetting" (*Laughter,* 3). He insists, therefore, that "the only reason people want to be masters of the future is to change the past. They are fighting for access to the laboratories where photographs are retouched and biographies and histories rewritten" (*Laughter,* 22). The despot retouches and rewrites in order, in Nietzsche's words, to "compel and constrain all that is past until it becomes the bridge leading to him"; the despot who can convince his subjects that his rule is preordained, that there is no alternative, will have succeeded in making his way the one way for all.

The despot is one danger to the past, according to Nietzsche, the mob another; yet, as Kundera stresses, the two are most dangerous when they work together. In relating the two, Kundera intertwines musical with political history in a story so intriguing that I cannot bear to condense it any more than I have, and so well told that only a fool would paraphrase rather than quote:

This is what my father told me when I was five: a key signature is a king's court in miniature. It is ruled by a king (the first step) and his two right-hand men (steps five and four). They have four other dignitaries at their command, each of whom has his own special relation to the king and his right-hand men. The court houses five additional tones as well, which are known as chromatic. They have important parts to play in other keys, but here they are simply guests.

Since each of the twelve notes has its own job, title, and function, any piece we hear is more than mere sound: it unfolds a certain action before us. Sometimes the events are terribly involved (as in Mahler or—even more—Bartók or Stravinsky): princes from other courts intervene, and before long there is no telling which court a tone belongs to and no assurance it isn't working undercover as a double or triple agent. But even then the most naive of listeners can figure out more or less what is going on. The most complex music is still *a language*.

That is what my father told me. What follows is all my own. One day a great man determined that after a thousand years the language of music had worn itself out and could do no more than rehash the same message. Abolishing the hierarchy of tones by revolutionary decree, he made them all equal and subjected them to a strict discipline: none was allowed to occur more often than any other in a piece, and therefore none could lay claim to its former feudal privileges. All courts were permanently abolished, and in their place arose a single empire, founded on equality and called the twelve-tone system.

Perhaps the sonorities were more interesting than they had been, but audiences accustomed to following the courtly intrigues of the keys for a millennium failed to make anything of them. In any case, the empire of the twelve-tone system soon disappeared. After Schönberg came Varèse, and he abolished notes (the tones of the human voice and musical instruments) along with keys, replacing them with an extremely subtle play of sounds which, though fascinating, marks the beginning of the history of something other than music, something based on other principles and another language.

If it is true that the history of music has come to an end, what is left of music? Silence?

Not in the least. There is more and more of it, many times more than in its most glorious days. It pours out of outdoor speakers, out of miserable sound systems in apartments and restaurants, out of the transistor radios people carry around the streets.

Schönberg is dead, Ellington is dead, but the guitar is eternal. Stereotyped harmonies, hackneyed melodies, and a beat that gets stronger as it gets duller— that is what's left of music, the eternity of music. Everyone can come together on the basis of those simple combinations of notes. They are life itself proclaiming its jubilant "Here I am!" No sense of communion is more resonant, more unanimous, than the simple sense of communion with life. It can bring Arab and Jew together, Czech and Russian. Bodies pulsing to a common beat, drunk with the consciousness that they exist. No work of Beethoven's has ever elicited greater collective passion than the constant repetitive throb of the guitar. . . .

The history of music is mortal, but the idiocy of the guitar is eternal. Music in our time has returned to its primordial state, the state after the last issue has been raised and the last theme contemplated—a state that follows history.

When Karel Gott, the Czech pop singer, went abroad in 1972, [Czech president Gustav] Husak [*the president of forgetting* (158)] got scared. He sat right down and wrote him a personal letter (it was August 1972 and Gott was in Frankfurt). The following is a verbatim quote from it. I have invented nothing.

> *Dear Karel,*
> *We are not angry with you. Please come back. We will do*
> *everything you ask. We will help you if you help us . . .*

Think it over. Without batting an eyelid Husak let doctors, scholars, astronomers, athletes, directors, cameramen, workers, engineers, architects, historians, journalists, writers, and painters go into emigration, but he could not stand the thought of Karel Gott leaving the country. Because Karel Gott represents music minus memory, the music in which the bones of Beethoven and Ellington, the dust of Palestrina and Schönberg, lie buried.

The president of forgetting and the idiot of music deserve one another. They are working for the same cause. "We will help you if you help us." You can't have one without the other. (*Laughter,* 179–181)

The president of forgetting and the idiot of music, the master of violence and the mob, "are working for the same cause": they work to make "everyone come together" through "a simple sense of communion with life": we are alike in that we all are alive, no one need be different, no one may be different. Our differences are obliterated when, and only when, our memories are erased. Such oblivion may seem joyful, and may be accompanied by laughter. This laughter can be Kundera's angelic laughter, which serves the despot because such laughter requires that everything make sense, and the despot's rewriting of history makes sense of everything: everything leads to him. But the laughter of oblivion may also be idiotic laughter, the laughter that erupts from those who conclude that nothing makes sense, so that it makes absolutely no difference what any of us do: "Life's a beach; let's party—somebody get a guitar." Angelic laughter is a symptom of religious nihilism, idiotic laughter, of radical nihilism; both work for the despot's cause.

Nietzsche, like Kundera, advocates neither angelic nor idiotic laughter, neither religious nor radical nihilism. Nietzsche laughs when he sees that things do not make the sense he had thought they made, but he does not conclude that they make no sense at all. We continue to make sense of them—better, we continue to make senses of them. But if we are so to continue, we must first avoid forgetting. We must preserve historical facts, not because preserving facts leads us closer to the one truth that ties all the facts into the one true interpretation, but rather because preserving facts is our safest defense against the domination of a single interpretation. Second, we must preserve ways of living—different ways—in part for the same reason but also, and perhaps more important, because preserving ways leads us closer to a different sort of truth, the truth that there are many ways of looking at things, the truth, perhaps, that we approach the only kind of objectivity we should desire by becoming aware of the variety of those ways. And there is a third reason for preserving ways, perhaps most important of all: "many nobles are needed and many kinds of nobility, *for there to be nobility.*

From the perspective of slave moralities, all human beings are base. From the Christian perspective, generally, all human beings are so vastly inferior to God that differences among human beings become insignificant in comparison (*Z*,IV:13.1; 356.15–20; also, *HH*,I:133). Nietzsche's transvaluation aims at a noble morality, a morality within which nobility is possible. But for there to be nobility at all, Zarathustra insists, there must be many kinds of nobility—a wealth of attempts to excel, to affirm, to live lives we can be proud of having lived. The one kind of putative nobility there cannot be— the one kind all other nobilities, of all kinds, must oppose—is that of the despot, which is that of the dogmatist—the kind of nobility that insists that it is the only kind, the kind of nobility that enslaves.

When God dies, his morality dies with him, albeit more slowly. When kings and courts die, their deaths may doom to decline a music that mirrors their intrigues, but also their privileges. As this morality and this music decline, it may appear that they can be replaced only by egalitarian uniformity or by anarchic chaos—and even these two may tend, progressively, to converge. Yet it is not as though the only musical alternative to Bach and Beethoven is the idiocy of the guitar. While not all rock musicians exhibit insight, daring, or innovation, the same may be said both of composers of "classical" music—Kundera says it of Tchaikovsky and Rachmaninoff— and of its performers. And Kundera recognizes, as his conjunction of Ellington with Beethoven reveals, that Europeans tired of listening only to each other can come again to life when they begin to converse with those who view and hear things differently.

The work to which Zarathustra returns at the close of Part IV is not the imposition of his yoke onto the thousand necks, the imposition of his way on all. The way that would be a way for all, he insists, is a way of the past— as of its kings, its court, and perhaps its music. We should not forget these things, he tells us, but neither should we worship them, nor should we regret their passing. His task is not to revive them in a new form, to construct a new world, but rather to contribute to the health of earth and humanity by cultivating nobility, which requires encouraging nobilities, and by allowing the development of worlds, which requires opposing despotism.

Not only a Stalin, but also a Charles Manson is a despot: both attempt to use others, to exploit, to oppress. Neither may be merely passed by, but Nietzsche's teaching is not that we should pass them by. On the contrary, Nietzsche gives us reasons other than the traditional moral ones for opposing their exploitation and oppression. To be sure, he does not show us, in detail, either how oppression is to be identified or how it is to be opposed; given its transformations over time, such demonstrations would be of limited aid to us in any case. Fortunately, many others continue to work on these demonstrations, exposing increasingly complicated forms of bureaucratic and economic oppression, and increasingly subtle forms of discrimination and prejudice. Nietzsche contributes little to work of this sort, but he supports it by giving us reasons for deeming it important.

9

Life Without Kitsch?

You are an important person, a rare individual, a unique creature. There has never been anyone just like you and never will be. You have talents and abilities no one else has. In some ways, you are superior to any other living person. The power to do anything you can imagine is within you when you discover your real self by practicing a few simple laws of success.

First law of success: Take inventory of your assets. Don't be modest or critical; be open and objective. Get a pencil and paper; write down every good thing about yourself you can think of.

Second law of success: Write a description of the person you would like to be. Describe your personal best: your home, your automobile, your desired occupation and income. Be honest. Now, go even deeper. Describe the inner person you'd like to be. Let your mind run wild. Assume you can become anything you desire; the fact is, you will become the person you honestly describe—you can't avoid it.

"Adventures in Success"; Will Powers

The Nietzsche I present in this book is less exciting, perhaps, than the more notorious Nietzsche who champions blond beasts and master races. As I read him, Nietzsche champions neither, but neither does he develop a powerful political alternative. On the contrary, my Nietzsche has little to say that is of political importance. I have argued that he presents us with reasons for respecting others and encouraging diversity, but he does not, in my judgment, illuminate our political action.

The most provocative teachings I find in Nietzsche are not political, but rather ethical; Nietzsche does not attempt to tell us how to save the world, but rather how to save ourselves—how to save ourselves from living lives that we will come to view with regret rather than with pride. And he teaches that we can do that without becoming supermen who blithely crush their supposed inferiors beneath their feet.

To the extent that my reconstruction of Nietzsche's teachings is convincing, I muffle, perhaps nearly silence, Nietzsche's thunder and fireworks. But what, then, do my Nietzsche's teachings boil down to? A bland combination of individualism and tolerance, easily digestible intellectually only because it provides so little food for thought, so little to challenge current preconceptions? Perhaps so; but if Nietzsche boils down to mental junk food, that is not because he offers us no intellectual nutrients, but rather because we will have boiled them away. Whatever is provocative or challenging in any philosophical teachings will be lost if the teachings are reduced to two words, be those words "individualism" and "tolerance," or any others. If one wants two words for my Nietzsche, these are better than "racist" and "fascist"; but they are also virtually worthless because, as words with histories, they are indefinable. And if we attempted to specify what they would signify with respect to Nietzsche, we would be forced to retrieve all that we boiled away to come up with them in the first place. Like any god worthy of his or her divinity, Nietzsche's god is in his details.

In this book, I have attended closely to some of Nietzsche's details. In so doing, I hope at least to have undermined the suggestion that Nietzsche has no more inspiring vision than that of having humanity follow him, in lock-step, across the bridge leading to the overman. Whatever his flaws may be, my Nietzsche does not succumb to what Kundera calls the kitsch of the Grand March:

> The fantasy of the Grand March . . . is the political kitsch joining leftists of all times and tendencies. The Grand March is the splendid march on the road to brotherhood, equality, justice, happiness; it goes on and on, obstacles notwith-standing, for obstacles there must be if the march is to be the Grand March.
>
> The dictatorship of the proletariat or democracy? Rejection of the consumer society or demands for increased productivity? The guillotine or an end to the death penalty? It is all beside the point. What makes a leftist a leftist is not this or that theory but his ability to integrate any theory into the kitsch called the Grand March. (*Lightness*, 257)

The teaching of the overman is a form of Grand March kitsch, but Nietz-sche himself undermines that teaching shortly after introducing it. More generally, the Grand March in all its versions presents us with lives that appear worth living only because they contribute to the attainment of a human existence that would follow the healing of what *The Birth of Tragedy* calls "the wound of existence"; Nietzsche unmasks all such presentations as life-denying, as variants of the Socratic delusion.

Nietzsche undermines the kitsch of the Grand March, but that is not to say that he avoids kitsch altogether. It might appear, on the contrary, that my attempt to present Nietzsche as a foe of totalitarians and dreamers has led me to portray, perhaps even to reveal him as an advocate of the "me-generation" kitsch derided in the song I quote in this chapter's epigraph. Without question, some of the song's phrases could trace plausible lineages from Nietzsche, as could, yet more clearly, the name taken by its singer. This is not surprising: Nietzsche's writings have, by now, been disseminating for one hundred years. Nietzschean phrasings begin to sound banal; even Silenian wisdom has become a bumper-sticker cliché: "Life is a bitch, and then you die." Nietzsche, it may seem, isn't telling us anything we didn't already know—even if it may be that we know it only because he started telling us one hundred years ago. Perhaps, however, we don't always know what we think we know: chuckling or groaning over bumper-sticker slogans is different from thinking about them, and from living on their terms. When the chips are down, as when they are up, we tend to turn not to thought, but to kitsch.

Kitsch, according to one of Kundera's definitions, is "a second kind of beauty," opposed to the Flaubertian beauty that "unveils a realm of reality that has not yet been revealed." The second beauty, kitsch-beauty, is not a beauty of revelation, but rather a "beauty outside knowledge":

> One describes what has already been described a thousand times over in a light and lovely manner. The beauty of "a thousand times already told" is what I deem "kitsch." And this form of description is one which the true artist should deeply abhor. And, of course, "kitsch-beauty" is the sort of beauty which has begun to invade our modern world. (Elgrably, 6)

To late twentieth-century readers who know Nietzsche only through excerpts, summaries, or cursory readings, he may seem to exemplify the "beauty of 'a thousand times already told,' " even if his manner does not tend to be "light and lovely;" his blunt and combative manner may itself be appropriate for the kitsch of "free, very free spirits." Nevertheless, I hope that I have demonstrated that Nietzsche's works themselves, like *Madame Bovary,* can continue to surprise through their power of unveiling. Those I have not convinced have ears, perhaps, for which I am not the mouth.

Nietzsche's "voice of beauty" is not the voice of "a thousand times already told," not, at least, to my ears. But even if Nietzsche, or my Nietzsche, is as free from this form of kitsch as from that of the Grand March, even then he may not escape kitsch altogether. Kitsch, Kundera tells us, "has its source in the categorical agreement with being" (*Lightness,* 256). He elaborates:

> The dispute between those who believe that the world was created by God and those who think it came into being of its own accord deals with phenomena that go beyond our reason and experience. Much more real is the line separating those who doubt being as it is granted to man (no matter how or by whom) from those who accept it without reservation.
>
> Behind all the European faiths, religious and political, we find the first chapter of Genesis, which tells us that the world was created properly, that human existence is good, and that we are therefore entitled to multiply. Let us call this basic faith a *categorical agreement with being.*

The fact that until recently the word "shit" appeared in print as s--- has nothing to do with moral considerations. You can't claim that shit is immoral, after all! The objection to shit is a metaphysical one. The daily defecation session is daily proof of the unacceptability of Creation. Either/or: either shit is acceptable (in which case don't lock yourself in the bathroom!) or we are created in an unacceptable manner.

It follows, then, that the aesthetic ideal of the categorical agreement with being is a world in which shit is denied and everyone acts as though it did not exist. This aesthetic ideal is called *kitsch*.

"Kitsch" is a German word born in the middle of the sentimental nineteenth century, and from German it entered all Western languages. Repeated use, however, has obliterated its original metaphysical meaning: kitsch is the absolute denial of shit, in both the literal and the figurative senses of the word; kitsch excludes everything from its purview which is essentially unacceptable in human existence. (*Lightness*, 247–48)

Kundera's genealogy, applied to Nietzsche, suggests two related questions: what is the nature of Nietzsche's "agreement with being"? And what about shit?

Shit

In a passage I have already cited more than once, Nietzsche accuses Christianity, grounded as it is in *ressentiment* against life, of "making of sexuality something impure," thereby "throwing shit on the origin, on the presupposition of our life" (*TI*,X:4). In *The Genealogy*, he expands his accusation:

On his way to becoming an "angel" (to employ no uglier word) man has evolved that queasy stomach and coated tongue through which not only the joy and innocence of the animal but life itself has become repugnant to him—so that he sometimes holds his nose in his own presence and, with Pope Innocent the Third, disapprovingly catalogues his own repellent aspects ("impure begetting, disgusting means of nutrition in his mother's womb, baseness of the matter out of which man evolves, hideous stench, secretion of saliva, urine, and shit [*Koth*]"). (*GM*,II:7)

Within the Christian-moral tradition, life itself appears as soiled by the shit that is a part of it. Disgust with this soiling is connected with the despising of the body and with denigration of the earth; on earth, soil remains, no matter how much asphalt we may spread.

Early on in *Zarathustra*, Nietzsche speaks explicitly to the despisers of the body and the denigrators of the earth. Much later, he relates earth and body to shit:

"To the pure everything is pure [*Dem Reinen ist Alles rein*]"—thus speak the people. But I say to you: to swine all things become swinish [*den Schweinen wird Alles Schwein*]!
That is why the swooners and head-hangers, whose hearts hang down as well, preach: "the world itself is a beshitted monster [*kothiges Ungeheuer*]."
For these are all of unclean spirit, particularly those who have neither rest nor peace [*nicht Ruhe, noch Rast*] except when they view the world from behind [*von hinten*]—the hinterworldly!
To these I say to their faces, even if it does not sound endearing: the world is like the human being in that it has a behind,—this much is true!
There is in the world much shit: this much is true! But that does not make the world itself a beshitted monster! There is wisdom in the fact that much in the world smells ill [*übel*]: disgust itself creates wings and forces that divine fresh waters [*quellenahnende Kräfte*].
Even in the best there is something disgusting; and the best is still something that must be overcome!—
Oh my brothers, there is much wisdom in the fact that there is much shit in the world! (Z,III:12.14, entire)

That there is shit in the world—in all worlds, on our earth—does not make the world, the earth itself a beshitted monster; we see what we look for, or what is visible from the perspectives we take. In conversing with the revolutionary fire-dog, whose true concern is with power rather than with human betterment (Z,II:18; 170.1–12), Zarathustra acknowledges that although the earth has its "skin diseases"—including both the fire-dog and humanity (168.15–17)—the "belly of things" (170.5) is not, as the volcanoes on the fire-dog's island lead it to believe, full of "ashes and smoke and hot mud" (170.19) that cause a "gurgling and spitting and griping of the bowels" (170.22–23) and that must, from time to time, be excreted or regurgitated, no matter how damaging the eruption. On the contrary, as another fire-dog—a revolutionary of a different sort—knows, "the heart of the earth is of gold" (170.25–26).
Although "there is much shit in the world," there is wisdom in its presence. Its presence is, perhaps, among the features that make the world a "humanly good thing." Although there is much shit in the world, Nietzsche insists, "the heart of the earth is of gold." Does he thereby acknowledge a categorical agreement with being?

Agreements With Being

Zarathustra affirms being. Immediately before describing his restoration to divinity of "Lord Chance," he announces:

I have become one who blesses and one who affirms: this is why I wrestled long and was a wrestler, so that once my hand would be freed for blessing.

And this is my blessing: to stand over every thing whatsoever as its own sky or heaven, as its rounded roof, its azure bell and eternal security: and blessed is he who thus blesses!

For all things are baptized in the well of eternity and beyond good and evil. (Z,III:4; 209.3–10)

Nietzsche, too, affirms being. His "experimental philosophy" presses on to "the reverse" of "a will to the No," on to "a Dionysian affirmation of the world as it is, without subtraction, exception, or selection" (N:16[32] / WP:1041). His *amor fati* requires "that one want nothing otherwise, not forward, not backward, not in all eternity. Not merely to bear what is necessary, still less to conceal it . . . but rather to *love* it" (EH,II:10).

Nietzsche's affirmation is, certainly, an acceptance. But an agreement? A categorical agreement? No, Zarathustra would insist, three times no! Zarathustra may "say yes as the open sky says yes," but he also says "no as the storm says no"; he says no, we have seen, to despotism, to dogmatism, and to mediocrity. And he knows that there is much shit in the world.

Categorical agreements with being, Kundera tell us, trace their origins to *Genesis*, with its myth of creation. In *The Birth of Tragedy*, Nietzsche insists that although we may find this myth "behind all the European faiths, religious and political," as Kundera has it, we do not find it behind the tragic disposition of the Greeks. There, we find the myth of Prometheus. According to the Promethean myth, human beings were created in the image not of an omnipotent god, but rather of a rebellious titan. Human beings initially find themselves, within this myth, not in a garden where all is provided, but rather in a desert where they must struggle to survive. The original sacrilege— the theft of fire, not of fruit—is then an act both necessary and courageous:

The presupposition of the Prometheus myth is to be found in the extravagant value which a naive humanity attached to *fire* as the true palladium of every ascending culture. But that man should freely dispose of fire without receiving it as a present from heaven, either as a lightning bolt or as the warming rays of the sun, struck these primitive men as sacrilege, as a robbery of divine nature. Thus the very first philosophical problem immediately produces a painful and irresolvable contradiction between man and god and moves it before the gate of every culture, like a huge boulder. The best and highest possession mankind can acquire is obtained by sacrilege and must be paid for with consequences that involve the whole flood of sufferings and sorrows with which the offended divinities have to afflict the nobly aspiring race of men. This is a harsh idea which, by the *dignity* it confers on sacrilege, contrasts strangely with the Semitic myth of the fall in which curiosity, mendacious deception, susceptibility to seduction, lust—in short, a series of pre-eminently feminine affects—were considered the origin of evil. What distinguishes the Aryan notion is the sublime view of *active sin* as the characteristically Promethean virtue. With that, the ethical basis for pessimistic tragedy has been found: the justification of human evil, meaning both human guilt and the human suffering it entails. (*BT*:9)

With "their need to invent [*anzudichten*] dignity for sacrilege, to incorporate [*einzuverleiben*] dignity within it," the Greeks "invented tragedy—an art and a joy that remain in their deepest essence alien to the Jews, despite all their poetic endowment and inclination [*Neigung*] toward the sublime" (*JS*:135).

The Promethean myth is a powerful alternative to the Jehovan, yet, I have argued, Nietzsche ultimately attempts to move beyond myth altogether. At the same time, however, he also comes to affirm being in a way that a Promethean could not. In so doing, does he abandon the Promethean perspective along with its myth, in favor, perhaps, of some form of the Edenic? Does his earth become the "garden" described by Zarathustra's animals? If it does, and if this garden is to replace Eden within a mythic basis for affirmation, then it must, according to Kundera, tell us three things: "that the world was created properly, that human existence is good, and that we are therefore entitled to multiply."

Nietzsche's earth does not become such a garden. First, Nietzsche insists not that human existence *is* good, but rather that it can be good. This is perhaps to say that there is nothing unacceptable in human existence; it is certainly to say that there is nothing *essentially* unacceptable therein. Kundera describes kitsch, expressing its "true function," as "a folding screen set up to curtain off death" (*Lightness*, 253). If mortality is essentially unacceptable then, Nietzsche agrees, life is essentially unacceptable; this is the judgment of the spirit of revenge. Nietzsche's alternative, based in the will to power, asserts that if life can be acceptable, so too must mortality be acceptable. "Let us speak of this, you who are wise, even if it be bad. Silence is worse; all truths kept silent become poisonous" (*Z*,II:12; 149.22–24).

If life were essentially unacceptable, we should refuse it; yet it is possible, paradoxically, to make life appear worth living precisely by deeming it unacceptable. Zarathustra sees this strategy at work in some of the most vociferous of life's deniers:

The small man, especially the poet,—how zealously does he accuse life in words! Hear it, but overhear with me the joy that is in all accusation!
...With all who call themselves "sinners" and "cross-bearers" and "penitents," overhear with me the lust that is in their complaining and accusing. (*Z*,III:13.2; 273.25–34)

To all who thus accuse life in words, Zarathustra issues a challenge:

There stands the bark [Nachen],—from there it goes over, perhaps, into the great nothing.—But who will board this "perhaps"?
No one of you will board the bark of death! How so, then, do you want to be tired of the world! (Z,III:12.17; 259.2–5)

If life were essentially unacceptable, then the only reason to continue to live would be cowardice (see 259.25–26). But Nietzsche denies, and I deny, that life is essentially unacceptable.

As a Nietzschean of my sect (of which I may be and may remain the only member), I judge that human existence can be good. Despite so judging, however, I do not accept the first presupposition Kundera finds behind the Biblical myth of creation: I do not view the world as having been created properly. I do not therefore view it as created improperly. On the contrary, I do not view it as created at all. Instead, I accept and applaud Zarathustra's restoration of Lord Chance.

The move beyond viewing the world as created or uncreated is the move beyond what I have been terming metaphysics—this, it seems to me, is the move that Kundera, for all his agreement with Nietzsche and his amplification of him, does not fully make. From the metaphysical perspective, and only from that perspective, the presence of shit on earth is an argument against the earth. Kundera writes, "Amid the general idiocy of the war, the death of Stalin's son"—who "laid down his life for shit"—"stands out as the sole metaphysical death" (Lightness, 245). A non-metaphysical world would not be a world without shit, but it might be a world in which there would no longer be any reason to lay down one's life for shit.

If God is dead, then we need not agree with him, categorically or otherwise; if we are aware of his death, we cannot agree with him. What remains after God's death is being, and with being there can be no agreement: being, unlike God, is not an eternal will working in and through all things (see Z,III:4; 209.19–20). Like human society, life itself is an experiment, not a contract or agreement (see Z,III:12.25; 265.22). Being is not something I agree or disagree with, it is rather something I accept or reject. In deciding whether to accept or reject being, I do not ask, "is being good"; I ask instead, "is it good enough"? Hic Rhodos, hic saltus, here is the rose, with its thorns, here we must dance, if we are to dance at all.

Child and Work

The Nietzschean makes no agreement with being, but rather, at least, accepts being; the Nietzschean judges not that life is good, but rather, at least, that it is good enough. But mere acceptance falls short of affirmation, and deeming life "good enough" is different from loving it. Marginal acceptance of life may give me reasons other than cowardice for continuing to live, but it cannot, I think, entitle me to multiply. If I have children, they may well suffer, and nothing I can do will preclude the possibility of their suffering so terribly as to wish never to have been born. If I am nonetheless entitled to multiply, nothing can provide the entitlement save my own judgment: if, viewing the human condition as thoughtfully and honestly as I can, knowing that I am exposed to countless pains and sufferings even when I am not beset by them, knowing that whatever I may do I will someday, perhaps today, die—if I then thank my parents for having multiplied, regardless of their entitlement for so doing, then I entitle myself to multiply; perhaps, depending on my perspective, I even obligate myself to do so. "From the ground up," according to Zarathus-tra—out of the earth, through trunk and branches—"one loves only one's child and one's work" (Z,III:3; 204.4).

To be admirable, to Nietzsche or to me, one need only love one's child (biological or, as for Zarathustra himself, otherwise) and one's work—from the ground up. Even some despots may be admired, but that is not to say that they should be emulated, or that they should not be opposed. In addition, the work one loves, if one is to be admirable, need not be as ambitious as that of most who are termed despots; to be admirable, one need neither found nor destroy empires, and one need have no other work than one's own life. It is enough to do what neither Kant nor Schopenhauer seems to have been able to do. It is enough if one can, thoughtfully and honestly, accept life on life's own terms:

Nothing offends the philosopher's taste more than human beings, *insofar as they wish*. If he views humans only in their doing, even if he sees this most courageous, most cunning, most enduring animal lost in labyrinthine distress [*Nothlagen*]—how worthy of admiration [*bewunderungswürdig*] man appears to him! He still likes man. But the philosopher despises the wishing human—also the human who is "wished for" [*wünschbaren*]—and altogether all wishables, all the ideals of humans. If a philosopher could be a nihilist, he would be one because he could find nothing behind all the ideals of humans. Or not even the nothing,—but rather only what is worthy of nothing [*nichtswürdig*], only the absurd, the sick, the weak, the tired, all sorts of dregs from the emptied [*ausge-trunkenen*] goblet of life. Humans, who are so worthy of respect [*verehrungswür-dig*] as reality—how is it that they deserve no respect when they wish? Must they do penance for being so capable [*tüchtig*] in reality? Must they balance their doing, the strain on head and will in all doing, by stretching their limbs in the imaginary and the absurd? The history of their wishables has been, until now, the *partie honteuse* of human: one must be careful not to read it for too long. What justifies humanity is its reality—that will justify it eternally. How much greater is the worth of the real human being, compared with any merely wished for, dreamed up, stinking, fabricated human being? With any ideal human being? And only the ideal human being offends the taste of the philosopher. (*TI*,IX:32)

Only the ideal, only the dreamed up, only the fabricated human being—only kitsch disgusts the philosopher. Yet kitsch, like shit, will always be with us: "none among us is superman enough to escape kitsch completely. No matter how we scorn it, kitsch is an integral part of the human condition" (*Lightness*, 256). The rabble, the small man, returns eternally, both within and without; even if the superhuman can be severed from the inhuman, its link with the all-too-human may remain. But even if kitsch is inescapable, it remains both possible and important to unmask forms of kitsch—including the various forms of totalitarian kitsch, which develop "whenever a single political movement corners power" (*Lightness*, 251), but also the insipid kitsch of situation comedies and the pretentious kitsch of Major Motion Pictures. The unmasking is important because "as soon as kitsch is recognized for the lie it is, it moves into the context of non-kitsch, thus losing its authoritarian power and becoming as touching as any other human weakness" (*Lightness*, 256).

Life without kitsch? Not on Nietzsche's earth—nor life without shit. But life, or lives, that can be loved—lives including, but not limited to the philosophical life.

Socrates, the prototypical philosopher, insists, "The unexamined life is not worth living"; he seems thereby to condemn as worthless the lives of the vast majority of human beings. Nietzsche, the exceptional philosopher, grants that to examine life may be noble, but insists in addition that "many kinds of nobility are needed, for there to be nobility." What justifies humanity, Nietzsche tells us, is its reality—not its self-examination. Neither the philosopher nor anyone else, then, is in the position to tell others how they must live their lives. The philosopher *is* in the position to talk to others about what is noble and what is desirable, but so are non-philosophers, both to the philosopher and to each other—the need for such talk remains, because to acknowledge that there can be many kinds of nobility, to advocate that there be many kinds, is not to say that all lives are noble. Because we are not provided with maps, moral or otherwise, through our labyrinth, we get along best within the labyrinth by sharing information about it.

In denying that we have maps that would show us the way through our labyrinth—in denying that there *is* a way *through* the labyrinth—I have, in this book, joined Nietzsche in rejecting both hinterworlds and moral absolutes. Most of my potential readers—educated, late twentieth-century Westerners—will, I suspect, already have relinquished dreams of hinterworlds; many, however, may continue to feel the attraction of moral absolutes. To reject such absolutes, many believe, is to invite disaster; if enough share the rejection, many believe, disaster is assured. I think not. I present this book, my work, in part for the sake of my children, to whom it is dedicated—my children, whom I, with questionable entitlement, have shared in creating, for whose very existence I am thus responsible. The responsibility can be heavy. It may become the heaviest of burdens. My sharing in bringing my children into existence was a throw of the dice, a step in my dance—like many of mine, a *pas de deux*—but one that allows them, too, the chance to throw their dice and to dance their dances. For their sakes, in part, I attempt to diminish, if infinitesimally, the likelihood of disaster, certainly not to increase it. I argue here for my version of Nietzsche's teachings because, I believe, the odds for my children's dice throws, and not for theirs alone, will be improved if we develop, on our earth, a less dogmatic, less relativistic, more Nietzschean world.

Endnotes

Notes to Chapter 1

Page 3, Nietzsche's inspiration of musicians. See David S. Thatcher, "Musical Settings of Nietzsche Texts," I (*Nietzsche-Studien* 4, 1975, pp. 284–323), II (*Nietzsche-Studien* 5, 1976, pp. 355–83), III (*Nietzsche-Studien* 15, 1986, pp. 440–52).

Page 3, Nietzsche as uninspired pseudo-philosopher. Thatcher, "Musical Settings" I, p. 285. Thatcher quotes Runciman's "Nietzsche and French Music" from *Saturday Review*, CI (3 March 1906), p. 266.

Page 4, Zarathustra's avoidance of deductive arguments. Laurence Lampert identifies "the only deductive argument made by Zarathustra in the whole book" as the argument for eternal return given in "Of the Vision and the Riddle" (Z,III:2.2; 200.15–33); the argument is invalid because it omits a premise supplied only later in the book (Lampert, *Nietzsche's Teaching: An Interpretation of Thus Spoke Zarathustra*, New Haven: Yale University Press, 1986, p. 166).

I follow Lampert above in part, I admit, for sake of dramatic effect. I note, however, that Zarathustra makes at least one other deductive argument (likewise invalid), one for the non-existence of God (Z,II:2; 110.11–13).

Page 9, Kundera interview. Jordan Elgrably, "Conversations with Milan Kundera" (*Salmagundi*, No. 73, Winter 1987), pp. 5–6.

Page 9, poets and philosophers. Readers who are convinced that there is indeed more to be learned from Bertrand Russell than from Marcel Proust are advised to read no more of this book; mine, I fear, is not the mouth for their ears—and neither is Nietzsche's.

Page 9, philosophy and poetry. Particularly given the venerability of the quarrel between philosophy and poetry, I hasten to acknowledge the incompleteness of the account I have just given. As I have indicated, this account is elaborated, at times elliptically, by what follows. I hope to consider the quarrel more fully and directly on another occasion. In the meantime, I refer interested readers particularly to Stanley Rosen's "The Quarrel between Philosophy and Poetry," contained in the book bearing the same title (New York: Routledge, Chapman and Hall, 1988), and to "Theory and Interpretation," in *Hermeneutics as Politics* (New York: Oxford University Press, 1987), esp. p. 148. On this as on many other matters, Rosen has powerfully influenced and stimulated my own reflections.

Page 10, what ails "us" moderns. Mark Warren's *Nietzsche and Political Thought* (Cambridge, MA: MIT Press, 1988), which I read only after completing a draft of this book, leads me to add an important qualification: the "us" whose ailment Nietzsche understands consists primarily of privileged Westerners. But Warren and I agree that Nietzsche's thought has potentially salutary consequences for the non-privileged as well; see Chapter Eight, below.

Page 10, my focus on *Zarathustra*. In concentrating as I do, I join those criticized by Tracy Strong (*Friedrich Nietzsche and the Politics of Transfiguration*, Expanded edition, Berkeley: University of California Press, 1988) and Ofelia Schutte (*Beyond Nihilism*, Chicago: University of Chicago Press, 1984) for ignoring Nietzsche's many troubling statements concerning such matters as slavery and breeding. I have provided my basic reason for doing so: I take my bearings from Nietzsche's assertion that his affirmative teachings are to be found in *Zarathustra* alone. There, I argue, the likes of slavery and oppression are not merely not supported, they are emphatically rejected.

Neither Schutte nor Strong acknowledges the centrality Nietzsche accords Zara-thustra; Strong indeed explicitly denies it, asserting that "in his commentary on each of his books in *Ecce Homo* [Nietzsche] makes no divisions" (p. 8). Whatever its reliability, however, the classification of *Zarathustra* as alone "yes-saying" and of the later works as "fish hooks" certainly divides Nietzsche's works. To be sure, Schutte and Strong are far from alone in ignoring this division; I find it simply bizarre, in light of Nietzsche's classification of his works, that not a single one of the fourteen essays included in the collection *Nietzsche as Affirmative Thinker* (ed. Yirmiahu Yovel, Dordrecht: Martinus Nijhoff, 1986) pays particular attention to *Zarathustra*.

I do not mean to suggest that I am the first to concentrate on *Zarathustra;* for lengthier arguments for its centrality within the Nietzschean corpus, see Chapter One of Harold Alderman, *Nietzsche's Gift* (Athens, Ohio: Ohio University Press, 1977); Gary Shapiro, "The Rhetoric of Nietzsche's *Zarathustra*," in Berel Lang, ed., *Philosophical Style* (Chicago: Nelson Hall, 1980), pp. 347–85; the Introduction to Laurence Lampert, *Nietzsche's Teaching* (New Haven: Yale University Press, 1986); and Robert B. Pippin, "Irony and Affirmation in Nietzsche's *Thus Spoke Zarathustra* (in Strong and Gillespie, eds., *Nietzsche's New Seas*, pp. 45–71).

Page 11, "metaphysical" and "postmetaphysical." These positions, as I sketch them, are caricatures. To be sure, some "metaphysical" readers do not present "metaphysical" readings of Nietzsche: Walter Kaufmann, for example, does not present Nietzsche as a totalitarian. Likewise, some (perhaps all) "postmetaphysical" readers avoid the absurdity of asserting that Nietzsche unambiguously teaches that there can be no unambiguous teachings. I allow my caricatures to stand because they clarify my own approach, and because I do not provide the detailed discussion that would be required to make of them more than caricatures. I make no attempt in this book to develop a hermeneutic theory; instead, I engage in hermeneutic practice, and I direct that practice to the writings of Nietzsche, not to those either of Derrida or Foucault, or of Danto or Müller-Lauter.

Page 13, Nietzsche's ideal readers. Karsten Harries examines this passage from *Zarathustra* in greater detail in "The Philosopher at Sea" (in Strong and Gillespie, eds., *Nietzsche's New Seas*, Chicago: University of Chicago Press, 1988, pp. 21–44); Harries opposes the philosophical self-confidence, or arrogance, exhibited by analytic philosopher Arthur Danto in *Nietzsche as Philosopher* (New York: Columbia University Press, 1965).

Page 13, justification for my interpretive strategy. What interpreters must do, in presenting their readings as interpretations of Nietzsche rather than as their own creations, is avoid discussing only passages that happen to support their readings while ignoring passages that might undermine them. Certainly, in what follows I ignore many passages that seem not to fit into my reading of Nietzsche, but my reason for ignoring them is that the doctrines they suggest do not develop within my reading of *Zarathustra*.

Notes to Chapter 2

Page 15, the history of uses of "nihilism." See W. Müller-Lauter's detailed treatment in "Nihilismus," in *Historisches Wörterbuch der Philosophie*, ed. J. Ritter and K. Grunder, vol. 6 (Darmstadt: Wissenschaftliche Buchgesellschaft, 1984), column 846.

Page 15, the importance of nihilism within plans for *WP*. See esp. N:2[100], 9[1], 9[127], 10[58], 13[3], and 13[4]; also 5[70], 5[75], 5[97], 6[26], 7[43], 7[64], 11[326], 11[328], 12[2], 13[1], 13[2], 14[114], 14[137], 14[156].

Page 15, the "standard version" of *WP*. I refer to the version edited by Peter Gast and Elisabeth Förster-Nietzsche, originally published in 1906; the Kaufmann-Hollingdale translation (Vintage, 1967) retains the numbering of this "standard" version.

Page 16, Heidegger's nihilisms. *Nietzsche* (Pfullingen: Neske, 1961), II:281: "Ecstatic nihilism becomes 'classical nihilism.'" See also pp. 35, 42, 88, (English translation (ET) by David Krell, *Nietzsche*, 4 vols., New York: Harper and Row, 1984ff, IV:5, 11, 50) and *Holzwege* (Frankfurt a. M.: Klostermann, 5th ed. 1972), p. 281.

Page 16, Deleuze's nihilisms. Gilles Deleuze, *Nietzsche and Philosophy*, trans. Hugh Tomlinson (New York: Columbia University Press, 1983), p. 148.

Page 16, Rosen's nihilisms. "Theory and Interpretation," *Hermeneutics as Politics*, p. 157.

Page 16, paucity of treatments of Nietzsche's use of "nihilism." One might expect careful treatment in Ofelia Schutte's *Beyond Nihilism*, but Schutte does not provide it. Schutte's confidence that she knows what Nietzsche means by "nihilism" is strong enough to allow her to assert, as early as p. 2, "In *Thus Spoke Zarathustra* Nietzsche identified nihilism as an emptiness that devours increasing amounts of life and yet fails to be satisfied with living." This assertion is not indefensible, yet in *Zarathustra*, the term "nihilism" does not even appear.

Schutte's confidence is far from unique; in their introduction to *Nietzsche's New Seas*, Tracy Strong and Michael Allen Gillespie announce summarily, "For Nietzsche, the meaning of nihilism is summed up in the dictum 'God is dead' " (p. 5). Similarly, although Robert Solomon criticizes others for using the term loosely, he himself makes no attempt to trace Nietzsche's uses of it ("A More Severe Morality: Nietzsche's Affirmative Ethics," in Yirmiahu Yovel, ed., *Nietzsche as Affirmative Thinker*, Dordrecht: Martinus Nijhoff, 1986, pp. 69–89).

One commentator who has not ignored the complexity of Nietzsche's references to nihilism is Richard Schacht, who, in "Nietzsche and Nihilism" (in *Nietzsche. A Collection of Critical Essays*, ed. Robert C. Solomon, Garden City, NY: Anchor Books, 1973, pp. 58–72) assembles most of the central passages from *The Will to Power* and the published works in order to respond, effectively, to Arthur Danto's charge that Nietzsche himself is a nihilist (see Schacht's references to Danto's *Nietzsche as Philosopher* on pp. 58–59).

Page 16, *Nachlass* notes distorted in *WP*. Most important among them:
2[131], much of which is omitted from *WP;* what is included in *WP* is divided among 69, 391, 856, and 1054.
5[71], divided in *WP* among 4, 5, 114, and 55.
7[8], contained incompletely in 113 and 8.
9[35], contained, in jumbled fashion, in 23, 2, 22, and 13.
9[107], divided among 37, 35, and 26.

Page 16, levels of nihilism. For further details concerning the subsidiary distinctions, see my "Nietzschean Nihilism: A Typology" (*International Studies in Philosophy*, XIX/2 [1987]), esp. pp. 35–37, 43.

Nietzsche's "first" nihilism, emphasized by Mark Warren, does not fit comfortably into my any of my three levels. This "first nihilism" is held by those who view life as too hard to be worth living. I treat this view in the following chapter, in my discussion of the "wisdom of Silenus." Warren, it seems to me, overstates its importance as a form of nihilism in three ways. First, he translates *erste*, "first," as "original," and then leans on the stronger sense of his term: "original nihilism is 'original' in the sense that European nihilism could only have developed because of its prior occurrence" (p. 18). Second, whereas Warren presents this first nihilism as a result of political oppression, Nietzsche often treats it as ontological rather than as political: Silenus reveals his wisdom not to a slave, but rather to a king. Third, Warren's Nietzsche presents a single account of origins; this strikes me as a dogmatism Nietzsche strives to avoid (see Chapter Four, below).

I appreciate Warren's emphasis of *N*:5[71] / *WP:*114 as evidence of Nietzsche's recognition of the importance of technological development. Because science has made life less "uncertain, contingent, senseless," we do not now need a hypothesis as powerful as God in order to overcome nihilism.

Page 16, the project of clarifying Nietzsche's "nihilism." In his references to nihilism in works he published or prepared for publication, Nietzsche himself is much more careful than in his notes: in the former works, "nihilism" is always pejorative, and usually refers to what I call "religious nihilism." It seems to me not overly fanciful to suspect that Nietzsche would have brought more order into the terminological chaos had he ever prepared *The Will to Power* for publication. In any case, I do not see my attempt at ordering as in any way antithetical to the spirit of Nietzsche's work.

I have attempted to take into consideration all passages in Nietzsche's works and notebooks where he uses the term "nihilism" or variations thereof (I have not examined the letters). I lacked the aid of a computerized index, so my list is probably incomplete, but I deem it unlikely that I have missed any of Nietzsche's extended treatments.

Page 16, *N:*11[99] / *WP:*12. The importance of this section for comprehension of Nietzschean nihilism is stressed by Heidegger (*Nietzsche* II, pp. 55–101, ET IV, pp. 24–67). In *The Will to Power*, it is given the title "Downfall of Cosmological Values," but Nietzsche's own title is "Critique of Nihilism." In an index made later, Nietzsche lists it under the title "Causes of Nihilism! Concluding Summary!" (12[1]).

Page 17, "religious nihilism." My use of this is, I stress, an adaptation; Nietzsche calls Buddhism a "nihilistic religion," but in my framework it may be better classed a form of radical nihilism; see *N:*9[35] / *WP:*23, quoted on p. 20, above.

Nietzsche's references to nihilistic religion and religions include *TI,*IX:21; *EH,*IV:2; *N:*VII:34[204]; 2[100] / *WP:*905; 9[35] / *WP:*23; 11[370] / *WP:*156; 11[371] / *WP:*153; 11[372]; 11[373] / *WP:*220; 14[10]; 14[13] / *WP:*152; 14[114]; 14[135] / *WP:*461; 14[137] / *WP:*401; 14[174] / *WP:*703. On the differences between Christianity and Buddhism, as the primary "nihilistic religions," see *A:*20 and *N:*2[127] / *WP:*1.

Page 20, conviction. See *A:*54, and *N:*11[48].

Page 20, passive nihilism. The context in which Nietzsche mentions the nihilism of *adiaphora,* indifference, (*N:*14[94] / *WP:*435) reveals that it is another form of passive nihilism; but in 14[102] / *WP:*45, Nietzsche suggests that there is in adiaphora an ambiguity similar to the one he finds in radical nihilism: *adiaphora* may be a sign of weakness or of strength.

Page 20, destruction and creation. To be sure, Nietzsche regularly teaches that creation always involves destruction; but that is not to say that destruction necessarily involves creation.

Page 21, "one cannot judge the whole." Nietzsche presupposes that the purpose, unity, or truth required by religious and radical nihilists would have to be outside our world of becoming, that is, that there could be no "whole" containing both the source of value and the world endowed with value.

Page 21, "complete" nihilism. For other Nietzschean uses of this term—some of which are in conflict with my adaptation of the term—see N:10[42] / WP:28, 10[43] / WP:21, 11[149], and 11[229].

Additional indications that Nietzsche seeks to move beyond nihilism are provided by the several references, in WP plans ignored by Gast and Förster-Nietzsche, to "the self-overcoming of nihilism": N:9[127], 9[164], 13[4]. In other plans, Nietzsche lists "Nihilism and its counter-image [Gegenbild]: those who return [die Wiederkünftigen]" (14[169]) and "Nihilism and its opposite [Gegenstück]: the disciples of the 'return'" (16[51]); these titles are, however, ambiguous, in that both Gegenbild and Gegenstück can signify either a likeness or an opposition.

Page 22, return to pre-nihilistic position. This similarity between the pre-nihilistic and the post-nihilistic may underlie Heidegger's introduction of "classical nihilism" as synonymous with Nietzsche's "complete nihilism" (Holzwege, p. 207). Nietzsche suggests such a connection in, for example, N:16[32] / WP:1041: "I sought in history the beginnings of this construction of reverse ideals (the concepts 'pagan,' 'classical,' 'noble' newly discovered and expounded)." But two additional points must be noted: (1) it is crucial that the ancient concepts be "newly discovered and expounded"; to adapt a Heideggerian phrase, the no-longer-nihilistic is not the same as the not-yet-nihilistic. (2) The context suggests that Nietzsche's seeking of the ancient ideals is a reaction—perhaps an extreme overreaction (see 5[71] / WP:55)—to the Christian negation of such ideals. If that is so, then the return to the ancient ideals remains on the level of radical nihilism. See my comments on 9[35] / WP:13, pp. 16–18, above.

Page 24, "becoming as a whole." I use "whole" here in the sense of "totality," leaving aside the question whether the totality in question is a true whole, or merely an all.

Page 24, the need for justification. My argument suggests that as of 1872, when Nietzsche publishes the first edition of The Birth of Tragedy, he remains a radical nihilist: he insists there that "only as an aesthetic phenomenon is the world justified," but that presupposes that the question of justification is a legitimate one. Looking back at The Birth of Tragedy in Spring 1888, however, he writes: "Art counts here as the sole superior counter-force against all will to the denial of life: as the anti-Christian, anti-Buddhist, anti-nihilistic par excellence" (14[17]). I consider The Birth of Tragedy's ambiguities in the following chapter.

Notes to Chapter 3

Page 26, Socrates. Throughout this book, my concern with Socrates is limited to Nietzsche's Socrates, just as the Platonism and Christianity I treat are those described by Nietzsche. That I do not view the Socrates of Plato's dialogues as subscribing to Nietzsche's "Socratic delusion," that I do not consider Plato to be a "Platonist," and that I am aware that many who have deemed themselves Christians reject central tenets of Nietzsche's "Christian-moral tradition," are not sufficiently relevant to this study to warrant development here. I stress in addition that Nietzsche's relation to

Socrates is far more nuanced than *The Birth of Tragedy*, and thus this chapter, suggests. For details, see Nehamas, pp. 24–34, and the references therein.

Page 27, disposition, *Gesinnung*. This is one of several terms Nietzsche uses as generally synonymous with "perspective"; *Optik* ("lenses"), introduced above, is another. I discuss Nietzsche's perspectivism in Chapter Four.

Page 27, sustaining the tragic disposition. In *Richard Wagner in Bayreuth*, Nietzsche insists that the most able guarantor of the tragic disposition is Richard Wagner. This is fully consistent with *The Birth of Tragedy*, although not with the "Attempt at a Self-Criticism." Given the centrality of my concern with *Zarathustra*, I attend particularly to a revision from *Ecce Homo* stressed by Lampert (p. 344, n116): "In all the psychologically decisive places [in *Richard Wagner in Bayreuth*] the talk is only of me—one may, without any reservation, insert my name or the word 'Zarathustra' wherever the text has the word 'Wagner' " (*EH*,IV:4). Of course, this may tell us little about what Nietzsche intended as he wrote *Richard Wagner in Bayreuth;* but it does indicate that long after he had given up on Wagner, Nietzsche continued to value the project he had once attributed to him.

Page 27, pessimism. Nietzsche later decides that "pessimism" is inappropriate as a description for the Greeks; see *TI*,X:4, quoted below, p. 162. As I have already indicated, Nietzsche rejects the pessimism / optimism dichotomy (*HH*,I:28, quoted above, p. 12, and the "pessimism" characteristic of radical nihilism.

Page 27, Indian pessimism. In terms introduced in the previous chapter: Buddhism is the most famous form of passive nihilism. I am not competent to assess the accuracy of Nietzsche's portrayal of Buddhism. I note, however, that despite *The Birth of Tragedy*'s apparent denigration of Indian thought, Nietzsche is not among those who would praise Greek "philosophy" to the detriment of Indian "religion" or "mysticism." In *The Genealogy of Morals,* for example, he identifies India and England as "the antithetical poles of philosophical endowment" (*GM*,III:7); he does not intend thereby to praise the English.

Page 29, Silenian wisdom. In *Anarchy, State, and Utopia* (New York: Basic Books, 1974, p. 337, n8), Robert Nozick cites an "old Yiddish joke" Nietzsche would have appreciated:

"Life is so terrible, it would be better never to have been born."
"Yes, but how many are so lucky? Not one in a thousand."

Nietzsche defines jokes as epigrams on the deaths of feelings (*HH*,I:202). At times, new feelings may obtrude—when, for example, one realizes that abortion statistics provide a more precise answer to the question posed in Nozick's joke's.

Page 30, morality as defense against goodness. In *The Genealogy of Morals,* Nietzsche develops this suggestion in detail, arguing that the "slave rebellion in morality" is led by those who are unable to attain goodness qua excellence or nobility, and who therefore redefine goodness as meekness or humility.

Page 33, Dionysus vs. the metaphysical. Indeed, immediately following the passage quoted above, he repeats the message "in the language of that Dionysian monster who bears the name of Zarathustra."

Page 37, Dionysian individuation. My distinction between the Silenian and the Dionysian provides a basis for rejecting the objections raised against Nietzsche's "Dionysian perspective" by Ofelia Schutte (*Beyond Nihilism*). Associating individuality exclusively with the Apollinian (17–18), Schutte identifies "the principal Dionysian truth, insofar as it affects the individual," as "the agony of individuation"; "Dionysian redemption promises," therefore, " 'the shattering of the individual and his fusion with primal being' " (p. 13; the Nietzsche passage is from *BT:8*). This "truth," dependent upon Schopenhauerian metaphysics, is what I have classed as "Silenian."

Even readers who remain skeptical with respect to my suggested distinction need not accept Schutte's contention that Nietzsche makes a lasting "decision not to give importance to the individual as such," a decision that "will be combined with the notion that all decadent life needs to be destroyed to make room for strong life" (16–17). I grant that Schutte finds passages to support these contentions; but I insist, and will argue, that a careful reading of *Zarathustra* undermines them.

Notes to Chapter 4

Page 39, Borges. Jorge Luis Borges, *Labyrinths* (New York: New Directions, 1964), p. 65.

Page 39, Calvino's lion. Italo Calvino, *tZero* (New York: Harcourt Brace Jovanovich, 1976), p. 97.

Page 41, the danger of overlooking history. See Chapter Eight, below.

Page 42, the impossibility of returning to earlier historical configurations. See *TI*,IX:43, titled "Whispered in the Ears of the Conservatives."

Page 47, belief in God not obligatory. To deny that a perspective is obligatory is not to deny that it is possible, or that it is desirable. On the contrary, Nietzsche insists that *no* perspective is obligatory; the question that results is, what kind of perspective shall I attempt to develop? The religious perspective remains open to the perspectivist, at least, I think, in principle. That Zarathustra doubts this openness, as of *Zarathustra*'s Prologue, is suggested by his refusal to speak to the saint of the death of God.

Page 47, religio-moral perspective no longer binding. That Nietzsche does not here assert that this perspective is false, but rather that it is "no longer binding on us," is consistent with, and indeed supports, the interpretation I suggest for the births of God. We are freed from the bondage of this perspective, but also deprived of its support, by our recognition that it is one perspective among many, or, metaphorically, by the death of God.

Page 48, selectivity as interpretation. My discussion of the importance of selectivity, and of Nietzsche's perspectivism, is deeply indebted to Alexander Nehamas's *Nietzsche: Life as Literature;* see especially his Chapter Two, "Untruth as a Condition of Life." Another sympathetic but critical treatment of Nietzsche's perspectivism is John Wilcox, *Truth and Value in Nietzsche* (Ann Arbor: University of Michigan Press, 1974). For an examination of Nietzsche's treatment of interpretation in his unpublished notes, and a relating of that interpretation to recent hermeneutics, see Johann Figl, *Interpretation als philosophisches Prinzip* (Berlin and New York: de Gruyter, 1982).

Page 48, citing and weeding. This last question indicates the sense in which deeds, as well as "facts," are interpretations; to write a book rather than weed the garden entails the interpretation of the former act as somehow preferable to the latter. To appropriate a post-Nietzschean formulation: there is nothing outside the text.

Page 49, Nietzschean exegesis. I do not present my exegesis of Nietzsche's exegetical example as the result of the application of Nietzsche's own exegetical art. Nietzsche's exegesis of 17 words from *Zarathustra* takes some 70 pages, say 15,000 words. If this ratio were maintained, the exegesis of the exegesis would run some 30 million words, perhaps 14,000 pages. The length would be decreased, of course, if one could isolate all the aphorisms contained in the Third Essay, and interpret them alone. Even then, the traditional disclaimer, which I hereby invoke, would obtain: such an exegesis would exceed the scope of the present study.

Page 52, "deepened vision." The German is *Vertieften Blick;* Kaufmann's "penetration" arbitrarily strengthens the sexual overtones of the "explosion" Nietzsche refers to later in the sentence.

Page 53, "priestly" asceticism. Nietzsche's location of the origin of priestly asceticism in reaction need not be read as dogmatic or empirical. It need not be the case that all who have been called priests and have been ascetic have been ruled by the will to revenge—any more than that all who have been deemed philosophers have avoided that form of will. The point, instead, is that asceticism can be rooted in reaction; in referring to asceticism of this sort, Nietzsche uses the term "priestly."

Page 55, the morality of the lowest common denominator. The analogy is Nehamas's, p. 214.

Page 55, women as work-slaves and prisoners. Readers appalled by various apparently misogynistic Nietzschean references to women should note this one as well. See also my note to page 142, on page 173, below.

Page 55, love of neighbor. For a more positive evaluation, see Chapter Eight, below.

Notes to Chapter 5

Page 62, Calvino's Diomira. Italo Calvino, *Invisible Cities* (San Diego: Harcourt Brace Jovanovich, 1974), p. 7.

Page 64, Calvino's misprinted book. Italo Calvino, *If On A Winter's Night A Traveler*, trans. William Weaver (New York: Harcourt Brace Jovanovich, 1981), pp. 25–27.

Page 64, identity and cosmological repetition. For a detailed examination, see Günter Abel, *Nietzsche. Die Dynamik der Willen zur Macht und die ewige Wiederkehr* (Berlin and New York: de Gruyter, 1984), pp. 217–46.

Page 67, Schopenhauer on eternal return. Arthur Schopenhauer, *Die Welt als Wille und Vorstellung* (2 vols., 8th ed. Leipzig: F. A. Brockhaus, 1891), section 58. Schopenhauer's view of life is shared by "good old Kant" (*GM*,II:6):

> The value of life for us, if it is estimated by that *which we enjoy*, is easy to decide. It sinks below zero; for who would be willing to enter upon life anew under the same conditions? Who would do so even according to a new, self-chosen plan (yet in conformity with the course of nature), if it were merely directed to enjoyment? (*Critique of Judgment*, #83n)

> [If the justification of divine goodness consists] in showing that in the destinies of men evils do not outweigh the pleasant enjoyment of life, since everybody, no matter how badly off he is, prefers life to death, . . . one can leave an answer to this sophistry to the good sense of each man who has lived long enough and reflected on the value of life; you have only to ask him whether he would be willing to play the game of life once more, not under the same conditions, but under any conditions of our earthly world and not those of some fairyland. (Kant, "On the Failure of All Philosophical Attempts at Theodicy," XI:110)

Samuel Johnson's judgment was significantly more negative. Boswell reports: "He used frequently to observe, that there was more to be endured than enjoyed, in the general condition of human life. For his part, he said, he never passed that week in his life which he would wish to repeat, were an angel to make the proposal to him." James Boswell, *The Life of Johnson*, edited and abridged by Christopher Hibbert (Middlesex: Penguin Books, 1979), p. 153; cf. p. 183. Be the offer from angel or from demon, Johnson's choice is clear.

Page 70, the "true" world. I take this example from Stephen Houlgate's *Hegel, Nietzsche, and the Criticism of Metaphysics* (Cambridge: Cambridge University Press, 1986), p. 80.

In *A Study of Nietzsche* (Cambridge: Cambridge University Press, 1979), pp. 160–61, J. P. Stern characterizes this movement of reappropriation of initially rejected terms as Nietzsche's dialectic. I diverge from Stern in arguing that many of the movements have more than the three moments of description, rejection, and reinterpretation. In *Zarathustra*, the overman is something like a reinterpretation of God— "All gods are dead—we now will that the overman live" (*Z*,I:22.3; 102.13–14)— but proves to be an insufficient one: "we [poets] set our motley puppets on the clouds and then call them gods and overmen. And are they not light enough for these insubstantial seats?—all these gods and overmen" (Z,II:17; 164.31–34). Similarly, the first reinterpretation of eternity, the literal, physicalist doctrine of the return, must itself be surpassed. For these reasons, I deny that Zarathustra continues to be the "prophet of the overman" throughout the book (Stern, p. 159), and that the doctrine of return articulated in "Of the Vision and the Riddle" is "the high moment of Nietzsche-Zarathustra's vision" (Stern, p. 163).

Page 71, multivocity of "eternal return." Assuming that there is textual evidence for the equivocity of "eternal return" within the Nietzschean corpus, the question remains whether that equivocity is intentional. This is a question that cannot, in principle, be answered; it is, therefore, of no importance.

Notes to Chapter 6

Page 72, García Márquez. Gabriel García Márquez, *Love in the Time of Cholera,* trans. Edith Grossman (Middlesex: Penguin Books, 1988), p. 165.

Page 72, "soul," for Nietzsche's commentators. See, for example, the *Historisches Wörterbuch der Philosophie,* where Nietzsche is presented in the article on the body (*"Leib, Körper"*) as reversing the traditional body-soul relation (Vol. 5, Col. 183), but is not mentioned in the article on that relation itself (*"Leib-Seele Verhältnis,"* Vol. 5, Cols. 185–206). Similarly, Thomas Altizer argues that "Zarathustra calls for the resurrection of the body" ("Eternal Recurrence and the Kingdom of God," in David Allison, ed., *The New Nietzsche,* New York: Dell, 1977, p. 232).

Page 72, the variety of Zarathustra's audiences. See Z,IV:1; 296.18–19. On the fitting of speech to audience, see also *HH,*I:374.

Page 73, Zarathustra addresses his heart. See (perhaps among others): Z.P:1, 14.4–5; Z,P:5, 18.25–26, 20.28; Z,P:7, 22.29–30; Z,P:9, 25.19–20; Z,II:1, 105.12–13.

Page 73, "O my soul." The failure of commentators to note the importance of the soul in "Of the Great Longing" and the following sections is a chief cause of the hermeneutical interment of Zarathustra's soul. To take one example: although we are told at the end of the immediately preceding section, "The Convalescent," that Zarathustra converses silently with his *soul,* Gustav Naumann, author of the first and most extensive German-language commentary on *Zarathustra,* reports that he converses with "himself" (*sich selbst*) (*Zarathustra-Commentar,* 4 vols., Verlag H. Häffel: Leipzig, 1899, III: p. 173). Worse yet, Naumann presents the central question in "Of the Great Longing" as "who is now to give thanks: is he to thank life, or is life to thank him?" (III: p. 173, cf. p. 180). It is only in the following section, "The Other Dancing Song," that life enters the conversation; in "Of the Great Longing," the word "life" (*Leben*) does not even appear. The question there is whether it is Zarathustra or his soul that owes thanks (Z,III:14; 281.1–3).

In "The Philosopher at Sea," Karsten Harries notes that "Of the Great Longing" is "Zarathustra's hymn to his soul," but he takes the earlier description of the soul as "something in the body" as definitive, and does not take the final songs to be those of Zarathustra's soul (p. 40). But these are not points on which Harries focuses.

Page 73, attention to detail. One commentator certainly not insensitive to details is Laurence Lampert, whose *Nietzsche's Teaching*—which appeared only after several versions of this chapter had been completed—is a major contribution that illuminates virtually every section in *Zarathustra*. For all but the most dedicated of scholars, however, I fear that Lampert provides too many details; more of the "abbreviating" and "omitting" Nietzsche describes as required in interpretation would have made Lampert's study less valuable as a reference work, but would have facilitated the emergence of a more persuasive reading of the text as a whole.

Lampert, unlike most others, notes many of Zarathustra's references to his soul (although not, for example, those in the Prologue or in Z,II:1), but he makes no attempt to interrelate them. He also inserts the soul where it is absent, although very rarely; for example (perhaps the only example), he describes the exchange reported in "The Stillest Hour" as a conversation between Zarathustra and his soul (p. 335, n106, to p. 153); that section contains no mention of Zarathustra's soul.

Page 76, the hinterworldly. The German is *Hinterweltler*. Kaufmann and Hollingdale use "afterworld," but that would be more appropriate for *Nachwelt*, which Nietzsche does not use in *Zarathustra*. The adjective *hinter* is spatial rather than temporal, meaning "behind" rather than "after." *Hinterwelt* can mean the country, as opposed to the city—compare the English "hinterlands"—but that is not, I suspect, why Nietzsche uses it. Instead, I take the term to point to the connection Nietzsche sees between Christianity and Platonism. Whereas the Christian emphasis is on an *after*life, a life to follow life on earth, the Platonistic underpinning is a world permanently present, somehow "behind" the world of appearance.

Page 76, the body's will to create. This creative will is the will to power; to create beyond oneself is to overcome oneself, and the will to self-overcoming is the will to power; see Z, II:12, esp. 147.34 and 148.16–18, discussed above, pp. 84–85.

Page 77, Zarathustra's "brother." The form of address "brother" should not be taken to indicate that Zarathustra here addresses the person to whom he speaks in "Of the Despisers of the Body"; Zarathustra generally addresses his companions as "brothers."

Page 79, the health of the pale criminal's body. The pale criminal's body is healthy, again, in that it wills to create beyond itself; this is the will that cannot be denied. If not allowed to express itself externally, as in the pale criminal, it will do so internally. Nietzsche examines the mechanisms of such internalization in *The Genealogy*, particularly in the Second Essay.

Page 79, body-soul harmony. The importance of agreement between soul and body is reiterated in "Of Child and Marriage": "You should build beyond yourself. But first you must yourself be built, foursquare (*rechtwinklig*) in body and soul" (90.14–15). In *Human, All Too Human*, Nietzsche identifies disharmony as essential to the "moral" teachings he opposes: "Within morality, man treats himself not as *individuum*, but as *dividuum*" *HH*,I:57); "In every ascetic morality man worships one part of himself as God and is thereby compelled to diabolize the other parts" (*HH*,I:137).

Concerning the adjective "foursquare," cited here and above (from 38.10): Colli and Montinari cite Aristotle, *Rhetorics* II.11.i, 1411,b26–27: "to say that a good man [*ton agathon andra*] is 'four-square' [*tetragonon*] is certainly a metaphor; both the good man and the square are perfect [*ampho gar teleia*]." Cope and Sandys (*The Rhetoric of Aristotle*, 3 vols., Cambridge: Cambridge University Press, 1877) comment: "*Tetragonos* comes from Simonides—or rather from the Pythagoreans, who by a square number or figure symbolized (or, as Aristotle tells us, *Met*. A, actually identified it with) completeness, and perfect equality in the shape of justice. It was their type of perfection." Included among their references are particularly interesting passages from the *Nichomachean Ethics*. Aristotle writes, "The happy man . . . is 'good in very truth' and 'four-square without reproach' [*tetragonos aneu logou*]" (1100,b21); at 1100b33, he describes this man as *megalopsychos*, great-souled (III: p. 125–26).

Nietzsche's relation to Aristotle is fascinating, and requires the thorough treatment that will be possible only following the publication of all the relevant Nietzschean texts. Broadly speaking, I view Nietzsche's opposition to the Western philosophical tradition as focused on the Platonistic stream within that tradition; I find much that would place Nietzsche within the stream flowing from Aristotle through Hegel.

Page 80, importance of the soul. I take my argument here to be sufficient to establish that Zarathustra does not reduce the soul to the body. Additional evidence, if it is needed, is provided by the description in "Of Old and New Tablets," 19 (261.12–24) of one kind of soul; that description is presented in *Ecce Homo* as "the concept of Dionysus himself" (*EH*,IX:6).

Page 80, sensual pleasure. On the whole, Zarathustra shares *The Genealogy*'s evaluation of asceticism. He does give a more positive account of sensual pleasure (*Wollust*) in "Of the Three Evils" (*Z*,III:10.2; 237.4–23), but there too he indicates the baseness of the life devoted merely to such pleasure: "I want to have fences around my thoughts and also around my words, so that swine and fanatics (*Schwärmer*) do not break into my garden" (237.21–23). Similarly, in "Of Chastity" he derogates men of the city, who "know nothing better on earth than to lie with a woman. Slime is at the ground of their souls" (*Z*,I:13; 69.6–9). As "Of Child and Marriage" makes clear, the baseness of the "men of the city" is revealed not by their "lying with women," but rather by their knowing nothing better.

Page 82, the writing rabble. Kundera provides commentary:

The proliferation of mass graphomania among politicians, cab drivers, women on the delivery table, mistresses, murderers, criminals, prostitutes, police chiefs, doctors, and patients proves to me that every individual without exception bears a potential writer within himself and that all mankind has every right to rush out into the streets with a cry of "We are all writers!"

The reason is that everyone has trouble accepting the fact he will disappear unheard of and unnoticed in an indifferent universe, and everyone wants to make himself into a universe of words before it's too late.

Once the writer in every individual comes to life (and that time is not far off), we are in for an age of universal deafness and lack of understanding. (Kundera, *Laughter*, 106)

On writing and immortality, see Chapter Seven, above.

Page 83, love of the overman. I find only one reference to love of the overman: "what would be my love for the overman and for all that is to come if I advised and spoke otherwise?" (Z,III:12.24; 264.23–25). In that this love is for "all that is to come," it is not exclusive in the way that Zarathustra's earlier affirmation of the overman seems to be.

Page 83, the "murder" of Zarathustra's youth. In "The Tomb Song," Zarathustra does not identify life itself as the murderer of his youthful dreams; instead, he speaks of nameless "enemies." But the following section, "Of Self-Overcoming," reveals that passage is a feature of life itself, not the result of acts of enmity.

Page 85, "everything deserves to exist." Two passages from *Twilight of the Idols* are sufficiently relevant to be quoted at length:

it is only in the Dionysian mysteries, in the psychology of the Dionysian state, that the *basic fact* of the Hellenic instinct finds expression—its "will to life." What was it that the Hellene guaranteed himself by means of these mysteries? *Eternal* life, the eternal return of life; the future promised and hallowed in the past; the triumphant Yes to life beyond all death and change; *true* life as the over-all continuation of life through procreation, through the mysteries of sexuality. For the Greeks the *sexual* symbol was therefore the venerable symbol par excellence, the real profundity in the whole of ancient piety. Every single element in the act of procreation, of pregnancy, and of birth aroused the highest and most solemn feelings. In the doctrine of the mysteries, *pain* is pronounced holy: the pangs of the woman giving birth hallow all pain; all becoming and growing—all that guarantees a future—involves pain. That there may be the eternal joy of creating, that the will to life may eternally affirm itself, the agony of the woman giving birth *must* also be there eternally. All this is meant by the word Dionysus. (*TI*,X:4)

The psychology of the orgiastic as an overflowing feeling of life and strength, where even pain still has the effect of a stimulus, gave me the key to the concept of *tragic* feeling, which had been misunderstood both by Aristotle and, quite especially, by our modern pessimists. Tragedy is so far from proving anything about the pessimism of the Hellenes, in Schopenhauer's sense, that it may, on the contrary, be considered its decisive repudiation and counter-instance. Saying Yes to life even in its strangest and hardest problems, the will to life rejoicing over its own inexhaustibility even in the very sacrifice of its highest types—*that* is what I called Dionysian, *that* is what I guessed to be the bridge to the psychology of the *tragic* poet. *Not* in order to be liberated from terror and pity, not in order to purge oneself of a dangerous affect by its vehement discharge—Aristotle understood it that way—but in order to be *oneself* the eternal joy of becoming, beyond all terror and pity—that joy which included even joy in destroying.

. . . Herewith I again stand on the soil out of which my intention, my *ability* grows—

I, the last disciple of the philosopher Dionysus—I, the teacher of the eternal recurrence. (*TI*,X:5)

Immediately following this passage, Nietzsche quotes *Zarathustra* III:12.29 in its entirety, thereby concluding the book.

Page 85, Zarathustra's minotaur. Whereas the size and strength of the Cretan Minotaur allows him—like the blond beast of *The Genealogy*—to conquer through deeds, the small, weak spirit of gravity, like the ascetic priest, can fight only with words, the leaden thoughts he drips into the ears of those who attempt to climb. Like the priest, the spirit of gravity must be clever.

Page 87, the dwarf and the moment. Heidegger effectively stresses that placement within the moment is what the dwarf cannot bear: Zarathustra ultimately questions the dwarf "from out of the moment. Such questioning, however, requires that the questioner be placed within the 'moment' itself, i.e., within time and temporality" (*Nietzsche*, Pfullingen: Neske, 1961, I: p. 297; ET II: p. 44). There can be decisive moments only for the one "who does not remain a spectator, but rather who *himself is* the moment, who acts into the future, thereby not dropping the past but rather taking it up and affirming it. . . . To see the moment means to stand within it. The dwarf, however, remains outside, squats by the wayside" (*Nietzsche*, I: p. 311–312; ET, II: pp. 56–57).

Page 88, eternal wakefulness. In that the thought is to "stay awake eternally," it is not something that is to be overcome; it cannot be the "over-dragon" that the overman would have to slay (*Z*,II:21; 185.19–20).

Page 88, *Rosenapfel*. My thanks to Dan Kaufman for identifying the "rose-apple" as a quince. Kaufman also reports having read that the quince has been taken to be the fruit from Eden's tree of knowledge.

Page 88, the animals respond to Zarathustra. Heidegger fails to note that the animals respond to Zarathustra's movement rather than themselves initiating the action (*Nietzsche* I: p. 305; ET, II: p. 51); this detail serves to distance Zarathustra from his animals.

Page 89, *Töne*. The German term, like the cognate "tones," is more closely related to music than is *Laute*, sounds, but I take Nietzsche to use "words and tones" here to emphasize that the words he describes are spoken rather than to distinguish between words on the one hand and musical tones on the other. The animals have, after all, uttered only words—they have not hummed or grunted—and, consistently in *Zarathustra* (at least until the end of Book III, and perhaps thereafter), "songs" have words.

Page 89, the other soul as hinterworld. This is yet another consequence of the fact that because there are too many facts, we must construct interpretations. Proust provides commentary:

It is one of the powers of jealousy to reveal to us the extent to which the reality of external facts and the sentiments of the soul are things unknown that lend themselves to endless suppositions. We imagine that we know exactly what things are and what people think, for the simple reason that we do not care about them. But as soon as we have a desire to know, as the jealous man has, then at once there is a vertiginous kaleidoscope in which we can no longer distinguish anything. (Proust, *Remembrance*, III:529; translation altered)

Page 89, perspectives. The Soothsayer's perspective, like the Christian perspective, is "false" only insofar as it purports to be the only possible perspective. Zarathustra neither can nor need disprove that it is a perspective that can be taken; he need only deny that it must be taken.

Page 90, the instant. The animals never speak of the moment [*Augenblick*], but only of the instant [*Nu*] (273.3, 276.16). The terms can be synonymous, but the sensory content of *Augenblick* makes it the more suggestive: "in an Augenblick" might often be translated as "in the blink of an eye," but the German *Blick* is a glimpsing, not a closing. For this reason, some translators have chosen "moment of vision."

Page 91, Heidegger. *Nietzsche*, I: p. 308; ET, II: p. 54. Alderman, a champion of the animals, quotes (with ellipses) the two first speeches of the animals, skipping over Zarathustra's reference to their jabbering and his remarks on language. He also ends the second speech with "The middle is everywhere" (p. 101), omitting the concluding sentence, "The path of eternity is crooked"—the very sentence that, as Heidegger points out, connects the animals' view to that of the dwarf. Alderman then ignores the form of address—"buffoons and barrel-organs"—reporting only, "Zarathustra responds to this voice of his animals by telling them in surprise that they knew all along what was required of him" (p. 101).

Page 91, lyres and hurdy-gurdies. The German musical terms Nietzsche uses in "The Convalescent" are suggestive in ways that English cannot reflect. The "hurdy-gurdy" song is, more literally, a "lyre song" [*Leier-Lied*]; if Zarathustra's reference to the "lyre song" is pejorative, we have reason to be suspicious of the animals' later suggestion that all Zarathustra needs is a "new lyre" [*eine neue Leier*] (275.22,24).
    Consultation of the entries for *Leier*, *Drehleier*, and *Drehorgel* in the *Wahrig Deutsches Wörterbuch* (Berlin: Bertelsmann Lexikon-Verlag, 1968, 1977) yields much more that is of interest. *Leier* can mean "lyre," but it is also short for *Drehleier*, "crank-lyre," an instrument similar to the "barrel-organ," the *Drehorgel*, itself a kind of "lyre case" [*Leierkasten*]. The *Drehleier* is a stringed instrument with a crank (requiring circular motion) that moves a pick (in linear motion) across the strings. The association of *Leier* with the *Drehleier* is sufficiently strong to make the *Leier* itself "an image [*Sinnbild*] of that which is constantly [*ständig*] repeated." Hence, the German idiom, *es ist (immer) die alte Leier*, "it is (always) the same old lyre," means, "it is always the same; I've often heard that before." The eternal return for which the *Leier* provides an image and the *Leier-Lied* a song is the eternal return envisaged by the dwarf and the Soothsayer; that doctrine is precisely what Zarathustra seeks to overcome.

Zarathustra does use *Leier* in a positive sense in "The Night-Wanderer's Song" (Z,IV:19.6; 399.20), but because he is there speaking to the "higher men" rather than to himself, I do not take the later passage to outweigh the etymological evidence. That evidence is further supported by the passage from Schopenhauer, quoted in Chapter Five (page 67), in which the meaningless, clockwork repetition of human life is described as a *Leierstück*.

Page 92, Heidegger and the animals. Although Heidegger is made suspicious of the animals' first speech by their retention of the terminology of the dwarf, he fails to note that in their second, they echo the radical nihilism of *The Joyful Science*'s demon. The animals announce, in their version of Zarathustra's death speech, "You teach that there is a great year of becoming, a monster of a great year: it must, like an hourglass, turn itself over again and again, so that it runs on and runs out from the beginning" (Z,III:13.2; 276.6–9). Compare the demon: "The eternal hourglass of existence is turned over again and again—and you with it, dust grain of dust!" (*JS:*341). The hourglass image is used in similarly nihilistic fashion by Schopenhauer (*World as Will and Representation,* I: p. 58).

Page 92, the animals' ignorance of the human. After his decision, at the beginning of Part III, to confront the thought of the return, Zarathustra takes a roundabout route back to his mountain; he may be motivated by his apprehension of the confrontation, but in any case he re-encounters, as he returns, all that has most disgusted him. We are told explicitly in "Of the Virtue That Makes Small" that Zarathustra wants to learn whether man has grown larger or smaller (Z,III:5; 211.7–10), something about which his animals would not even wonder.

It is also relevant to note that in Part IV, we learn that the animals cannot cope even with the higher men (Z,IV:11; 346.22–347.2), who, despite their shortcomings, are indeed higher than many encountered earlier by Zarathustra.

Page 93, Zarathustra's lack of response to the animals. In his summary, Heidegger omits the passage indicating precisely that Zarathustra *did not hear* what his animals had said about his going-under; instead, he writes, "When Zarathustra heard these words of his animals' 'he lay still' " (*Nietzsche,* I: p. 315; ET, II: p. 59).

Page 93, Zarathustra eludes his animals. Even this does not shake Alderman's faith in the animals; he comments, "After a brief, bantering exchange, Zarathustra leaves for greater solitude on the mountain top" (p. 116), later adding, "the first section [of Part IV] shows the animals parodying Zarathustra by quoting him to himself (in their pre-theoretical innocence, they have always known what Zarathustra so arduously learns)" (p. 116).

Page 93, "pre-theoretical innocence." Such innocence would be the innocence of Part IV's ass, who "says only yes and never no" (Z,IV:17.2; 389.13) (Nietzsche's ass brays "I-A," a German "hee-haw" homophonic with an extended "*ja,*" "yes"). The ass's kingdom is "beyond good and evil" because it is his innocence "not to know what innocence is" (389.18–20). That the "higher men" are capable of resurrecting

God in the ludicrous form of the ass suggests to Zarathustra that they are still capable of resurrecting themselves; but he does not acknowledge asininity as a desirable final goal.

Page 93, the reliability of the animals. I am certainly not the first to discount the testimony of Zarathustra's animals. Paul Valadier, in "Dionysus Versus the Crucified" (in *The New Nietzsche*), also does so (p. 254), but is not led to consider a radical reinterpretation of eternity (see p. 260, n26). Gilles Deleuze also rejects the authority of the animals (*Nietzsche and Philosophy*, trans. Hugh Tomlinson, New York: Columbia University Press, 1983, p. 72), but continues to interpret the eternal return as a cosmological doctrine; according to Deleuze, the animals err chiefly in making the return comprehensive rather than selective (see pp. 48, 68–69, 86, 103). Nehamas notes that Zarathustra never acknowledges the animals' speech (*Nietzsche*, p. 147), but does not discuss Zarathustra's conversation with his soul.

Page 93, end of Part III. I take Zarathustra's development to be complete by the end of Part III. Nietzsche did not originally plan for a fourth part, and in the fourth part he later wrote Zarathustra undergoes no unanticipated transformations (the anticipated one is described in Z,IV:20; 406.24). Lampert provides a detailed discussion, with which I am in substantial agreement, of the status of Part IV (pp. 287–91). In *Nietzsche's Zarathustra* (Philadelphia: Temple University Press, 1987), Kathleen Higgins valiantly attempts to establish the importance of Part IV by relating it to *The Golden Ass*, but I have not been persuaded by her treatment.

Page 94, twilight. As Thomas Burke has pointed out to me, my use of "twilight" for both *Zwielicht* and *Dämmerung* strengthens the case for my interpretation somewhat artificially; I have bridged a gap that should not, perhaps, be simply ignored. *Dämmerung*, like "twilight," refers to times of transition between night and day. *Zwielicht* is more complicated: the *zwie* is from *zwei*, "two," and the *licht* cognate with "light." So, *Zwielicht* is a mixing of light from multiple sources. This is not inappropriate as a reference to times of twilight, if one thinks (for example) of candles being lit as the sun rises or sets. But Nietzsche may have had something else in mind; "for every soul, every other soul is a hinterworld."

Page 95, *Kahn, Nachen*. I take the "bark" [*Kahn*] of Z,III:15 to be the "boat" [*Nachen*] of Z,III:14.

Page 95, "Once More." The title is provided in the penultimate section of Part IV, where the song is sung to the "higher men" who have sought Zarathustra out on his mountain, and is accompanied by a commentary for their benefit.

Page 95, life's fathomability. As we have seen, *The Birth of Tragedy* presents the belief that existence is *ergründlich*, that we can get to the bottom of things, as an essential feature of the Socratic delusion.

Page 96, life as woman. With only one exception that I have found, Zarathustra feminizes "life," using the feminine pronoun (*sie*, she) even though the noun, *das Leben*, is neuter. The only section in which Zarathustra use the grammatically expected pronoun *es*, it, is "Of Self-Overcoming." I am intrigued by this detail, but I do not know what to make of it.

Page 99, dice throws. Deleuze makes much of the "dice throw," but insists, without textual support, that there is but one throw of the dice (*Nietzsche and Philosophy*, pp. 25–27). I suggest, on the contrary, that to live is continually to throw the dice. In addition to the arguments provided below, consider Nietzsche's admonition to the higher men, which I deem clearly to refute Deleuze's interpretation:

> Timid, ashamed, awkward, like a tiger whose leap has failed [*missrieth*]: thus, you higher men, have I often seen you slink aside, you higher men. A *throw* had failed [*missrieth euch*].
> But, you dice-players, what does that matter! You have not learned to play and to mock as one must play and mock! Do we not sit on a great table for play and mockery?
> And if great things have failed for you, does that make you—failures? And if you yourselves have failed, has humanity thereby failed as well? And if humanity has failed: well then! come on! (*Z*,IV:13.14; entire)

Page 99, Dionysus as redeemer. Nietzsche's Dionysus offers not the release from life on earth, but rather reconciliation with it. Or, as redeemer Dionysus informs Ariadne in the poem "Ariadne's Complaint," "I am your labyrinth" (*Dionysian Dithyrambs; KSA* 6:401.25). This poem is quoted nearly in entirety by the Magician in *Zarathustra*'s Part IV (*Z*,IV:5), but Dionysus's response to the complaint is not included.

Page 99, growth and pain. Similarly, at the beginning of the book Zarathustra is described as descending from his mountain in order to free himself of the wisdom of which he is overfull (P:1, 11.16–21). On the pain involved in growth, see *TI*,X:4, quoted above, p. 162.

Page 102, the pale criminal's view of his deed. Given the ease with which perspectivism is confused with relativism, it may be worth stressing, again, that although the pale criminal's identification of himself as "the doer of one deed" is "true for him" in that he accepts it, in fact it is *false*. Its falsity is visible through the lenses of life. If the pale criminal were to judge, "my doom is sealed, because this one deed will send me to eternal perdition," he might be right—who could prove him wrong? But he might also be wrong. He would certainly be wrong if he were also to judge, "this is the only way to view my deed, as one that damns me forever." That judgment would be false. Recognition of its falsity would lead to the appropriate question, how am I to attempt to view the deed?

Page 102, responsibility for forgetting. Nietzsche argues in *The Genealogy*'s Second Essay that we are responsible even for our forgetting: granted that it is not in my power to remember everything I say, do, or suffer, it nevertheless is in my power, in the great majority of cases, to remember whatever I deem sufficiently important. My allowing myself to forget something is a consequence of my deeming it not worth remembering.

Page 103, passing by. This principle is presented to the "fool" known as "Zarathustra's ape," a caricature who castigates the masses in Zarathustrian terms but who remains in the city because he can do no more than condemn.

Page 104, accurate anthropology. We *all* "return eternally," in the sense I have developed; not all of us, however, explicitly recognize that we do so, and not all of us who recognize that we do so can will to do so.

Page 104, no one way. In terms Foucault has introduced, Nietzsche's transvaluation involves a reversion from the emphasis on codes of behavior—specific laws and rules—characteristic of Christian morality to an emphasis on "forms of subjectivation" or "practices of the self," comparable to that found in classical Greece (see *The Use of Pleasure*, vol. 2 of *The History of Sexuality*, New York: Vintage Books, 1986, p. 29).

Notes to Chapter 7

Page 105, Calvino's same and different books. Italo Calvino, *If on a Winter's Night a Traveler*, p. 197.

Page 107, Calvino on life's architectural order. Italo Calvino, *Mr. Palomar* (New York: Harcourt Brace Jovanovich, 1985), p. 124.

Page 107, my treatments of Nehamas and Kundera. As should go without saying by this point—as should be clear from the length of the accounts to follow as well as from the general principles articulated above—my treatments of Nehamas and Kundera are exhaustive neither as summaries nor as critiques; I view them as supplements to the works they consider, certainly not as substitutes.

In the remainder of this book, I continue to cite *Zarathustra*, but I attend less closely to specific contexts, particularly in terms of Zarathustra's development. Instead, I rely on the context provided by my account of Zarathustra's deepest teachings. Passages from anywhere in the book that are consistent with those teachings, and that expand or clarify them, I take to be aspects of Nietzsche's affirmation; passages contradictory to them I take as preliminary, or as audience-specific. Again, I acknowledge that this is not the only way to proceed. The most that I or anyone else can do, in explaining a manner of reading, is to provide my reasons for doing what I do.

Page 108, dyadic oppositions. The description of Nietzsche's position in terms of avoidance of dyadic or binary oppositions points in the direction of an important investigation I hope to pursue elsewhere. A basic poststructuralist objection to "metaphysical thinking," and thus to what is often taken to be all of Western philosophy, is that this thinking relies on binary oppositions. Nietzsche is beyond such reliance and, therefore, a "poststructuralist." But so too is Hegel (see my *Absolute Knowledge*). The relation between Hegelian and Nietzschean thought requires much more careful treatment than it has received to date, although Stephen Houlgate's *Hegel, Nietzsche, and the Criticism of Metaphysics* introduces a number of issues important within this relation. For a brief presentation of my reservations about Houlgate, see my review in *The Owl of Minerva* Vol. 21 (Fall 1989), pp. 91–96; Houlgate has responded in *The Owl* Vol. 21 (Spring 1990), pp. 227–30.

Page 112, Proust and eternal return. To clarify Nehamas's use of Proust, I cite the paragraph from which the quotation above is drawn:

> The life of Proust's narrator need not have been, and never was, Nietzsche's own specific ideal. But the framework supplied by this perfect novel which relates what, despite and even through its imperfections, becomes and is seen to be a perfect life, and which keeps turning endlessly back upon itself, is the best possible model for the eternal recurrence. (168)

Page 113, music vs. literature. *HH*,I:626, "Without Melody," describes a strikingly non-"literary" way of living as worthy of emulation. See also 611.

Page 114, living in order to be paid.

> You want to be paid as well, you who are virtuous! Do you want reward for virtue and heaven for earth and eternity for your today?
> And are you now angry with me because I teach that there is no reward-giver and no paymaster? . . .
> You love your virtue as the mother her child; but when was it heard of a mother wanting to be paid for her love? . . .
> Ah, my friends! That *your* self be in the action, as the mother is in the child: let that be *your* maxim of virtue! (*Z*,II:5; 120.11–15, 121.3–4, 123.9–11)

Page 116, literary lives. "Good" lives also often make for poor literature. Of course, as Nehamas is aware, "literary" characters are not always evaluated in terms of the extent to which their acts express "one will." An alternative some would take to be Nietzschean (wrongly, as I am confident Nehamas would agree) is embraced by Xavier, creation of Kundera's poet Jaromil:

> He was repelled by the pettiness that reduced life to mere existence and that turned men into half-men. He wanted to lay his life on a balance, the other side of which was weighted with death. He wanted to make his every action, every day, yes, every hour and minute worthy of being measured against the ultimate, which is death. That was why he wanted to lead the file, to walk the tightrope over the abyss, his head illumined by a halo of bullets, to grow in everyone's eyes until he has become as immense as death itself . . . (Kundera, *Life is Elsewhere*, p. 82)

In *Human, All Too Human*, Nietzsche warns against another "literary" pitfall:

> *Man as bad poet.*—Just as bad poets, in the second parts of their verses, seek thoughts that will rhyme, human beings tend in the second halves of their lives, having become more anxious [*ängstlicher*], to seek the acts, positions, and relations that will fit with those of their earlier lives, so that everything seems harmonious: but their lives are no longer ruled by strong thoughts and determined anew again and again; in the place of such thoughts enters the intention of finding new rhymes. (*HH*,I:610)

Page 119, melody and goal. Nehamas quotes this parable, p. 198; yet it supports the "art without artifact" interpretation more than the "life as literature" alternative.

Page 120, suicide. My question concerns suicide in the narrow sense, excluding both (1) the sort of self-sacrifice involved in, for example, a soldier's throwing himself on a live hand grenade in order to save the lives of his companions, and (2) the choice of "death with dignity" made by the sick or aged. On the latter, see *HH*,I:80, 88, *Z*,I:21, and *TI*,IX,36, "Morality for Physicians."

Notes to Chapter 8

Page 125, what Kundera thought when he was young. Kant is a striking example of one who thinks, as Kundera thought when he was young, that "the good of the world" requires the precedence of angels over devils, and thus that reason and purpose banish Nietzsche's playful "Lord Chance":

> [S]ince the philosopher cannot assume in the great human drama that mankind has a rational purpose [*Zweck*] of its own [i.e., one we pursue consciously], his only point of departure is to try to discover whether there is some natural purpose in this senseless course of human affairs, from which it may be possible to produce a history of creatures who proceed without a plan of their own but in conformity with some definite plan of nature's. (Kant, "Idea for a Universal History with Cosmopolitan Intent," Introduction)

> In the teleological theory of nature, an organ that is not intended to be used [*das nicht gebraucht werden soll*], an organization [*Anordnung*] that does not achieve its end, is a contradiction. If we stray from that fundamental principle [*Grundsatze*], we no longer have a lawful but an aimlessly playing [*endlos spielende*] nature, and unconsoling chance [*trostlose Ungefähr*] takes the place of reason's guiding thread. ("Idea," First Thesis)

> [If we were to conclude that our natural capacities are not destined to develop fully,] all practical principles would have to be given up [*aufheben*], and nature, whose wisdom serves as a fundamental principle in judging all other arrangements, would in the sole case of man have to be suspected of *childish play*. ("Idea," Second Thesis)

Page 125, "Lord Chance." An untranslatable pun: the phrase *von ohngefähr* means "by chance," and that is how Kaufmann renders it. But, as Hollingdale points out, Nietzsche personifies chance as "the oldest nobility," nominalizing *ohngefähr* by means of capitalization. The *von* then becomes ambiguous: preceding a proper name, it indicates nobility.

Page 125, Lampert's "good and just" and "free spirit." In my earlier terms, Lampert's "good and just" are passive nihilists, his "free spirits," active nihilists.

Page 126, *Nutzen*. Another untranslatable pun: the "I" Nietzsche here describes seeks its *Nutzen* in the *Nutzen* of the many. In both cases, *Nutzen* can mean "profit" (Kaufmann) or "advantage" (Hollingdale). The "I" who finds its own profit in what profits the many could appear to be "the origin of the herd," but this "I," according to Nietzsche, is sly or devious rather than altruistic; it is in fact the beginning of the end for the herd. The turning point from origin to decline is the second *Nutzen*, which can be read as a nominalization of the verb meaning "to use." In my translation, I emphasize the second sense, which identifies the relationship as one of exploitation; Nietzsche wants both senses, I think, but I see no way to put both into English save through a footnote.

Page 127, foothill. My thanks to Campbell Connell for bringing the foothill reference to my attention.

Page 128, *Sucht*. Nietzsche makes a similar play in the term *gottsüchtig*, Z,I:3; 37.28. Here as elsewhere, the source of my information on German etymology is the *Wahrig Deutsches Wörterbuch;* for English supplementation, I consult the *Oxford English Dictionary.* Throughout, my etymologies are intended to be accurate rather than Heideggerian.

Page 128, premature answers. Nehamas writes, "Socrates believes that not enough questions have been asked, while Nietzsche is afraid that too many answers have been given" (p. 26). Both Nietzsche and Socrates, however, aim the most persistent of their questions at beliefs that are taken to be truths, that is, that are no longer recognized as provisional answers to questions; both, it seems to me, believe both that not enough questions have been asked, and that too many answers have been given.

Page 128, earthly heaven. *Erdenhimmel;* as I have noted, *Himmel* names sky as well as heaven, but Nietzsche's *Erdenhimmel*—which, I judge, may well be his coinage— is reminisent of *Himmel auf Erde,* heaven on earth.

Page 130, PhD programs. This assumes further that there is an important connection between philosophy or contemplation and PhD programs—another dubious assumption.

Page 131, reasons. Again, the question is not whether one can produce reasons that are logically compelling. Even if that could be done, they would be influential only on the relatively few who are compelled by logic.

Page 134, classical music. Concerning music, Kundera adds: "But even in the tower where the wisdom of music reigns supreme we sometimes feel nostalgic for that monotonous, heartless shriek of a beat which comes to us from outside and in which all men are brothers. Keeping exclusive company with Beethoven is dangerous in the way all privileged positions are dangerous" (*Laughter,* p. 181).

Page 135, reasons for remembering. A fourth reason, fully consistent with the three I present as Nietzschean, is implicit in the following passage from Foucault:

> I prefer the very specific transformations that have proved to be possible in the last twenty years in a certain number of areas that concern our ways of being and thinking, relations to authority, relations between the sexes, the way in which we perceive insanity or illness; I prefer even these partial transformations that have been made in

the correlation of historical analysis and the practical attitude, to the programs for a new man that the worst political systems have repeated throughout the twentieth century. (Foucault, "What Is Enlightenment," p. 47)

On memory and forgetting, see also Italo Calvino, "Dinosaurs." In *Cosmicomics*, trans. William Weaver (New York: Harcourt Brace Jovanovich, 1968), pp. 97–112).

Page 135, Rachmaninoff. See Kundera, *The Art of the Novel* (New York: Harper and Row, 1988), p. 135.

Page 136, forms of oppression. Mark Warren argues convincingly that Nietzsche recognizes only a narrow range of forms of oppression, missing, most importantly, the ways power is exerted through markets and bureaucracies; see Chapter Seven of *Nietzsche and Political Thought*, esp. pp. 243–46.

Notes to Chapter 9

Page 137, Will Powers. Lynn Goldsmith and Sting, "Adventures in Success," Adrenalynn Music (BMI) / Reggatta Music / Illegal Songs Inc. (BMI), Island Records, Inc., 1983.

Page 138, Nietzsche and the Grand March. In arguing similarly, Lampert quotes *Richard Wagner in Bayreuth*, following Nietzsche's later suggestion that "Zarathustra" or "Nietzsche" replace "Wagner" (see above, p. 155): "May sane reason preserve us from the belief that mankind will at any future time attain to a final ideal order of things, and that happiness will then shine down upon it with unwavering ray like the sun of the tropics: with such a belief Nietzsche / Zarathustra has nothing to do, he is no utopian" (*WB:*11; quoted Lampert, p. 218).

Page 140, Pope Innocent. Colli and Montinari were unable to locate a source that would have confirmed these as Innocent's words; see *KSA*,14:379.

Page 141, viewing the world from behind. Nietzsche's scatology is developed in his description of the hinterworldly as the *After-Weisen* (Z,III:10.2; 239.31), literally "the anally wise," and their wisdom as *After-Weisheit*, anal wisdom (239.28). Kaufmann and Hollingdale, translating in the days of s– – –, render *After-Weisheit* "sham-wisdom." Kaufmann uses "sham-wise" for *After-Weisen*, whereas Hollingdale omits the paragraph in which this term occurs, inadvertently, I assume.

Page 141, wisdom that there is shit in the world. This conclusion holds even from Zarathustra's final perspective, where value is no longer placed on disgust.

Page 141, skin diseases. Zarathustra's identification of humanity as one of the earth's skin diseases may seem life-denying, yet just as the revolutionary fire-dog has as its counterpart another fire-dog, rather than an "over-fire-dog," there may be another humanity, which likewise is not a disease.

Page 141, wrestler. The German words for "wrestler" and "wrestle" are *Ringer, ringen;* another meaning in the pocket "ring."

Page 142, the "feminine affects" dominant in the Semitic myth. "Feminine," too, is a pocket into which many meanings have been put. Many avowed feminists are as critical of traditional "femininity" as is Nietzsche.

As has recently been stressed by others, the status of woman within Nietzsche's work, and especially within *Zarathustra,* is complex and fascinating. Traces of this theme have recurred throughout my earlier chapters, from "suppose truth is a woman," through women as forced to become "work-slaves and prisoners," to Zarathustra's favored women, life and wisdom (his "stillest hour" is another). I hope to develop this topic more fully elsewhere. Here, I note only—in addition to what I have noted above—that although Zarathustra's followers seem to be exclusively male, his deepest teachings are addressed, equally, to women. Two particularly revealing passages are contained in successive subsections of "Of Old and New Tablets." In the first, Zarathustra announces, "Thus do I want man and woman: the one able to wage war, the other able to bear children, but both able to dance with head and with legs" (Z,III:12.23; 264.2–3). Women, like men, should dance with head and with legs, with body and with soul. Men should be warriors, but Zarathustra often insists that men must bear children as well (e.g., Z,II:2; 111.4–9). Might it not be that women should also be warriors?

In the subsection immediately following, Zarathustra considers the ethics of marriage and adultery:

> Your wedlock [*Eheschliessen*]: see to it that it not be a bad locking [*Schliessen*]. If you lock it too quickly, there follows wedlock-breaking [*Ehebrechen*].
> Better wedlock-breaking than wedlock-picking [*Ehe-biegen*], wedlock-tricking [*Ehe-lügen*]. Thus said a woman to me: "Indeed I broke my marriage [*Ehe*], but only after marriage had broken me." (Z, III:12.24; 264.8–13)

In this passage, Nietzsche combines the prefix *Ehe* (marriage, matrimony, wedlock) with four suffixes, each a verb in its own right. The first two of the resulting compounds are ordinary-language terms, the third and fourth, Nietzschean coinages. Normally, no doubt, a German-speaker confronted with the term *Ehebrechen* would think of adultery without thinking directly of the "breaking"—any more than speakers of English, hearing the term "wedlock," normally think directly of the "locking," or Germans, the *Schliessen* in *Eheschliessen.* But with the very first sentence, Nietzsche forces us to think of the locking, the *schliessen,* by using it both with and without its prefix. Similarly, he forces the German reader explicitly to think the *Bruch* in *Ehebruch,* by using it separately, twice ("I broke the marriage after it broke me").

So: does *Ehebruch,* here, mean adultery? Or does it mean, more literally, breaking or destroying the marriage, getting out of it entirely (abandonment, divorce, etc.)? To decide, we must note that it is opposed to, more literally, "marriage-warping" (wedlock-picking) and "marriage-lying" (wedlock-tricking). Could not both of those refer to adultery? Not necessarily, perhaps: if a good marriage "releases the woman in woman" (along with, perhaps, the man in man), then a marriage that entraps, enslaves, or otherwise "breaks" a woman would be a twisting or warping; it might also, I suppose, be a lying, a deception. But adultery also might well qualify as twisting or lying.

At the very least, it should be noted that Zarathustra is criticizing certain kinds of marriage, not the women who break those marriages. Also noteworthy is that whereas "breaking," destroying, is a characteristic of the warrior, and traditionally masculine, both lying and twisting are often, from androcentric perspectives, taken to be characteristically feminine. Lying and warping are also the options, I suspect, most often open to women living in cultures where, to adapt Zarathustra's formulation, the men are not sufficiently masculine that they may allow the women to be feminine. And just as being sufficiently masculine involves the feminine trait of giving birth, albeit in a metaphorical sense, the passage we are now discussing suggests that the "masculine" trait of breaking may be required of women who are to become women, at least under certain conditions.

I stress again that more is to be said concerning Nietzsche and woman; recent treatments include Maryann Bertram, " 'God's Second Blunder'—Serpent, Woman, and the *Gestalt* in Nietzsche's Thought," *Southern Journal of Philosophy*, Vol. 19 (1981), pp. 259–77; Jacques Derrida, *Spurs. Nietzsche's Styles* (Chicago: University of Chicago Press, 1979); Sarah Kofman, "Baubô: Theological Perversion and Fetishism," in Gillespie and Strong, eds., *Nietzsche's New Seas*, pp. 175–202 and Michael Platt, "Woman, Nietzsche, and Nature," *Maieutics*, Vol. 2 (1981), pp. 27–42.

Page 143, Nietzsche's move beyond myth. My contention is supported by the fact that, according to the indices both of Colli-Montinari and of Schlechta, *Joyful Science* is the last book in which Nietzsche even mentions Prometheus. Colli and Montinari identify a note from April–June 1885 (*N:*VII:34[112]; see *KSA* 11:457–58) as Nietzsche's final reference to Prometheus.

Page 143, poets. Zarathustra, too, is a poet, as is Nietzsche (see Z,II:17). Poet Kundera's treatment of lyric poets in *Life is Elsewhere* casts light on Zarathustra's judgment.

Page 143, accusation and complaint. The joy that can accompany complaint and accusation is another form of kitsch. Like laughter, tears are ambiguous. Like Kundera, Nietzsche warns us against certain kinds of tears. In "Of the Great Longing," Zarathustra asks his soul, "Is all weeping not a complaining? And all complaining not an accusing?" (Z,III:14; 280.3–8). Tears of complaint and of accusation against life suggest a categorical disagreement with being: things are not as they should be, God has not done right by us. How sad it is that we die; how noble this makes our continuing to live! Kundera writes: "Kitsch causes two tears to flow in quick succession. The first tear says: How nice to see children running on the grass!" How sad it is that we all shall die! "The second tear says: How nice to be moved, together with all mankind, by children running on the grass!" Or by mortality, or by human endurance in the face of mortality! "It is the second tear that makes kitsch kitsch" (*Lightness*, p. 251).

What makes Nietzsche's romantic poets' tears of complaint and accusation kitsch is the joy that accompanies them. But Nietzsche recognizes, within *Zarathustra*, that not all first tears are followed by second ones, and that not all weeping is a complaining or an accusing. The saint who lives in the foothills of Zarathustra's mountain weeps, but in praise and in joy, perhaps in appreciation—but not in self-congratulation (Z,P:2; 13.29–31). In the section following "Of the Great Longing," "The Other Dancing Song," Zarathustra and life weep together (285.15–16), and there is nothing to suggest that kitsch-tears are involved. At the end of the book, when Zarathustra receives the sign indicating to him that his "children are near," he weeps again (Z,IV:20; 406.32–407.2), in joy and in relief.

On Zarathustra's earth, it remains possible to weep over the past without complaining and without accusing. That we age and die is sad, perhaps, but it is no basis for complaint or accusation: with whom would the complaint be lodged? Against whom would the accusation be made? Certainly, there may be bases for complaint or accusation in *how* some of us die, or in *how* some of us are forced to live; these are also bases for "saying no as the storm says no," for resistance both in word and in deed. But these would be complaints, accusations, and resistances against oppression or exploitation, or against stupidity; they would not be against life or being.

Page 144, *Hic rhodos, hic saltus.* On Rhodes and roses, jumping and dancing, see the Introduction to Hegel's *Philosophy of Right.*

Page 145, wishing. I use "wish" for the cognate *wünschen;* Kaufmann uses "desire," which is, I believe, deeply misleading. Nietzsche regularly insists that desire is something that human beings can never avoid; the priestly ascetic ideal is the result of the explicit attempt to avoid desiring, but Nietzsche unmasks it as itself another form of desire. Wishing is something else; it here suggests, in German as in English, a longing for life under conditions altogether different from the ones we know.

Page 146, unmasking kitsch. In a more fashionable idiom, "unmasking forms of kitsch," particularly totalitarian kitsch, might be described as deconstructing, particularly deconstructing totalizing discourses.

Works Cited

Abel, Günter. *Nietzsche. Die Dynamik der Willen zur Macht und die ewige Wieder-kehr.* Berlin and New York: de Gruyter, 1984.

Alderman, Harold. *Nietzsche's Gift.* Athens, Ohio: Ohio University Press, 1977.

Allison, David (editor). *The New Nietzsche.* New York: Dell, 1977.

Altizer, Thomas. "Eternal Recurrence and the Kingdom of God." In *The New Nietzsche.* Edited by David Allison, Pp. 232–46.

Aristotle. *The Rhetoric of Aristotle.* With commentary by E. M. Cope, revised and edited by J. E. Sandys. Three volumes. Cambridge: Cambridge University Press, 1877.

Aristotle. *Nichomachean Ethics.* Translated by H. Rackam. Cambridge, MA: Harvard University Press, 1926.

Bertram, Maryann. "'God's Second Blunder'—Serpent, Woman, and the Gestalt in Nietzsche's Thought." *Southern Journal of Philosophy.* Vol. 19 (1981). Pp. 259–77.

Boswell, James. *The Life of Johnson.* Edited and abridged by Christopher Hibbert. Middlesex: Penguin Books, 1979.

Calvino, Italo. *Cosmicomics.* Translated by William Weaver. New York: Harcourt Brace Jovanovich, 1968.

———. *If On A Winter's Night A Traveler.* Translated by William Weaver. New York: Harcourt Brace Jovanovich, 1979.

———. *Invisible Cities.* Translated by William Weaver. New York: Harcourt Brace Jovanovich, 1974.

———. *Mr. Palomar.* Translated by William Weaver. New York: Harcourt Brace Jovanovich, 1985.

———. *tZero.* Translated by William Weaver. New York: Harcourt Brace Jovanovich, 1976.

Danto, Arthur. *Nietzsche as Philosopher.* New York: Columbia University Press, 1965.

Deleuze, Gilles. *Nietzsche and Philosophy.* Translated by Hugh Tomlinson. New York: Columbia University Press, 1983.

Derrida, Jacques. *Spurs. Nietzsche's Styles.* Chicago: University of Chicago Press, 1979.

Elgrably, Jordan. "Conversations with Milan Kundera." *Salmagundi.* No. 73 (Winter 1987). Pp. 3–24.

Figl, Johann. *Interpretation als philosophisches Prinzip.* Berlin and New York: de Gruyter, 1982.

Foucault, Michel. "What Is Enlightenment." In *The Foucault Reader.* Edited by Paul Rabinow. New York: Pantheon Books, 1984. Pp. 32–50.

Foucault, Michel. *The Use of Pleasure. The History of Sexuality,* Vol. 2. New York: Vintage Books, 1986.

Harries, Karsten. "The Philosopher at Sea." In *Nietzsche's New Seas.* Edited by Strong and Gillespie. Pp. 21–44.

Heidegger, Martin. *Holzwege.* Frankfurt a. M.: Klostermann, 5th ed. 1972.

———. *Nietzsche.* 2 vols. Pfullingen: Neske, 1961. English translation (ET) by David Krell, *Nietzsche,* 4 vols. New York: Harper and Row, 1984.

Higgins, Kathleen. *Nietzsche's Zarathustra.* Philadelphia: Temple University Press, 1987.

Houlgate, Stephen. *Hegel, Nietzsche, and the Criticism of Metaphysics.* Cambridge: Cambridge University Press, 1986.

Kant, Immanuel. *Werkausgabe.* Edited by Wilhelm Weischedel. 12 vols. Frankfurt: Suhrkamp, 1981.

Kofman, Sarah. "Baubô: Theological Perversion and Fetishism." In *Nietzsche's New Seas.* Edited by Gillespie and Strong. Pp. 175–202.

Kundera, Milan. *The Art of the Novel.* Translated by Linda Asher. New York: Harper and Row, 1988.

———. *The Book of Laughter and Forgetting.* Translated by Michael Henry Heim. New York: Penguin Books, 1980.

———. *Life is Elsewhere.* Translated by Peter Kussi. New York: Penguin Books, 1986.

———. *The Unbearable Lightness of Being.* Translated by Michael Henry Heim. New York: Harper and Row, 1984.

Lampert, Laurence. *Nietzsche's Teaching: An Interpretation of Thus Spoke Zarathustra.* New Haven: Yale University Press, 1986.

Lang, Berel (editor). *Philosophical Style.* Chicago: Nelson Hall, 1980.

Müller-Lauter, Wolfgang. "Nihilismus." In *Historisches Wörterbuch der Philosophie.* Vol. 6, column 846.

Naumann, Gustav. *Zarathustra-Commentar.* 4 vols. Leipzig: Verlag H. Häffel, 1899.

Nehamas, Alexander. *Nietzsche: Life as Literature.* Cambridge, MA: Harvard University Press, 1985.

Nietzsche, Friedrich. See "References to Nietzsche's Works," pp. xiii–xiv, above.

Nozick, Robert. *Anarchy, State, and Utopia.* New York: Basic Books, 1974.

Pippin, Robert B. "Irony and Affirmation in Nietzsche's *Thus Spoke Zarathustra.*" In *Nietzsche's New Seas.* Edited by Strong and Gillespie. Pp. 45–71.

Platt, Michael. "Woman, Nietzsche, and Nature." *Maieutics,* Vol. 2 (1981). Pp. 27–42.

Proust, Marcel. *Remembrance of Things Past.* 3 vols. Translated by C. K. Scott Moncrieff and Terence Kilmartin. New York: Vintage Books, 1982.

Ritter, Joachim, et. al. *Historisches Wörterbuch der Philosophie.* 10 vols. Darmstadt: Wissenschaftliche Buchgesellschaft, 1971ff.

Rosen, Stanley. *Hermeneutics as Politics.* New York: Oxford University Press, 1987.

———. *The Quarrel between Philosophy and Poetry.* New York: Routledge, Chapman and Hall, 1988.

Schacht, Richard. "Nietzsche and Nihilism." In *Nietzsche. A Collection of Critical Essays.* Edited Robert C. Solomon. Garden City, NY: Anchor Books, 1973. Pp. 58–72.

Schopenhauer, Arthur. *Die Welt als Wille und Vorstellung.* 2 vols. Eighth edition. Leipzig: F. A. Brockhaus, 1891. References are to sections, not to pages.

Schutte, Ofelia. *Beyond Nihilism.* Chicago: University of Chicago Press, 1984.

Shapiro, Gary. "The Rhetoric of Nietzsche's *Zarathustra.*" In *Philosophical Style.* Edited by Berel Lang. Pp. 347–385.

Solomon, Robert. "A More Severe Morality: Nietzsche's Affirmative Ethics." In *Nietzsche as Affirmative Thinker.* Edited by Yirmiahu Yovel. Pp. 69–89.

Stern, J. P. *A Study of Nietzsche.* Cambridge: Cambridge University Press, 1979.

Strong, Tracy. *Friedrich Nietzsche and the Politics of Transfiguration.* Expanded edition. Berkeley: University of California Press, 1988.

———, and Michael Allen Gillespie (editors). *Nietzsche's New Seas.* Chicago: University of Chicago Press, 1988.

Thatcher, David S. "Musical Settings of Nietzsche Texts." I: *Nietzsche-Studien,* Vol. 4 (1975). Pp. 284–323. II: *Nietzsche-Studien,* Vol. 5 (1976). Pp. 355–83. III: *Nietzsche-Studien,* Vol. 15 (1986). Pp. 440–52.

Valadier, Paul. "Dionysus Versus the Crucified." In *The New Nietzsche.* Edited by David Allison. Pp. 247–262.

Warren, Mark. *Nietzsche and Political Thought.* Cambridge, MA: MIT Press, 1988.

White, Alan. *Absolute Knowledge*. Athens, Ohio: Ohio University Press, 1983.

_____. "Nietzschean Nihilism: A Typology." *International Studies in Philosophy.* XIX/2 (1987). Pp. 29–44.

_____. "Review of Stephen Houlgate, *Hegel, Nietzsche and the Problem of Metaphysics.*" *The Owl of Minerva* (Fall 1989). Pp. 91–96.

Wilcox, John. *Truth and Value in Nietzsche*. Ann Arbor: University of Michigan Press, 1974.

Yovel, Yirmiahu (editor). *Nietzsche as Affirmative Thinker*. Dordrecht: Martinus Nijhoff, 1986.

Index